Participatory **Design Thinking** in Architecture & Urban Planning

JOHN ODHIAMBO ONYANGO

Table of Contents

Chapter 5: Discussion and Conclusions

Preface

The book offers a study of participatory design thinking methodologies used in architecture and planning through vehicles called 'Urban Design Laboratories' UDL, from the western world: USA, Spain and Denmark. It looked into their origins and some of the ethical issues that rise out of participation in the design thinking processes and policy issues decisions and how these affect the outcomes of the projects so undertaken. It critically examined how the historical socio-political context of the 1960s contributed to the movements that led to the formation of UDLs and the participatory design thinking methodological practices of the UDLs for a sustainable place-making of the built environment. The research in the book examined the methodologies and practices of UDL's, that initially started in the USA coming on the heels of the civil rights movements and how it later appeared throughout Europe.

It looked at the historical and social circumstances that drove the participation processes where they existed, the ethical approaches to design and how they influence the methods and strategies used. It used comparative analysis of 3 distinct UDLs in the USA and Europe to suggest a model for such laboratories in developing world for sustainability of designed places. The work of the book was limited to work of the UDL at Carnegie Mellon University in Pittsburgh, USA, Laboratori d'Urbanisme de Barcelona (LUB) at Universitat Politècnica de Catalunya and Royal Danish Academy of Fine Arts in Denmark through work of the founder Jan Gehl. It looked the ethical and moral values that are introduced by the pedagogical methods and approaches followed in the three selected cases. It assessed the various methods and approaches used by the laboratories in addressing the complexities of urban design education and practice. The book finally suggests aspects that have universal application that that may be incorporated in the use of the urban design laboratory model as a tool for educating future urban designers.

It is the first book that fills the urgent need to analyze the processes that are used in the participatory design thinking methodologies in the UDLs from the western world of similar age and how they can to sustainable place-making. Competing books have used case studies are from one part of the world only, while the *Participatory Design Thinking in Architecture and Urban Planning* looked at several projects from different parts of the western world. It provides examples of how these techniques and methods can be universally applied with contextual modification. The ethical and moral values discussed in the books are important to many of schools of architectural and architectural practices in the USA, the UK and in many developing countries. The materials and methodologies can easily be adopted for course work in many schools of architecture and can be translated into Spanish for wider market in Central and South America; to French for west African market.

CHAPTER 1

Urban Design: Theories & Methods

1.1 Introduction and Overview

This chapter deals with the literature on the subject of urban design, urban design laboratories and the theoretical and historical context that framed them. It gives a narrative of the how the urban design theories developed, and critiques that led to them. The chapter takes a sweep at the social architecture, developments of community architecture and participatory design thinking engagement and how these affected the approaches to learning. It concludes by looking at impacts on architecture and urban design education and the genesis of urban design laboratories.

The creation of the built environment is complex involving very many players including the professional designers, the developers, government organizations, and many others. According to Carmona *et al*

"...Most concerns today are located in the critiques of the role played by the various professionals in the building industry itself..." (2003, p.12). The roles played have been framed by the force emerging from the modern movement that impacted on policy-making and place-making (Lang,1994). In addition, architects and planners who are in charge of improving spatial and physical forms have questioned on their sole abilities and responsibilities.

However, the questioning began much earlier at the beginning of the Twentieth Century and is very much tied to the transformations that were in the quality of the environment in cities due to the industrial revolution. They developed in the late 1930s, giving rise to the new vision of civic design as a means of joining up fragmented sets of professions and of restoring or giving qualities of coherence and continuity to individual developments. This was thought to result inevitably in improved overall quality of the built environment and the making of better places. Mumford suggests that urban design has its "...intellectual roots in the late *Congres Internationaux d'Architecture Moderne* (CIAM) and especially in the work and ideas of Sert, Kahn and others..." (2009, p.viii). This book follows the historical events leading to the formation of urban design as a discipline and how they influenced the methodologies adapted by the three urban laboratories identified later in the chapter as case studies. However, before proceeding, it would be worth examining how the theories of urban design came about and what were the driving forces that led to them.

Most urban design theories are normative and focus on the various competing interests and preferred values. They assess value judgement system about their desirability, dealing with things *as they ought* to be rather than *as they are* [emphasis mine]. Herson (1984) points out that normative theories are in essence a political debate, therefore, are used to plead a cause or to convince others about a cause. They work on identity and relationships between logical classes, means and ends or cause and effect. The normative theories have descriptions of reality leading to the logical conclusion that if things or phenomena are described as they are, then one is likely to agree on changes that will reconstruct things as they ought to be. However, one challenge with such a view is that a distorted description is likely to lead to a warped solution.

Urban theories deal with the object of study at different scales with some focused on the struggle between classes at the production of spaces. In mind are the Neo-Marxist theories concerned with the relationship between the lived space and the individual (Sennett, 1977) and (Lefèbvre, 1991). The Neo-Marxists describe how the socio-psychological impacts on the individuals and lived spaces and how it affects socio-spatial relations as seen in everyday life.

The process of place creation can thus be analysed from an evolutionary theoretical perspective of social formations produced. Literature reveals that the forms of spatial settlement are the footprints of the modifications of social construction (Castells, 1972). The current urban design theories have their sources in works of four influential writers of the late nineteenth Century and early Twentieth Century: Max Webber, Georg Simmel, Walter Benjamin and Henri Lefèbvre. Their contributions to the understanding of the city even though varied had a common thread through them. They all took the 'city as an object of critical reflection', thus a laboratory or field for study (Parker, 2004). The city was the object or place for consumption and production [capitalist economy]; and a place for culture, spectacle and space. The important link between the four writers is rooted in how they studied the city as a microcosm for modern society. The following sections discuss the urban theories from the perspective of the four writers and the relationships between them.

1.1.1 Max Weber

Max Weber (April 1864-June 1920) was an important German Sociologist and political economist. He contributed to the understanding of rationalization and the disenchantment associated with capitalism through development of a systematic methodology for historical sociology. He was against the positivists' empiricism thinking that was applied to almost all fields of knowledge from the 1890s to 1920s. It included the new vision espoused by the modernists and proponents at the Bauhaus as is discussed later in the chapter.

Parker (2004) asserts that Weber contributed to the historical understanding of the transition of society through the various economic systems in the formation of cities. His emphasis was on the territorial and historical aspects of the social phenomena highlighting the essential characteristics of urban form that were related to western civilization. He drew from 'a multi-dimensional, idealistic typical approach' (Parker, 2004).

Weberian city had three important characteristics; firstly, it was a collection of one or more separate dwellings but was a relatively closed settlement where inhabitants lived off trade and commerce rather than agriculture. Secondly, city generated money capital through trade in agriculture, manufacturing and through the extraction of rent. Its link to outlying areas and other cities were important. Thirdly, it's formation and running depended on the politics of governance through the opportunities for *civic participation and especially democratic participation* [emphasis mine] (Parker, 2004). The key aspects of interest to this book from Weber is the opportunities that must be available to all residents in the politics of making decisions about the developments that affected them including place- making. Weber thus pointed to the importance of historical analysis in the understanding of cities, by tracing their trajectories for future growth. The formation and the development of the cities occur through the politics of class division and production, a theme picked up and expanded on later by other historians.

1.1.2 George Simmel

George Simmel (March 1858–Sept.1918) was a sociologist, colleague and contemporary of Max Webber. He contributed to the ant- positivists questioning of definition of society and introduced the methodology of analysis of the society from a moral philosophical approach in contrast to the positivist one of other Anglo-American researchers. However, he acknowledged the existence of a transformation power of modernity [art and aesthetics] visible in the modern metropolis and urban culture (Parker, 2004).

For Simmel, capital and money were the key to all exchanges in urban centres that allowed for the dissociation of power, securing of goods without the need for coercion of the medieval society. This provided the affordances of independence from the will of all others in power and created the new consciousness in the fight for social justice. However, capital and money also created the realignment of class division hence replicated the power structure.

Simmel's and Weber's conception of the city are similar because both used historical analysis: to construct the genesis from observation of micro-behaviour. However, Simmel used an anthropological or social psychological approach rather than systematic analysis of Weber and placed his focus at the individual level. In the previous section, Weber had pointed to the importance of freedom that trade and commercial activities brought about by allowing for participation in the governance, while Simmel argued that urbanization is associated with emancipation from the traditional forms of social dominance that persisted until the Eighteenth Century (Parker, 2004).

According to Simmel, the city was a place that liberated from the traditional social structure, from the economic and political domination by the elite that is noteworthy. The emancipation led to desire for freedom that set the foundation for the democratic aspiration, the desire to contribute to the changing or the making of one's built environment. As pointed earlier the flip side of the emancipation was that once the traditional social structures and centres of power were dissolved, new ones emerged, replicating themselves in a similar manner. The new elite, the merchant class used their wealth and positions acquired through it to accrue benefits that propagated the *status quo.*

1.1.3 Walter Benjamin

Walter Benjamin (July 1892-Sept. 1940) was also a German philosopher and sociologist among other things. He was also linked with the Frankfurt School where he contributed to critical theory. His work was different from Webber and Simmel in that he took a positivists position to critiquing the changing society. Benjamin's approach to the city was exegetical and involved an extensive and critical interpretation of the city as text on the basis of what it provided. The work was the interpretation of the data collected from the field and laboratory of the city.

Benjamin's work was different from the contemporary empirical sociologists (Webber and Simmel) after Marx as he dwelt on the philosophical dialogue on the nature of truth, morality and human conditions of Kant and Nietzsche. He argued that private life was permeated with communal life, where the home became the exhaustible reservoir from which they flooded out (Demetz, 1978). It was thus imperative that the individual had the right to participate in the creation of the public realm because the private and public realms within the city are closely intertwined.

Benjamin's work talked about the important issues that affected the civic participation and democracy asserting the importance of the individual right. This has not only to be acknowledged by those already in positions of authority but also need to be nurtured for effective participation; in other words, capacity building.

1.1.4 Henry Lefèbvre

Henry Lefèbvre (June 1901-June 1991) was a French sociologist who was very influential in the radical thinking of the 1960s and was concerned with the critique of the *rights to the city* for the citizens. He was involved with a European avant-garde movement based between COBRA, (Copenhagen, Brussels and Amsterdam) and the Situationist International (SI).

For Lefèbvre, a complex of social forces affecting the spatial practices and meanings produced space. His views are opposed to those of Weber and Simmel where space is mainly a creation of economic force or capital. The Lefèbvre's space is a product of political contest because it served as a tool of thought and action, thus, became a means of control and dominance. In essence, he argued that the production of the public realm was contextual and particular because it was shaped by societal force of historical events [political, cultural, social etc.].

Lefèbvre was critical of the contemporary town planning theories that were predominant in 1960s because they were dominated by what he saw as "... an empirical ideology that often-used concepts and methods of other disciplines and was understood as science of space and not time..." (1976, p.30). This was problematic because the resulting planned space was viewed as objective, neutral and not influenced by the political contexts. This meant that space making would be a result of the physical elements that contained it and was positivist in regard to the community. In addition, the civic participation was closely tied to the local historical and political context.

However, before proceeding to look at the critiques and developments that led to the new design thinking in architecture and urban design, it is worth examining some of the definitions associated with the field. This is followed by the examination of the critiques of those theories and how they led to the ideas of community participatory design thinking and formation of the urban design laboratories.

1.2. Definition of Urban Design

The term 'urban design' has been around since the 1950s, having its origin in North America to replace the term 'civic design' that was deemed narrow. The latter term had its origin in the City Beautiful Movement that focused mainly on the location and design of major civic buildings such as the city hall, museum, opera houses, etc., and their relationship to the open spaces. Prior to the 1950s, urban design was predominantly concerned with the aesthetic of building morphology and the spaces in between.

Other definitions include an '...attempt to change spatial organizations and social relations to the city...' In response to the complex and sometimes antagonistic interests (de Souza, 2006; p.327). The state apparatus, as an agent, tries by means of persuasion, co-option and if necessary, by oppression to co-ordinate these competing interests. De Souza's definition sees urban design as concerned primarily with the form of urban space regardless of the origins, of the aims; that is social reformation, formalizing space, environmental ends etc. It is very much concerned with the distribution and use of resources and the politics of why.

Today, Urban Design is seen as the "process of making better places for people" than would otherwise be produced, (Carmona *et al.,* 2003; p.3). It highlights important themes related to it: firstly, that it is concerned with the creation and enhancement of communities; i.e., for people and about people. Secondly, the places so created have value and are significant to those communities. Thirdly, the design process occurs in the real world, is multi-disciplinary and multi-faceted. Therefore, it is constrained and bound by competing social, economic and political realities. Finally, it is important to see the design is a process (means) rather than a product (ends). The process is iterative problem-solving approach, involving constant reflection, glancing back at the historical forces that influenced it and responding to them as they change, hence carried best carried out through design thinking.

The definitions are vague, as pointed out by Madanipour (1996), Carmona *et al* (2003) and Tibbalds (1988a) who argued that it is everything visible outside the window increasing the ambiguity in meaning further. Gosling and Maitland (1984) define it in terms of the fields it falls under: the interface between architecture, landscape architecture and town planning. The difficulty in the definition comes from its history in the modernist split between architecture and planning, affecting both the academia and the profession.

The ambiguity continues as illustrated in *Table 1.1* below that reveal that the definitions oscillate between the product and process themes. However, it is important to note that of the seven definitions, only two are product oriented while the rest are focused on the process. This highlights the importance of the process to the place-creation. The book will therefore focus mainly on the design thinking methodologies used to create places at the case study urban laboratories.

The European Union recognizes urban design as:

> '...Concerns an *inclusive* and *participatory* [emphasis mine] planning, design and management *process* that: aims at creating "beautiful", healthy, socially integrated and inclusive places; promotes equitable economic development; conserves land; looks at towns and cities in relation to one another and their hinterlands; ensures the strategic location of new developments in relation to the natural environment and transport systems; ensures development is mixed and of appropriate density; includes a well-developed green structure and a high quality and well- planned public infrastructure and respects and builds upon the existing cultural heritage and the social capital'. (European Commission, 2004, p.2).

In the UK, it is taken as the art of making places for people and includes the way places work and matters such as community safety as well as how they look (the aesthetics). Therefore, concerned with the *connections between people and places,*

Table: 1.1: Developed from Madanipour (1996, pp.93-117).

ACTIVITY	PRODUCT or PROCESS?
Level of Focus (larges scale as region as opposed to single building)	PRODUCT
Visual qualities of the urban environment or broad organization and management of urban spaces	PRODUCT
Transformation of spatial arrangements or ethical issues	PROCESS
Production of the urban environment or the process of its production	PROCESS
Reserve of architects, planners, landscape architects (elitist)	PROCESS/ PRODUCT
Public or private activity (capitalist view)	PROCESS
Objective-rational process (science) or an expressive-subjective process. that was criticized by Lefebvre, (1976, p.30).	PROCESS

movements, urban form, nature and the built environment and the *processes* for successful villages, towns and cities DETR and CABE (2000, p.8).

There are three traditions or schools of thought within which urban design is researched and practiced that arise from the differing ways of conceiving and perceiving design and the products of the process of the design. These are: the visual-artistic, the social-usage traditions and the third place-making having emerged since 1970s drawing strengths from the first two approaches (Jarvis,1980). The later takes into account the fact that urban design encompasses both the product and processes involved in crafting the place.

1.2.1 The Visual Artistic Tradition

This tradition is characterized by emphasis on the product- rather than processes- involved in creating places. It focuses more on the visual qualities of urban design and the aesthetic experience (delight) of the spaces produced with other factors such as economical, socio-cultural and political receive less emphasis. The visual-artistic traditions in the modern historical period have their roots in the works and writings of Camillo Sitte (1889); Unwin (1909); Le Corbusier, (1970 edition) and Cullen (1961).

The principles are underpinned on the works of Sitte (1889), which have been criticized for its deterministic tendencies. However, within the definitions of urban design so far, they are spot on. Sitte was following on the traditions laid down by the Renaissance and Baroque masters of the Fifteenth and Sixteenth Centuries. Le Corbusier on the other hand in his book *Vers Une Architecture* (1923) (later translated as *Towards a New Architecture*) was against artistic adornment that had no functions, a view that he shared with fellow modernist of the period. To him the form of the city should follow the functions that he saw espoused visual qualities of town planning (the name urban design was also known by). He argued that thc visual qualities should be arrived at only from "...geometry as a means to perceive the external world and expressed the world within..." (1928, p.1). He saw geometry was the means to create order in design of modern cities of tomorrow. It is a view that is also deterministic in that it believed that the ordered physical world would create an orderly social and economic world in contrast to the chaos experienced during his time and the period after the Second World War.

Cullen's approach was equally visual, aesthetically and stylistic, but fundamentally the same as Sitte's and Le Corbusier. The main difference was in the "...style and the impressionistic sketches that replaced the formal prose and precise drawings..." (Jarvis, 1980; p.53). His methods were personal interpretations of the visual space. Cullen placed emphasis on the pictorial approaches of perspectives, the frontispiece design and compositions similar to those used in the Renaissance and Baroque periods. However, all the views by the three had one thing in common; they ignored the perceptual aspects of the users and contribution by users to the design process.

The townscape movement and methods rose from the "philosophies of conservation, anti-scrape and surrealism in 1930s and 1940s Britain" (Macarthur, 2009; p.387). The reasons given are attributed to the owner and editor of the Architectural review (AR) Hubert de Cronin Hastings who promoted the popularity of architectural modernism and attacked the *Tabula Rasa* approach of the CIAM promoted by Le Corbusier and others. He wanted to portray the idea that irregular planning had their origins in England, in the picturesque and in what the AR called the functional tradition.

According to Macarthur, townscape movement saw "history as analysis and kind of imagination to be practiced with the surprising conjunction of old buildings and new building" (2009, p.388). This is very much in line with the rationalist ideas that were prevalent in Italy. Adherents of the townscape methods saw cities as made by the contingencies of history and according to no overall principles. Here, they acknowledged the ideas of Webber and Simmell of historical development of cities previously discussed. Because cities were seen to be less formed in comparison to the buildings in it, there was a difference that allowed for experience through visual view points of the snap shots of history.

Townscape movement built on the ideas of Sitte, however suggested according to Macurther "...That the urban fabric might be not merely humble and indifferent but actually bad, in poor taste and in styles and ideologies at odds with its architectural re-framing..." (2009; p.389). In a sense, it was a critique of the formalistic of the methods of Sitte, though both agreed on the visual aspects of analysis and representation of cities.

Ray Lucas describes Gordon Cullen's work as based on:

> "...Serial vision, which is a simple proposition that consisted of a series of sketch perspectives arranged in a sequence along a path and accompanied by a plan indicating the points along the paths where the perspectives are taken..." (2009, p.1)

Cullen's methodology of perception is therefore analytical and shows the various patterns and variations within the space. It allowed the representation of what the space might look like when built. It has however been criticized by Jarvis (1980) and Vernez-Moudon (1992).

Jarvis argues that it fails to consider the collaborative approach to design and is elitist in that it is based on the eyes of the designer alone to conceive and represent the place created. He pens:

> "...The essential value of Cullen's approach lies in its uninhibited, personal and expressive response to space. For instance, Cullen mingles aspects of spatial analysis with poetic evocation..." (1980, p.26)

The meanings are ascribed to the space in the process that may not be of same value to the users of the place and in that sense, shares the same problems of designing urban places as those of the modernist period. Vernez-Moudon on the other hand found the method shallow as a tool for analysis especially if used in education of students. She argued that it was deterministic and places too much focus on the product end of the scale, thus ignoring the process. She posits it is good for "... maintaining a high profile for the beginning student of urban design but does not sustain well a more rigorous and deep investigation..." (1992, p446).

1.2.2 The Social-Usage Tradition

The social usage tradition grew out of the contexts of a new research approach by the sociologists at the Chicago School of Sociology. The most influential years of the Chicago School ran from 1918 to 1932. Their way of thinking about social relations was heavily quantitative, rigorous in data analysis, and, most importantly, focused on the city as a social laboratory (Ackerman and Lutters,1996; p.1). The city became the site for field study, a place that is up close and personal where research on urban studies could be carried. It thus became the laboratory of controlled environment where artificial specimens yielded generalities that are true elsewhere as argued by Gieryn (2006). The city now provided opportunity for distant and objective analysis that provides its credibility.

The central theme of the Chicago School was that naturalistic observation of urban and social phenomena is best done through quantitative methodologies. The city when used as a laboratory created opportunity for ethnographic closeness to the rich and deep data that helped in understanding the relationship between the social structure and the activities of the city and how they are impacted by the production of urban forms and the process of production. The methodology has been criticized for lacking the faces behind the numbers, ignoring the individual's relationships to the historical contexts.

Urban design is concerned with places and people and its success is measured by people's usage. This second school of thought was driven by the way space is consumed and colonized. The perceptions and meanings of spaces are as important to the tradition as places that, it is argued, acquire meanings from it. (See Lynch, 1960; Tuan 1976; Canter,1977a and others).

The view of the importance of social-usage tradition on the design of urban spaces is supported by Gehl (1971), Whyte (1980), Alexander (1987). Christopher Alexander's theory identified the failures of existing design theories based mainly on the visual- tradition but have ignored the contexts that frame them. He pointed to the importance of the relationships between the activities and places and goes farther in his 'A Pattern Language' (1977) to sketch out patterns of the minimal framework of essentials necessary that are then to be refined by the designers.

Lynch's seminal work '*Image of the City*' (1960) is claimed to have sparked an interest in the way the public perceived and thus the used urban spaces. He acknowledged the importance of visual methods of designing and representing space, however points out that "...the pleasure users get from cities is a common place experience shared by different people..." (1960, p.1). Hence all can appreciate urban environment and that the pleasure or sense of good urban environment is not exclusive to, and the concern of only the elite.

Therefore, he suggested that the city is experienced through the everyday events and association both past and present in relationship to other things. His work is important to urban design theories and caused a paradigm shift in the understanding of urban spaces. It introduced new ways of appreciating the urban environment and thus changed the study of cities from being an objective thing examined using scientific knowledge methods of analysis to that of user perceptual experience and behaviour.

Relph (1976), Tuan (1977) and Canter (1977a) all concur that the relationship between place and *place-ness* is determined by three elements; the physical, the activities and the meanings. According to Canter, place is conceived by the user differently hence the importance of considering the user perspective in their creation. This stems from what he saw as the influence of physical attributes on psychological and behavioural processes. Others contributing to the tradition are Jane Jacobs and Allan Appleyard whose arguments are underpinned on the socio-economic aspects of the city seen in the activities on the streets, sidewalks and parks.

1.2.3 The Place-Making Tradition

A shift in the thought in urban design occurred since 1980s with emphasis now on 'making places for people' as pointed out by Carmona *et al* (2003, p.7). This is due to re-examination of new definitions from Gibberd (1953), Jacobs (1961) and Buchanan (1988). Gibberd postulated that the design of towns ought to be functional as well as pleasurable in appearance. His work combines both the visual-artistic and social-usage traditions. It began to recognize the complexities of designing and creating places in terms of the physical arrangement of buildings, but also the subjective quality of beauty. This was not any different to Vitruvius thinking on building having commodity and delight.

Jacobs on the other hand argued that a wider contextual approach to urban design as if it were an architectural problem would be similar to substituting art for life. Therefore, sole architectural solutions will not solve urban problem because they are not sole determinants. While Buchanan pointed out that place-making was essentially what urban design was about, arguing that spaces become places because of the logical relationships to the meanings assigned to them by the activities and events a view supported by Bohl (2002).

Therefore, the place-making tradition is a fusion of the visual-artistic and social-usage approaches that looks at urban design as 'an aesthetic entity and a behavioural setting' (Carmona *et al.,* 2003; p.7). It is very much interested in how well the physical built environment affords functions and activities that take place in them. This shifts the focus of urban design to include the management of the public realm making it the public face of the building; the spaces between frontages, activities taking place in and between the spaces and the management of all the activities that are affected by the buildings (Gleave, 1990).

1.3 The Critiques of Urban Design up to 1960s

As previously, discussed, normative theories are by their nature prescriptive. It is interesting to note that the three fundamental schools of thought in urban design; the visual-artistic, the social-usage and the place-making traditions are all normative. They have varying degrees of prescription with Lynch's work being the least prescriptive. Carmona *et al* (2003, p.11) argue that the urban designer should be less prescriptive about the urban form because of the various degrees of appropriateness in response to the social, cultural, economic and political contexts that frame it.

The period after the Second World War heralded the questioning of the acceptance of normative thinking within the social sciences. Scholars pointed to the atrocities of the war especially in Nazi Germany and Stalin's Russia as the origins of the questioning (Fromm, 1955; Lyotard, 1984). Erich Fromm was a major psychoanalytic thinker, sociological theorist, and public intellectual during the 1940s and 1950s. He was critical of the sociological relativist position that "...each society is normal in as much as it functions..." (1955, p.12). In his view, a society is deemed sane on the basis of comparison to another by implication there must exist a set of universal criteria for measuring the sanity. However, this he points can be problematic in that it leads to a deterministic view that "...human nature is malleable and can be influenced by decisive environmental factors..." (1955, p.13).

Jean-François Lyotard a French philosopher questioned the foundation of the republican ideals pointing to the *differend* that he saw in politics. He argued that:

> "...In a republic, the pronoun of the first-person plural is in effect the linchpin of the discourse of authorization. Substitutable for a proper name, We, the French people ..., it is supposedly able to link prescriptions (such as articles in codes, court rulings, laws, decrees, ordinances, circulars, and commandos) onto their legitimization "in a suitable way." The republican regimen's principle of legitimacy is that the addresser of the norm, y, and the addressee of the obligation, x, are the same. The legislator ought not to be exempt from the obligation he or she norms. And the obligated one is able to promulgate the law that obligates him or her ...We *decree as a norm that it is an obligation for us to carry out act a.* This is the principle of autonomy..." (1988, p.98)

His analysis of the above statement revealed that there was a difference in the application of the decrees in that the one who spoke the law and the one to whom the law was spoken were not the same person. It was declaration that propagated the continued inequality of capitalist class division. The normative thought here suggests in like manner to Fromm's view that value system of one sector of society is applied to the other for purposes of all being normal.

This is perhaps the view that was taken by a lot of the designers in 1930s and 1940s with a belief that if a good environment were provided, then the social problems would be solved because better human beings would result. The thought is based on assumptions of opposite dialectics; right or wrong existing for every human problem without necessary examining the societal context. The right or wrong is presumed to be values of the normal society imposed on the abnormal society.

However, the atrocities of the Second World War revealed the fallacy of the concept in what Fromm saw as "consensual validation...Where it was assumed that if majority of people shared certain ideas, then they must be valid..." (1955, p.14). A view supported by Wood *et al.* (1996) positing that past research found that recipients agreed with majority group positions and resisted minority group positions on direct measures of influence. They see the cause as desire to "...align with valued majority and to differentiate from the derogated minorities because of normative pressures" (1996, p.118).

The contexts for questioning continued to interrogate power relationships within the capitalist societies. Therefore, an antagonism existed between what was viewed by majority as normal versus what actually defined it leading to emergence of new thinking within psychology circles (see Deleuze, 1968; Laing, 1966 etc.). Keith Ansell Pearson points to Deleuze's lecture of 1960s on Bergson's Creative Evolution that argued that we have to think beyond the existing human conditions making references to Nietzsche philosophical "story of how the "true world" finally became a fable, which is also a story of the devaluation of the highest values and the advent of nihilism" (2007, p.2). It challenged the human thought to seek reconnection with the universal consciousness beyond the relativism, as had been the norm. Deleuze began the philosophical search for a new thinking within the individual, the site for questioning of the true human condition as revealed by the upheavals of the Second World War, the Vietnam War that was going on and the at the same time the inequalities that the individuals could see. The media of course played a great role in revealing what was happening elsewhere.

The new thinking began to create influence in the design field when Jane Jacobs (1961) among others questioned the trends in renewal and development that were destructive of the environment. They asked where were the rights of the individuals to participate in the design decisions that affect their livelihood. Across the USA, the design students and professional faculty actively started to support the minorities to protest by offering services to design alternative proposals to those of the establishment. Two examples are highlighted below, the students at University of California, Berkeley and Columbia University in New York.

Ward (1993) posits that the actions of the Free Speech Movement at University of California, Berkeley in 1968 were a starting point of the design thinking process. The students had "...devised a compromise plan to diffuse the confrontations of the People's Park by forging agreement for the city to lease land from the University..." Ward (1993, p.8). The student protests movement had actually begun in 1964 over "...political activity and speech, but then stimulated complaints about education..." As pointed out by Meyerson (1966, p.714). This also coincided with the student activism at Columbia University in New York.

The student unrest at Columbia University started in April 1968 and it involved both students and none students alike who had been swept into the wave of action as pointed out by Slonecker penning:

> "...Tom Hayden was not a student at Columbia University. Still, at two o'clock on the morning of April 26, 1968, he found himself "joining a silhouetted wave of students surging across Columbia's grounds and entering, with a key volunteered by a graduate student..." (2008, p.967).

The Students for a Democratic Society (SDS) and the Students Afro-American Society (SAS) had coordinated protests to gain maximum support from most students. Slonecker (2008) points out that the students had several grievances that included issues of institutional racial inequality in dealings with community, involvement with Vietnam War through provision of research support to the Department of Defence and issues related to disciplinary processes when dealing with students.

The media reports created further support for the students from other activists' groups such as the Student Non-Violent Coordinating Committee (SNCC), the Congress for Racial Equality (CORE) as well as the residents of the area. The events at Columbia highlight the importance of coalition between the racially divided student body and the ethical issues of politics and culture that they had to deal with.

Slenecker (2008) argues that the coalition at Columbia had two important significances; firstly, it revealed that the New left counter-culture was not confined to the west coast (Berkeley area) as had previously been thought of and despite the tense relationships between the black and white activists suggest it may have been possible to have a single social movement under the right conditions. However, this was never to be despite various attempts in mid 1960s.

The problem of the Morningside Park however had a long history. Columbia University had planned to have a gym in it as early as 1920, but lack of finances did not allow it. However, in 1961 it was able to lease the 2.1 acres of the park from the New York City authorities and embarked on the process of fundraising. The City had required the university to provide a facility that was accessible to the Harlem residents as pointed out by Slonecker (2008).

The Morningside Heights was a mixed community of minorities from working class black, Chinese and Puerto Ricans. The park even though did not provide much in recreation amenities; it served as a buffer between the community and the white Ivory Tower of Columbia University, the epitome of class division. The lease of the property in 1961 turned the Columbia University president into "the biggest slum lord in Harlem" (Slonecker, 2008; p.970); and by 1968 almost 85% of the seven thousand evicts were from minority backgrounds.

It is not surprising that a climate of resistance developed mainly due what Slenecker (2008) identified as "inept communication and competing visions" for the Morningside Park between the community. This revealed that participation of the community in the design decision-making process about their place is strongly dependent of the level and quality of communication channels used.

John Lindsay, a local candidate for Mayor in 1965 brought the issue to the political campaign when he opposed the development because "...the immediate neighbourhood had not been sufficiently involved in the process..." (Slenecker, 2008; 970). It was the start of opposition to development from various groups in 1966,

West Harlem Morningside Park Committee in January, CORE Columbia chapter in February, SDC among others.

The protesters at Columbia employed a unique strategy of using different activist groups to occupy different locations on campus but networked to form one single voice. In particular, the architecture students questioned the existing tense relationship between the university and the neighbouring Harlem community. The activism stemmed from two influential academics, Peter Prangell (had left by 1968 to join University of Toronto) and Herman Hertzberger who had promoted the idea of subversive architecture that served the community.

The students resolved that:

> "...The University should adopt an expansion policy that doesn't overrun adjacent areas; that the University should make a conscious effort to recruit more black and Puerto Rican students; [and] that the administration should give greater recognition to students and community groups in the formulation of University policy..." (Slenecker, 2008; p.974).

The students were commenting on the modernist urbanism of expansion into adjoining areas for social engineering reasons as well as the urban renewal programs promoted in the US during that period. They were also taking an ethical stand, calling for equal opportunities for all and for a voice in matters that affected their lives while at the university and challenged the relevance of education to the problems of the world. These were issues of justice, equality, and participatory design processes and democracy.

The architecture student did not stop at making resolutions but saw their role as designers to include meditation of community conflicts. The process they used in collaboration with other students in their building (Avery Hall) and "...held a "design-in" to create a blueprint for gym construction on land already owned by the University, illustrating a unique enthusiasm for proposing alternative solutions to protest conflicts..." (Slonecker, 2008; p.981). The design-in came about using a design thinking process that came out of the new consciousness.

The activities of the New Left counter-culture occurred both in the east, mid-west and west of the United States at most important institutions of higher learning. The student's actions during the riots of 1969 at Berkeley were part of the period of student radicalism against a host of issues including anti-Vietnam military actions, drafts, against undemocratic university regimes and perhaps environmental injustices and inequality.

Peter Allen points out that there was more: "...it was a conflict *over competing visions of urban space* played out at the People's Park..." (2007, p.i) [emphasis mine]. He identifies that the counterproposal was done through a collaborative design thinking processes between the professionals and students drawing on the new consciousness that was emerging. Therefore, it became a test bed for community design theories.

Allen links the protests to the actions of the elite through the different organizations that used endowments to promote the principles espoused by the modern movement. He points to the campus planning publications of the Ford Foundation's Education Foundation Laboratories (EFL) formed in 1958 whose purpose:

> "...Was to help schools and colleges maximize the quality and utility of their facilities, stimulate research, and disseminate information useful to those who select sites, plan, design, construct, modernize, equip, and finance educational structures and the tools therein" (Marks, 2001; p.1).

Allen concurs and argues that EFL "...advocated for modern architecture and planning on American universities, and in critical countries such as Germany..." (2007, p.4). Many universities across USA developed links with EFL to meet the physical needs of expansion in education to the demands of the baby boomers. It was through this relationship that U.C. Berkeley had proposed the demolition of the large residential neighbourhood south of the campus.

The area had previously been designated for urban renewal from as early as 1957 that under federal law could only happen if the area was blighted but was silent on the process of determination. It was not surprising that the Berkeley Planning Department therefore shortly issued another report titled, "The Problem of Blight in Berkeley" which both revealed an interest in social transformation of the area through modernist design principles.

Therefore, I argue that the People's Park was a site of confrontation and contestant of competing ethos of community building and how it was to have been carried out, either through design thinking process or normative process. Allen aptly asserts that:

> "...It presented with two conflicting paradigms of design and governance... Those in power saw social disintegration in events like those at Berkeley, while those at the bottom saw the rebirth of a new kind of community power to protest the unjust imposition of an urban order..." (2007, p.6).

This view is in line with one by Lyotard's (1988) questioning of the foundation of the republican ideals pointing to the *differend* that he saw in politics.

Manuel Castells makes the argument that in a capitalist society, "... the state through various organs has holds over the problems associated with the environment..." (1972, p.1). These he sees as arising out of interrelated actions of class division through social and political practices. In other words, he saw a strong correlation between the social injustices, ethical problems and the political ideologies held by those societies. The constituent authorities rejected the proposals by the students at the University of California, Berkeley and the Columbia University in New York.

In all the places where the student riots had begun in the Denmark, France, Spain and US, an underlying theme was the rights to determine and participate in how the built and natural environment was carried out. Perhaps they tie in with a growth in environmental movements in 1960s because of the perception of the harm that man caused to the environment. (For more on this see work by Dunlap and Mertig, 1992 titled "American environmentalism: the U.S. environmental movement, 1970-1990").

The impacts of the radical social theories of Goodman, Laing, and others who had continuously questioned the existing theories and actions on society and lambasted the scientific methods that was dominant at that time. What was at clear from the historical events of the period is the issue of the right to the participatory processes in democracy: what Ward calls:

> "...The power of self-determination, the power to shape one's own environment, the power to define the terms of reference of one's own destiny, and all of this was encapsulated in a struggle for the power to determine meaning..." (1993, p.9).

The 1960s was therefore a period that embodied the hope for democracy, equality, social justice and the possibility to transform the world by young people and toppling of the older generation. It is however interesting to note that the drive for new thinking came from the academic emigrants who had been at the Frankfurt School. The next section will look at the development of what is known as social architecture and how that led to community design and participatory design thinking processes.

1.4 Social Architecture

The growth of social responsibility was manifested in the new consciousness expressed by the students in alternative proposals at Berkeley and Colombia campus riots. There was collaboration between not only the professionals but also the students to work with the communities to build their capacities to ask questions and offer alternative views to that of the elite. In this sense, Social Architecture is also known as "Socially Responsible Design" that is achieved through design thinking process between the various participants (professionals, student and users).

Most definitions of social responsibility are from social and political perspectives of cultural context as pointed out by Ward (1993) who observes:

"...That the issues of equality, justice, the redistribution of resources, ownership of the means of production, civil rights, participatory democracy, critical citizenship were more evident in the work of design students in 1960s and 1970s than today..." (1993, p.6).

He blames the absence of emancipator of post-modernism for the demise of the radical thoughts and points out that in the 1960s, knowledge was recognized as ideological and had the purpose of conservatively maintaining the existing hierarchical structures of power and authority. This led to the continued sustenance of the existing orders of resource distribution. Bourdieu supports this view and points out that "knowledge is situated in space and time" (1977, p.2) hence it is tacit as opposed to practical and is of and about the social world.

Social architecture also grew out of the CIAM's desire to respond to urban problems of appropriate and affordable housing shortages in the industrializing Europe. The 1929 CIAM 2 at Frankfurt had focused on the design of minimum housing as part of what Mumford described as "...the effort to standardize and rationalize dwelling units within the smallest volume..." (2000, p.31). However, the main driver seems to have been the searches for radical urbanism solutions based on the *dom-kommuna* or communal house; ideas coming out of the Marxist Soviet Union (Mumford, 2000). It was seen as a deterministic tool for transforming society to the acceptance of a more collective mode of life that Moisei Ginzberg founder of the OSA Group (Organization of Contemporary Architects) and others saw as "... socially superior mode of life..." (Quoted in Mumford; 2000, p.38).

The first image (*Figure 1.1*) illustrates how the propaganda of photo montage was used to promote the idea that CIAM's architecture would result in much better life than in traditional European cities at that time. It shows a couple relaxing in their balcony suggesting liberated people in recreation within confines of their dwelling away from the polluted streets. The emphasis was on the qualities perceived to be essential for biological functions of humans: light, air and opening (*licht, luft, oeffnung*).

The second image (*Figure 1.2*) showed plants brought into living areas in tandem with the living in the sky philosophy. It was to demonstrate how the high-rise buildings would transform lives by bringing pleasures close to living areas. The two images are critical in understanding the context within which CIAM propaganda operated especially after the Second World War.

The horrors and the inhumanity of post Second World War created the need for resettlement. Massive rebuilding efforts ensued that led to the interrogation of the place and meaning of dwelling in relationships to the society and humanity. CIAM advanced an ideology that appeared inclusive. Within CIAM an international forum of professionals and educators called Team X emerged and began the campaign for

Figure 1.1: Liberated Living.
Mumford (2000, p.32)

Figure 1.2: Urban Garden in Sky.
Mumford (2000, p.35)

the reconstruction that would include both the contexts of the social structures and cultural traditions.

Team X was composed of loosely organized individuals, however the core group consisted of Jaap Bakema, Georges Candilis, Giancarlo De Carlo, Aldo van Eyck, Alison and Peter Smithson and Shadrach Woods (Heuvel and Risselada, 2005). The individual members had joined meetings CIAM at different dates. They were vocal enough to have changes made to involvement of younger persons. It is however difficult to establish the exact date when the group began because of the type of organization it was.

In addition, the generational gap between the older CIAM members and younger new ones caused tensions leading to the formation of Team X after the tenth congress in Dubrovnik in1956. The group's major departure from CIAM ideology was their belief in Utopia which had social dimensions that allowed for both the individual and the collective identities. They saw the *importance of context specific response in design process rather that the use of universal solutions to social problems* [emphasis mine]. This saw an opportunity for a new beginning that had a moral imperative towards to society (Heuvel and Risselada, 2005).

Bakema had argued that a new approach underpinned by the life of the community was needed pointing out that:

> "...The study of techniques and aesthetics are not of primary use, but rather the study and understanding of a new structure of society. Regulations

> being made now for the reconstruction must be based on ideas about life... The modern architect must be able to communicate with people...Beauty has to express openness in human relationships to make a new style."
> [1946, quoted in Harrison (1998, p.10)]

Accordingly, Bakema was in essence criticizing the approaches by the visual-artistic tradition architects and pointing to the importance of the transformation in the society that arose from the modernity, and industrialization.

The state of urban design today and its history is related to the ways the professional and institutional settings changed after Second World War. It firstly established itself as a field in the academic arena in the US Universities before the rest of the world then later took hold in the professional arena (Vernez-Moudon, 1992).

However, at its root is the modernism that grew after the war led by CIAM, and the Green City Movement, GCM (Jacobs and Appleyard, 1987). Both movements proposed responses to the ills of the industrial city in very different ways, one resulting in the suburbs and the other in the destruction of both the suburb and the inner-city housing to create the vertical high density functional city. The ills have been discussed previously under heading "critiques of urban design".

Even though the movements grew out of concern for people, the proposed solution did not seem comprehensive enough in approach to examine the pros and cons of values such as the environment, public-ness, the community, and further, as Jacobs and Appleyard make the assertion, "...they threw the baby out with the bath water..." (1987, p.114).

The concern for the social meanings and other issues ignored during the heights of CIAM and GCM marshalled the birth of community design and advocacy movements. It has to be pointed out that there were other factors that also contributed to its growth such as the civil rights movement, urban social movements. The concern of the community design and advocacy movements have centred on the social groups who were negatively impacted by the urban design as promoted and practiced by CIAM and modernism. This was especially true with the rebuilding of cities through demolitions and destruction of existing communities without regard for the positive values in social, cultural, political and economic aspects that they contributed to the built environment.

David Harvey (2003) argued that the right to the city raised several questions; who's right and whose city; how are these rights to be exercised? The issue is contentious especially if one is to take the history of the city from the Marxist point of view as dominated by the accumulation of capital. How then can a socially just city be created if the capitalist economic engine allocates disproportionate power to the ruling class? Robert Park argued that aptly:

> "...If the city is the world which man created, it is the world in which he is henceforth condemned to live. Thus, indirectly, and without any clear sense of the nature of his task, in making the city man has remade himself..." (1925 quoted in Harvey, 2003, p.939).

Since man has no choice in location of place to live, he surely must have the rights to control of that environment. The connection between man and the environment is closely tied than one would imagine that there exist within society the collective desires or will to make the changes together that would not be injurious to all. Harvey agrees with Park and asserts, "...the right to the city is not merely a right of access to what already exists, but a right to change it after our heart's desire..." (2003, p.941).

Perhaps the way forward to the collective rights can be asserted through the development of a new consciousness as viewed by the Surrealist Benton who posits: "...it gave birth of a new movement with an even greater power of liberation..." (1948, p.46). I argue that the new consciousness that led to clamour for advocacy and participatory design thinking developed because of the several events that framed it. The events like the new thinking that I pointed to earlier in the book, of questioning of the way the world is perceived. The questioning of normality, the inequalities post Second World War and many other circumstances. The next section looks at the rise of meaning of participatory engagement within urban design and what is involved.

1.5 Community Engagement

Before interrogating the meaning of community engagement, it is important to frame how the term community is understood within the book. The term community is nebulous, hence equally raises questions on who can and should participate in the new consciousness of transforming their environment. This is not new because there has always been a struggle between two views espoused by those who support individual rights versus those who support the collective rights.

Gusfield (1975) defined a community as the geographical and territorial aspects, and the quality of human relationships irrespective of the location. McMillan and Chavis (1986) building on the above saw the community to have explicit and identifiable characteristics. Such as membership or sense of belonging, influence in the sense of having a voice to make a difference, integration, which relates to the first and finally having a shared emotional connection. Therefore, community means a group of people that identify with the territory or geographical location and have claimed the rights to make perceptible influence to its management and are emotionally tied to the location through the various activities and relations.

Ancient Greek builders used *'tektons'* a process or learning by making in their design processes for testing or prototyping of the materials (Tepavčević, 2017). This continued in the renaissance with the new ways of seeing things through architectural representation. In the 20th Century, there have been great architects who have followed the methodology of working using prototypes: Antonio Gaudí, Frei Otto, Peter Zumthor and Herzon & de Meuron among others that have been able to realize very complex design solutions.

Various authors have attempted to define design thinking as consisting of "...a productive mix of both analytical and intuitive thinking..." (Martin & Euchner, 2012), driven by the use of the historical context while using contemporary data to make decisions. It is seen as both reaching back to time and forward to the future that is imagined. It is a process that comes from "...failure-friendly, iterative prototyping immersible social research..." Tokinwise (2011). It involves problem identification and definition and solution finding through a co-evolution by all those affected and includes both the expert designers and the community. It is "...concerned with not only the products and wide range of tools..., but also the ...methods, the processes from other disciplines driven by concern for human experiences..." (Gobble, 2014). Others have seen it as "a human centred approach to problem solving (Brown, 2008). The various definitions and understandings is well summarized as "...a discipline that uses the designer's sensibility and methods to match people's needs with what is technologically feasible and what is a viable business strategy that can convert into customer value and market opportunity..." Gobble (2014).

Design Thinking (DT) was initially started by David Kelley of Stanford University and popularized by Tim Brown of IDEO and Barry Katz from their consultancy work that is creative innovation driven to develop products (Katoppa & Sudradjat, 2015). However, the term DT has been widely used writhing research design from the early 1970s by Cross,1972, Kimbell, 2009 and Doorst, 2010. Central to the DT argument of Brown are: collaboration, focus on human needs, innovation and sustainability. These occur in three spaces of Inspiration (where problems are identified, defined and opportunities for solving them); Ideation (development of ideas, tried through prototyping,) and Implementation (where comprehensive vision is developed and produced for the users).

Various authors have attempted to define design thinking as consisting of "...a productive mix of both analytical and intuitive thinking..." (Martin & Euchner, 2012) driven by the use of the historical context while using contemporary data to make decisions. It is seen as both reaching back to time and forward to the future that is imagined. It is a process that comes from "...failure-friendly, iterative prototyping immersible social research..." Tokinwise (2011). It involves problem identification and definition and solution finding through a co-evolution by all those affected and includes both the expert designers and the community. It is "...concerned with not only the products and wide range of tools..., but also the ...methods, the processes from other disciplines driven by concern for human experiences..." (Gobble, 2014). Others have seen it as "a human centred approach

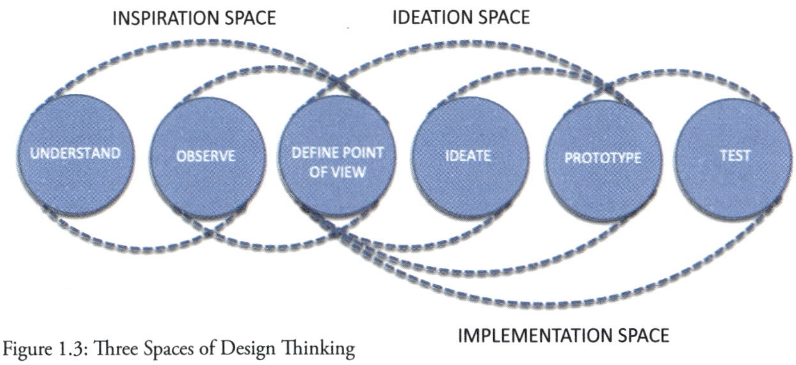

Figure 1.3: Three Spaces of Design Thinking (Katoppa & Sudradjat, 2015; pp. 122).

to problem solving (Brown, 2008). The various definitions and understandings are well summarized as "...a discipline that uses the designer's sensibility and methods to match people's needs with what is technologically feasible and what is a viable business strategy that can convert into customer value and market opportunity..." Gobble (2014).

Community design, as a design thinking process used by urban design laboratories has its history in the 1950s as Advocacy planning; then in the 1960s became known as Community Design. It has its roots in the period of awakening and acknowledgment of human rights in the world (Toker and Toker, 2006). The ideas are rooted in the works of Davidoff (1956), Lefèbvre (1967) and Harvey (1973). Today it is seen as a new idea yet it was in the mainstream many decades ago. The understanding of the concept and the terms "community design" and "participatory design thinking" has changed over this period and this has had an impact on the practice and theory of urban design. Toker and Toker point to studies by Arnstein (1969) and Wulz (1986) that revealed the changes from the ideological phase to the pragmatic phase in the 1980s and 1990s.

Participatory urban design thinking is more about a *process* of a design than design as a *product*, the *process* of creating the vision of a community. It is concerned with community building, and designing for the community (Sanoff, 2008). It places the emphasis on the *participants and stakeholders* at the centre of decision making rather than the expert professional.

Both Sanoff (2000) and Wates (2000) define community design as an interdisciplinary movement with the focus on involvement of local people in the design thinking process and management of their built environment on the basis that the professional's technical knowledge is often inadequate for the resolution of social problems. Therefore, the process adds a moral and political content to the professional practice and education. It is a movement for discovering how to make it possible for people to be involved in the shaping and management of their environment.

There are seven main aims of the participatory urban design thinking (Hester, 2006). They are aimed firstly, at creating the everyday environment in which people spend most of their time. Secondly, meeting the unique needs of people who will use the particular built environment in the design and planning process; thirdly, empowering the voiceless communities and peoples. The fourth, addresses the environmental inequalities; fifth, the creation of environmental justice, sixth, environmental injustices and last one the participation in the design and planning decision making. The tasks align with the key issues of the movements from the 60s i.e., to provide people with a voice, civil rights and advocacy. It is not surprising that the initial phase of the community participatory design thinking process is advocacy planning where the designers act as the community organizers and advocates for empowerment and progress (Davidoff, 1956; Arnstein, 1971 and Alinsky, 1972).

Participatory design thinking methodology is action based, i.e., a way to understand knowledge by doing. It relies on the traditional, "the tacit and often invisible ways that people perform their everyday activities" as pointed out by Spinuzzi (2005, p.163). Therefore, it has its own articulated methodological orientation, and techniques and draws on several methods such as ethnographic, observations, interviews, and analysis of artefacts and sometimes protocol analysis. The methods are used to construct the emerging design through an iterative process. The participant's interpretations are important to the process not just to the confirmation of the design as a common vision.

The participatory design thinking process has Marxist underpinnings and attempts to examine the tacit and invisible aspects of human activities by the designer and the community through partnership of co-designing the artefacts (urban design framework or building). The process is ITERATIVELY so that the designer and participant stakeholders can *develop and refine their understanding of the activity* (emphasis mine). Pelle Ehn (1993) supports the view arguing that it steers a course between the traditional and transcendence, the community's tacit knowledge and the designer's abstract analytical knowledge.

The citizen's power for self-decision making is the foundation of the participatory design thinking process and has taken different forms during various periods as seen from the literature on processes from the 1960s to the present date. Arnstein's (1971) ladder of citizen participation (*Figure 1.4*), reveals that the process begins to fall from top rung 7 or 8 (the delegated power and citizen control) to 4 or 5 (the consultation and placation stages). Interestingly, the 1990s was the more of collaborative decision-making that was approach was likened to lace creation. The changes within the participatory design thinking processes are thus on the "area of focus rather than the field" (Toker and Toker, 2006). The participatory design

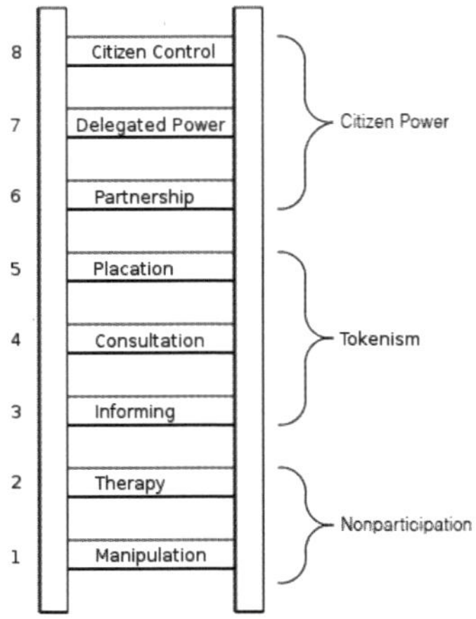

Figure 1.4: Eight levels of participation. French students. (Arnstein; 1969, p. 218-219)

Figure 1.5: A poster painted by rebelling. (Arnstein; 1969, p. 218-219)

thinking process becomes partly false or takes the pretence mode as illustrated by poster carried by protesting French students during the May 1968 riots (*Figure 1.5*). It reads "I participate, you participate, he/she participates, we participate, you participate...they profit" hence the scepticisms in the process and is likely to lead to failure. The community must buy into the process for its success.

Wulz (1986) conducted a study that revealed a shift from an advocacy approach to a continuum approach. In the latter, the power relations of the citizens in the decision-making ladder are reduced from one condition to another without abrupt changes being noticed. The citizens′ power is reduced from one of "maximum say to a minimum say" starting from self- decision, to a co-decision between the participating stakeholders and the designers, then alternative solutions being offered either by the designers or representatives of any of the stakeholder groups, regionalism, where regional solutions are pushed as the best alternative and finally one achieved through dialogue.

Toker and Toker (2006, p.158) have also pointed to a study that identified key issues. Leaders and priorities on participatory design thinking indicate that the process has now moved to the mainstream of urban design and the lines of thought being used have mutated. The idea of genuine participation is still supported, but the new focus on pragmatic consensus building rather than on idealistic advocacy that has allowed approaches by Congress of New Urbanism, CNU, *charrette* to borrow the terminology.

However, the new urbanism has been criticized by score of scholars as leaning towards spatial determinism (Sorkin 1998, Talen, 1999, and Hayden 2003), while the *charrette* approach has been criticized for being composed of information sessions termed participatory design thinking meetings where the designers do not act as facilitators. The term facilitator, as used in the book refers to an expert who leads the *charrette* to provide the technical know-how, clarify the problems identified and help build the capacity of the group to participate effectively.

The move towards a consensus building approach rather than advocacy shifts the focus away from citizens' participation (place creation theoretical paradigm) to social-usage and visual-artistic theoretical paradigms. The genuine participatory design thinking approach is still possible and should be focused on local communities having control of the decision-making about issues that affect the whole community. Secondly, the approach should include all stakeholders, particularly the minorities; thirdly, should be used to generate goals and strategies through maximum participation possible and consensus building. The fourth is that the action comes at the end of the process (detailed designed occurs after this stage).

1.5.1 Participatory Design Thinking Processes

Participatory urban design thinking process relies on the tacit knowledge of the community, on what are important objectives, linkages and visions. The designers do not possess the tacit knowledge, as they are not immersed in the community through either work or residence and therefore, they possess only abstract knowledge. Participatory design thinking on the other hand is founded on the constructionist theory that explicitly resists the notion that knowledge can be completely compartmentalized. In this theory, knowledge is acquired through a constructive process in which the participant learner builds an internal and personal illustration of the knowledge, but is continually open to modification. The structure and linkages form the ground on which another new knowledge is attached (Bednard *et al.,* 1995).

The conceptual growth in knowledge in the participatory design thinking process comes from sharing the various perspectives held by the stakeholders and users and at the same time the simultaneously changing of the internal representations in response to the perspectives held by others during the dialogue and cumulative experience. Spinuzzi (2005) sees this knowledge as a complex of artefacts, practices and interactions, therefore interpretive.

Therefore, the knowing and learning take place in a dynamic system of people, practices, artefacts, communities and institutional practices (Mirel, 1998). The knowledge in participatory design thinking process is about being involved, having the practical understanding that comes from the experience as opposed to theoretical reflection. The process oscillates between the *discovery* of tacit knowledge held by the community and stakeholders which the designers and participants *critically reflect* before proceeding to the next phase.

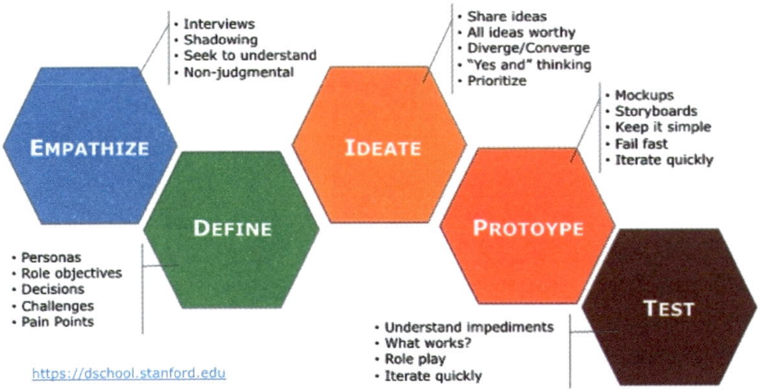

Figure 1.6: Design Thinking Process (Stanford, 2018)

In participatory design thinking process, the community's tacit knowledge is valuable and therefore the focus of the process is on exploring that and is taken into account when developing the design framework. The tacit knowledge is described (in community meeting, a collaborative process) so that it can be used to develop the framework and shared community vision through a process that empowers them. As pointed out earlier, the paradigm in participatory design thinking process is constructivist; the knowledge is a condition of the context. A common language is thus essential to be a bridge between the world of the designer and the community (stakeholders) that is comfortable to all.

The methodology is derived from participatory *action research*, i.e., practice research; "involving the practical interventionist investigations" (as opposed to the traditional method of gathering data) and parallel theoretical reflections (as opposed to posterior) as argued by Ehn (1989, p.13). It has a political-ethical connotation of empowering the community to take control of their built environment with the designer acting as a facilitator and not a decision maker. The success of the process is dependent on the level of emphasis placed on CO-RESEARCH (the Inspirational phase) and CO- DESIGN (the ideation & Implementation spaces) as illustrated in *Figure 1.7.* The conclusions must be found in conjunction between the designer, and the stakeholders (community).

The participatory design thinking process aims to ground changes to the community by empowering all its participants, involving all the participants to build the community. It has been criticized for not lending itself to "radical" changes that sometimes characterize a new system of doing things. The gradual tendency can lead to tunnel vision in which particular stakeholders are served while others are left out, as pointed out by Spinuzzi (2005, p.166). The second criticism is the danger of the participants losing focus on the broad objectives and bogged down in details of the

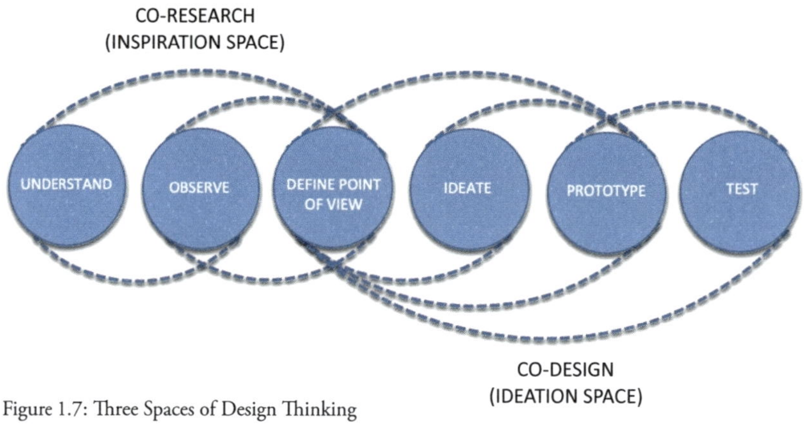

Figure 1.7: Three Spaces of Design Thinking (Katoppa & Sudradjat, 2015; pp. 122).

artefacts rather than the community visioning. This normally manifests itself in the form of arguments over the colour of buildings (because of how they are represented during the community meetings), details of door or windows, issues of style etc. The third limitation comes during the migration of the design methodology from one context to another across socio-economic, cultural and political borders. The difficulties could arise in maintaining the methodological tenets that requires a focus on democratic empowerment. This could turn it into a tool for the powerful to advocate for the consumptive goods at the exclusion of other marginal stakeholders.

1.6 Approaches to Learning/education

Before proceeding further, it is worth looking at impacts of the new consciousness on education starting with the questioning of the definition of normative social and cultural contexts that resulted in the new consciousness in education pedagogy (Goodman, 1960; Illich, 1971; Freire, 1972). The proposals by Illich and Freiri are briefly looked and their impact on architectural education. However, work of Goodman has not been reviewed and I refer readers to (*The Society I Live In Is Mine*, 1962 and *Compulsory Mis-education*, 1964).

The radical schooling movement of the 1960s and early 1970s was critical of the existing educational model because they "...failed to achieve their stated purposes..." (Gross and Gross, 1969). The proponents of radical schooling suggested alternative models that were voluntary rather than compulsory to allow for freedom (Goodman, 1964) and ones that promoted opportunities for abstract learning through networks that supported it (Illich, 1970). The arguments of the proponents of the radical movements were underpinned on the power relationships between the teacher and the learner.

The student unrest witnessed in the late 1960s was seen as result of failure in the system of education. However, Keesbury argued that it was caused by "...frustration and anger because the crusade against war, poverty, and racism had failed and used the schools as a vehicle to vent this anger and frustration..." (1981, p.216). To the radicals there was an urgent need to modify the educational model, from the organization, the curriculum to the pedagogy if the societal ills were to be cured. John Dewey supported the view arguing that, "...unless the local communal life can be restored, the public cannot resolve its most urgent problems to find and identify itself..." (Quoted in Kaplan; 1970, p.7). Keesbury (1981) disagreed arguing that the society needed to change first before drastic changes in the education model that would contradict the societal value system.

Paulo Freiri in *"Education for Critical Consciousness"* (1973) argued that education gained through critical consciousness was emancipating. He saw this as: "...dynamic and rooted in the historical process by which the oppressed struggled unremittingly to remove the slave consciousness which the oppressors had interjected in the deepest recesses of their being..." (1973, p.viii). Therefore, education as a learning activity liberated both the student and the teacher. This happens in non-instrumental problem-solving exercises by defining the problem through the social, cultural, and political historical context that allows for transfer of tacit knowledge between the two before solutions are suggested. It is a reflective practice where all participated in dialogue discourse. Even though Freiri's ideas are utopian, they grow out of experience with the oppressed groups in the process of the struggle, where he was participant observer.

Freiri (1973) suggested a method for liberating literacy that included; the educator engaged in participant observation of the context of the student; followed by co-search (both learner and teacher) of the generative at the language level and the experiential level. The generative world is then transformed into visual language that allows for participants to submerge into the context and emerge as conscious makers of own culture. This is followed by de- codification of the new culture guided by the expert- novice in dialogue with novice-expert cyclic learning process and finally a new creative codification that has critical reflection embedded.

Ivan Illich also in *"Deschooling Society"* (1970) was critical of the traditional schooling model in which students are passive recipient of knowledge from the teacher. This view was in agreement with Freiri who also saw the teacher in the traditional model as authoritarian custodian of societies' rituals. Illich proposed an alternative learning model that is an emancipator in that the citizen developed through learning under guidance of the master facilitator. In his model, the learning occurs through the dialogue process in three ways; between the master and the student; between the students themselves (peer learning), through reflective discourses and through real life experience that integrates theory and practice.

1.7 Architectural Design Education and Urban Laboratories

This section looks at the methods used in architectural education starting with the Beaux Arts model, tracing its developments and the changes that led to the new visual thinking through the modernism and New Bauhaus. It concludes by looking at the growth of participatory-based urban design thinking education model that urban laboratories are underpinned on.

1.7.1 The Ecole des Beaux-Arts and Architectural Education

In order to understand the Beaux Arts model of education, one has to go back to the Seventeenth Century French education system. Vitruvius in his *"Ten Book on Architecture"* posited that an architect required competency in both theory and practice. The practical gained through the real experience on the job, working with hands while the theoretical through ability to reason and explain the development of the design. This view is supported by recent authors such Mohamed Awad who argues that "architecture is both an intellectual practice and pragmatic discourse that responds to the conception and production of buildings" (2002, p.77). Therefore, the educational system that he advocated required the learners to be engaged with the everyday life experiences in some form or the other within the course of learning.

One would imagine that the approach of education of an architect used at the Ecole de Beaux Arts would echo the Vitruvius' model. The methods used in the Ecole des Beaux Arts can be understood from its history (Cret, 1941). He points out that in France, prior to the Seventeenth Century, arts education was not taught within its own facilities, but was carried out under apprenticeship system in workshops and homes of master craftsmen. Therefore, arts and crafts were taught together and the students would learn from the several masters within a particular guild that they belonged to.

Selby (1972) argues that even master masons that led the guilds did not necessarily have the kind of education advocated today. The intellectual, reasoning and practical occurred while the student followed the master. She posits:

> "...It does not appear that literacy was a necessary accomplishment for a mason to become a master of his craft, for clerks were readily available to provide whatever reading and writing skills that might be needed in the transaction of business and the keeping of records in building construction..." (1972, p.397).

However, these were in the days when the process of production of buildings was not conveyed through voluminous sets of drawings. This is evident from the drawings that Renaissance architects like Bernini used to convey instructions for construction of a building like Palazzo Montecitorio in Rome (*Figure 1.8*).

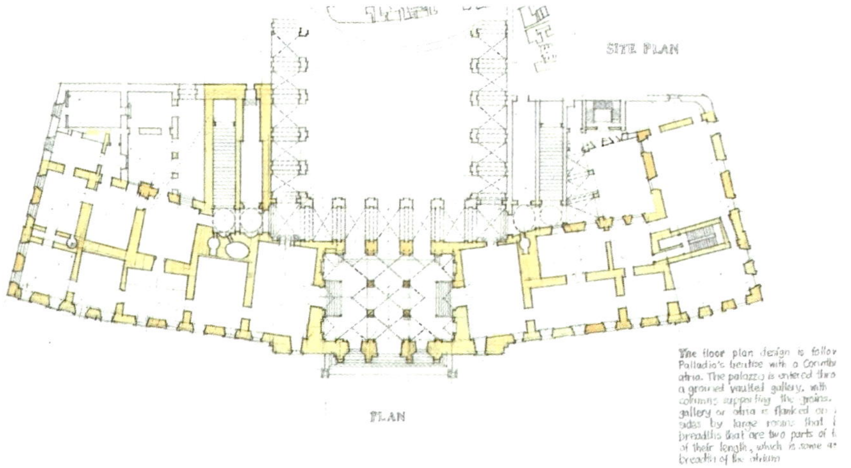

Figure 1.8: Plan of Palazzo Montecitorio

The Figure above is an illustration of how the drawings used in the construction of a prestigious building, as Palazzo Montecitorio were very basic. The work was carried out on instruction of the master mason Carlo Fontana; Bernini himself probably may not have even gone to the site to supervise.

During the renaissance, a transformation occurred that allowed the artists to be freed from the guild system as well as the fine arts from the craft. Moore aptly points to the change positing that:

> "...Beginning of the Renaissance, at which time architects began to seek a social distinction between themselves, as practitioners of the liberal art of decoration, and practitioners of the mechanical art." (1996, p.259).

In Moore's view, the transformation was driven by social rather than technical reasons because of the capitalist class production. Architecture of course was very much tied to the elite aristocrats and the ruling courts. This removed the architect from the actual physical work on the ground thereby rupturing a vital part of the training method. Similar views were expressed by influential architect/ builder Alberti's work *De re aedificatoria* (*On the Art of Building*) of 1450 translated into Italian, French, Spanish and English by the Eighteenth Century. The "...an architect was not a carpenter or joiner and that manual work was not any more instrumental to an architect in his ability to complete the work..." (Moore, 1996; p.259). The perception that the practical work that Vitruvius had previous argued for was beneath the station of one with such a title as well as that there was no much learning to be gained from the endeavour that would have increased his knowledge.

It is not surprising that a crisis in the education of the architect occurred after this period. Literature reveal that his view had support in France as pointed out by Wilkinson (1977) who suggests that Philibert Delorme (1510-70) defined the spheres of appropriate to the patron, the architect and the workman and their relationship. She posits:

> "...The architect was something different, a man who combined the practical experience of the master mason with the knowledge of the amateur, a man schooled not only in books but long experience..." (1977, p.125).

As in most cases, the architect was dependent on a patron to continue his practice and to influence changes in the professional settings. By the Seventeenth Century, the French national government had got involved with the formal training of architects by setting up academy, first within the French Academy of Painting and Sculpture in 1648, later in the Royal Academy of Architecture. 1671 the Royal Academy of Architecture was set up in 1671 with support of the Secretary of State. The students at the academy were instructed in "...construction, geometry, mechanics, military architecture and other required branches..." (Crete, 1941; p.4),

However, even though the model of education was in transformation, it was not until the Nineteenth Century that the École des Beaux Arts (1807) in the form it has been known established itself. The training up to this time was still based on the apprenticeship system lead by either academicians or winners of Prix de Rome who carried out the teaching.

1.7.1.1 The System of Education

The Beaux Arts curriculum had two parts, the first class and the second class arranged in themes as explained later in the book. The courses were not in a neat telescopic order as seen in today's schools. The student had to earn credits by completing all the required courses over the period of stay, generally around five years. The only restriction was that the age to enter an atelier was set at 18 years and one had to complete by the time they were 30 years old.

Weismehl (1967) reveals that the Ecole Beaux de Arts model was organized into ateliers (workshops or studios), in not much different to the guild systems of old. A patron supervised each atelier and an architect approved or sponsored by the administration would run it. However, from 1807 onwards, the architect would normally have been a winner of the prestigious Prix du Rome.

In order to enter the first class, one had to pass a series of examinations, in both oral and written form. The entrance to the Ecole Beaux de Arts was through competition held twice a year for the limited places. Weismehl gives an account of the entrance system that was in two parts; the first was on

> "...General study and the presentation of a solution of a simple building and the second on several written examinations in mathematics, geometry, architectural history etc...." (1967, p.2).

The construction examination was most feared. Prentice (1985) points out that oral examination was held in a lecture theatre where all the 15-20 students were asked questions at random from a name drawn from the hat of the professor.

Prentice gave an account of the events pointing out that one started by joining an atelier to prepare for the entrance examinations with each student placed in own cubicle supervised by the guardians (1985). The examinations were taken over 12 hours and during that period if one left the area they would not be allowed back in and to ensure that was the case, the drawings were stamped and only those were accepted. He also points out that only about 10-12 percent of the students who sat for the examinations were accepted, highlighting the how competitive it was to join the school.

Once a student was accepted to the Beaux Arts School, they would continue learning at the atelier, operated by the students, however supervised by the prominent architects, called *anciens*. These probably were previous winners of Grand Prix and who supported learning of the students without pay but rather out of pride and interest (Prentice, 1985). The atelier members were close and supported each other even though they were in competition among themselves. They identified with the atelier against others elsewhere and hence had a collegial support for one another.

In the atelier system, the student did not receive any direct teaching as is typical of the schools of architecture today. The *anciens* provided critics and Prentice suggests:

> "...It operated on apostolic succession and when the senior students required help on his drawing or his chassis or whatever, he would shout "un nouveau" and a nouveau would run up and offer his services..." (1985, p.385).

However, the students who preferred to spend time working on their projects rarely attended other courses offered at the Academy.

The students had the freedom of choosing an atelier, however, because of the nature of the competition for the Prix du Rome, they had to be strategic in the selection with the view of success depending very much on the leader of the atelier's credentials. However, Weismehl points to the lack of complete independence positing: "...influence of certain atelier' heads on the combined student judging is, nevertheless, a strong factor in the students' selection..." (1967, p.1).

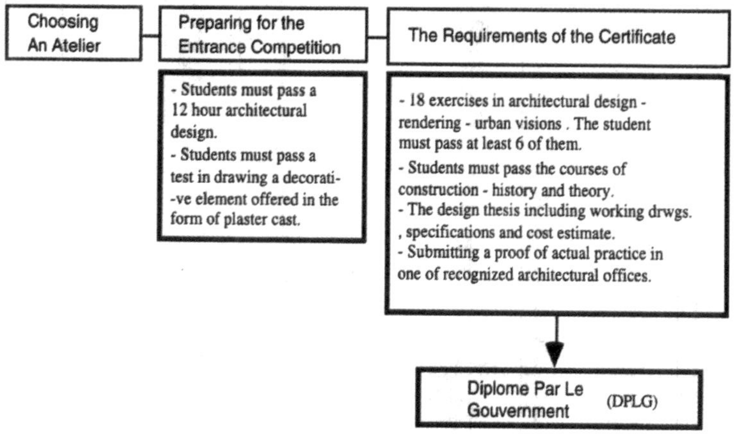

Figure 1.9: Structure of Learning at Beaux Arts.
Salama (1995, p.48).

The reasons according to Carlhian (1979) were in contrast to the strict nature of the system; tenure of the teachers at the Ecole was very difficult and teaching method was rigid. However, Carlhian notes that a master with:

> "...Forty students, selecting an architect as their teacher would ensure the latter to be accepted as a full-fledged member of the teaching body, and eventually of that crucially important ruling body, the architectural jury, which made all decisions on a student's progress as a designer..." (1997, p.1).

This indicates the symbiotic relationship between the master and the student in achieving and propagating the practice to maintain the prestige.

For completion of the course of study, the student was required to pass at least a third of the set exercises in addition to design thesis and working drawings as summarized in *Figure 1.9* above. They also had to prove that they had spent time in practice in one of the recognized offices. This was therefore an essential driver to choosing an atelier as opportunities to gain experience would be enhanced and by the time, they had been at the academy for 5 years.

The curriculum consisted of a series of exercises on five different themes; analytic, scientific, construction, artistic and project (Weismehl, 1967). The Analytic would have involved studying in details the design of existing or formally existing building through copying (*Figure 1.10*). Many modernist scholars have criticized the method used at Beaux Arts; *mimesis* is distinct from copying. According to

Figure 1.10: Analytic Project at Ecole Beaux de Arts.
Moore (1977, p.166).

Calquhoun, "...habit and imitation were the methods by which all artefacts were made, whether these were mainly utilitarian or mainly religious..." (1969, p.71). His arguments were that the artefacts were objects of cultural exchange and as such had both use and exchange value.

In the Beaux Arts system of education, mimesis was of existing or formerly existing building, plaster cast of models, and ornaments. The artefacts were selected for their iconic or important social values within the given society, as religious objects, buildings of importance or decoration that adorned important buildings. One would argue that the mimesis process allowed for teaching of ethical values to the students.

However, I will not go into the debates of the merits of the method except point to its historical significance later. [For debates on imitation versus copying, see book by Samir Younés (1999). *The true, the fictive, and the real: the historical dictionary of Quatremère de Quincy*].

The Beaux des Arts model of education relied on a system called *dessin au trait,* i.e., outline drawing. Its purpose Moore points out was to:

> "...Teach the artist to see planimetrically in terms of the single wholeness of the contour *exterieur*, rather than in terms of a multiplicity of details, the contours *interieurs*..." (1977, p.146).

The method was innovative in that it allowed for the three sides of an object to be viewed on three different planes at right angles (orthographic projection). Hence the plan was a representation that reduced structure to pure form. This method became the point of criticism of the Beaux Arts method of teaching in that it ignored all other forms of representations.

Paul Zeichner echoes the criticism pointing out that the new students:

> "...Were restricted to copying for several years with the expectation that the formal elegance of the ancient and renaissance masters would be internalized by the time they began to work from life themselves..." (2008).

The image in the precedent page (*Figure 1.10*) is a representation of the temple of Hercules at Corinth. The compositional arrangement is definitely well done, allowing for representation of the essential elements of the temple at different scales to be seen at one glance. The drawing is composed in such a manner that the front elevation of the temple is shown at a smaller scale within a frame as if one was looking at it from a distance via a window or from a portico.

However, the things that stand out in the drawing are the details the columns, the *entablature* and the pediment that allows for simple yet clear identification of the typology as Doric. The learning by copying existing fragments of previous enables the level and the number of details to be shown. It is through this technique that the student would have become familiar with the proportioning system, arrangements and compositional issues related to the analytic techniques.

The second theme in the exam was in scientific subjects of importance to architecture such as geometry, mathematics, materials, forces, drawing and representation techniques in perspectives, etc. The third exercise built on the second; was practical application of the theory of materials and forces carried out through model building and analysis of force paths through the building. The fourth theme was exercises in freehand drawings using charcoal of various plaster cast models of statues and ornaments. It taught not only presentation skills but also observation skills and attitude to detailing. The final theme was a project done once a year. All students were required to pass at least one project a year to meet the requirements.

According to Middleton (1982) and Prentice (1985), the students received a programme that defined the subject of study. This would typically be the design of a monument or most commonplace of buildings such as public lavatories, butcher's shops, telegraph towers, and railway stations. The student had 12 hours to prepare the rough outline also called *esquisse,* that developed into the project over the allocated time.

The final project had to be close to the *esquisse* and if it looked too different it would be rejected. The student developed strategies for preparing outlines that were rough enough yet easy to develop to final solution. The project presented in as style called *pompier,* consisting of columns, pilasters, arches, cornices, pediments, *cartouches*, finials, and cupolas (*see Figure 1.10*).

The students would then work continuously until last minute and deliver the project to the cart called *charrette* pulled by *un nouveau*. Jury composed of the patron and others from different ateliers judged the projects and allocated three possible grades; "medal, mention and *foor*" according to Prentice (1985). The work given *foor* earned no credit and the student repeated in the following year.

The significance of the exercises and sequence is revealed from the view held by François Blondel (1618-1686) who considered the mission of the academy as one of "...to work for the "rétablissement de la belle architecture'..." (1941, p.6). He was pointing to the Roman architecture that had been lost from the period when the Gaols, the Visigoths, the Vandals, and Ostrogoths sacked Rome several times in 387, 410, 455, and 546 BCE that left it in ruins.

The competition system for success and the views held by the masters drove the methodology, which placed great emphasis on presentation skills as pointed out by Weismehl:

> "...The student must *attract* the jury's attention (during the few minutes devoted to his work) by means of a *well-executed presentation in an acceptable manner of rendering*. Although his solution or idea may be imaginatively or thoughtfully conceived, he will very likely *fail with a poor or even mediocre rendering*. The converse is not necessarily detrimental to his entry; a well-delineated and clever arrangement of a mediocre or copied idea will very often gain a positive vote..." (1967, p.3).

The focus could not have been clearer than as expressed above revealing that the presentation and rendering of the projects had to be in a manner` acceptable to the jury. The student had no choice but to stay within the straight jacket provided by the former winners of Prix du Rome. This is corroborated by Cret who suggests that the competition system: "tended to place emphasis on what is most likely to please the judges hence... Hence the undue importance given to the presentation of drawings..." (1941, p.12).

The analytic of plans of existing building as part of the course of study ensured that the students were adept at abstraction and analysis and in finding out a required number of solutions to a problem before selecting the best. This system relegated the importance of using elevations and sections in the analysis placing emphasis on plans. Cret points out that by end of Nineteenth Century, "...students had almost lost interest in all questions of architectural forms; the main elevation still received a modicum of attention..." (1941, p.13). (see Figure 1.10 on analytic of Temple of Hercules at Corinth).

Fundamental to the Beaux Arts model was that the learning that occurred in the studio as well as in practice. The two spheres of influences where critical on formulating a well-rounded architect despite the criticisms labelled at it on the restriction of artistic freedom. The next section will examine how the critiques of the Beaux Arts system led to the development of a new consciousness. It will also make an argument that the new vision also failed in addressing some of the critiques that had been raised.

1.7.2 Enter the New Consciousness: Bauhaus

In the context of the western countries, the Bauhaus as a cultural initiative was very influential "...as a seed for the crystallization of a new practice of art and culture of form..." (Wick, 2000; p.11). It's effect in the Twentieth Century is visible in the history of art and as a genesis of modernism. According to Naylor (1985), the ideas of the Bauhaus were not as innovative as it has been claimed penning: "...other schools of art, design and architecture in Germany had experimented with preliminary courses and interdisciplinary approach..." (1985, p.9). Also, contemporary with the German movements were similar approaches in Russia, Holland and England.

However, Naylor acknowledges that the Bauhaus stood out because: its ideologies epitomized the changing concepts concerning the nature and purpose of design in the early Twentieth Century. He argues that:

> "...It *inherited*, reinterpreted and then rejected the craft ideas of the Nineteenth Century; it attempted to discover the laws of art that could be related to the design and architecture seeking a universal language of form that would represent the *elimination* of social as well as national barriers..." (1985, p.9) [emphasis mine].

Another aspect in which Bauhaus was unique in comparison to other schools in Germany was that the leaders and teachers (Itten, Van Duisburg, Moholy-Nagy, Gropius) were *artists* and constantly attempted to define and redefine its programme. It was thus progressive and responsive to the changing circumstances in the society. They constantly had to defend the ideals of the school due to public pressure as evidenced by the publications about their work to describe and justify the approach of the school [see *Idee und Aufbau des Staatlichen Bauhauses in Weimar* (1923); *New Architecture and the Bauhaus* (1935), *Bauhause* 1919-1928 (1938) among others].

1.7.2.1 The Social History of the Bauhaus

Naylor (1985) points out that the Bauhaus was founded by Walter Gropius in April 1919 and closed in 1933 by the National Socialists. Historically the school operated during the period of the Weimar Republic that ended with the coming to power of the Nazi regime of Adolf Hitler in January 1933. The school was driven by a new consciousness, a new kind of popular as opposed to elitist art.

It was utopian in approach and attempted to respond to the social and political problems of the time especially the emerging Modern Movement that demanded a new language of form for a new age. Naylor argues that the Bauhaus attempted to relate "...creativity and the changing concepts of craftsmanship to the demands of industrial production..." (1985, p14), in other words, it was driven by the advancements in technology.

The school had a very short life span indeed in Germany, but was very influential worldwide and Wick attributes its success to the "...outstanding abilities of Gropius to organize and coordinate..." (2002, p11). He strove to create a balance between a new expressionist art practice and the ideals of craftsmanship of the Middle Ages. The Bauhaus was therefore a meeting place of ideas that fused the practical with the functional ideals that also responded to the emerging surrealist art movement.

The Surrealism as a movement sprung up in France in 1919 from a small circle of literate friends; Andre Breton, Louis Aragon, Philippe Soupault, Robert Desnos, and Paul Eluard (Benjamin, 1978). The movement embodied the dreams of the artist; it represented freedom from the power and domination of the bourgeois patron. Breton pointed out that Surrealism could not be defined solely from constructive or destructive points but from the events in life of the period. It was about "...degree of resistance that determined the more or less certain flight of the mind toward a world at last inhabitable..." (1969, p.125). In this sense, surrealism advocated for the total liberation of man and the immediate social consequences that it would entail, and finally, a revelation of the unknown. The Bauhaus ideal followed on these new consciousnesses that were emerging around the turn of the Twentieth Century.

Bauhaus was seen as the genesis of modernism, however despite this, it had roots to an earlier period of the Industrial Revolution, hence romanticism as pointed out by Wicks (2000). The desire to reconstruct the unity of art and culture of production that had broken down during the industrialization process drove the ideal. It also wanted to connect art to the everyday life through the design of household items. The Bauhaus idea was therefore Utopian or Surreal.

1.7.2.2 The Pedagogy at the Bauhaus

The Bauhaus idea of the art school for modernism has its roots in the historical context of transformation movements of the surrealists, Jugendstil etc. Wicks identify the movements as the medieval mason's lodges and circles around ideas for arts reform by Morris, Semper and the arts and crafts movement. Gropius who in a speech to the German State Parliament in 1920 acknowledged this view positing: "... the Bauhaus was not an experiment, not an original idea, but the logical realization of reform ideas typical of our age..." As farther, pointed out by Wick (2000, p.56). This alludes to the existence of other voices calling for not only the reformation of the art and technology, but also perhaps other schools of art had started trying out the reforms as discussed early in this section of the book.

The Bauhaus ideal was therefore an attempt to unify the fine arts of the old academy system with the applied design system that was emerging in the new arts and crafts schools (*Kungstgewerbeschule*). Wicks (2000) argues that regardless the differences in the how the reforms were to be characterized, five points of agreements emerged. The first, the existing academy system (Beaux Arts model) was outdated; secondly, failures of the old academy led to defensive posturing by its proponents. Thirdly, the use of the idea of workshop training to unite arts and crafts (design and making); supported the fusion of both the fine arts training of the academies with the vocational training of applied design in the architectural study. Fifth, the need for basic course or foundation course that gave all students opportunities to explore and experiment to find their best talent before specializing. The five points are looked at in detail in the sections that follow.

The model of the academy was seen as outdated because it was not responsive to the contextual forces of the society. It had failed to change with the industrialization and advancements of technology leading to the loss of economic benefits to both the tradesmen and the artist in a mass production economy. The proponents of the Bauhaus called for a complete de-linking from this model; however, in public they were timid of the public response. This was seen from Gropius address to the German parliament (quoted previously) and several publications released during the period toning down the perception that the Bauhaus was an experimental system of education.

However, the supporters of the Beaux Arts model argued that any reforms must be underpinned on the craft system that existed pre-industrial revolution. It had responded to the social needs of the society by allowing for the cottage industries to grow and the economic status of the community to develop. Hence, they called for the revival of the handicraft as the basis of the foundation for all the students. In pedagogical terms; they argued, "...art cannot be taught; only techniques from the crafts could be taught and learned..." Wicks (2000, p.58). The Bauhaus proponents agreed with this as they viewed technology as a solution to the social and economic ills of the society. This is a deterministic view that has continued to haunt architecture to date.

The above view led to the development of a pedagogy that would be carried out in the workshop where techniques and working methods of various materials were experimented on. The old academy system was viewed as an idle work that was not productive especially in difficult economic circumstances. Hence, in the new proposal, the students would work on projects, designs and prototypes for industry and for sale to the public.

Wicks (2000) points out that the pedagogical role of the workshop remained vague, limiting the criticism from the old academy supporters. It had the workshops in the craft industries but lacked direct connection to the production process that the Bauhaus now introduced. It is not surprising that the teaching workshop system was dominant at the between 1919 and 1930 when Mies Van De Rohe was the director discussed later.

It is interesting to note that even though the initial idea of starting the new educational model was the elimination of the old academy system of education, the proponents of the Bauhaus were still very much interested in the fine artistic training. Therefore, it developed into an art school where the synthesis of fine arts and applied design met or were unified into a coherent whole. Behrens posits this aptly: "...priority is to consolidate all branches of artistic activities that belong to the visual arts into a single pedagogical entity from shared starting level onwards..." Wicks (2000, p.59). From this developed a collaborative training of architects, artists and building engineers. The key aspect of the reform was the inclusion of architecture in the new unified art school, in the university of design elevating it above the other arts as applied activity that was taught in technical schools.

One of the goals of the reform was the artistic freedom that was integrated with the training in technical methods. The foundation stage or school provided the "...beginning student with the self-experience and self-knowledge to allow them to explore their creative abilities..." Wicks (2000, p.60). It seems rather contrary to the second argument that artistic skills and creativity could not be taught. I would argue that the Bauhaus ideals could easily have been implemented within the existing academy model had it not been for the lack of democratic process of tenure that had existed.

Having looked at the criticisms of the old academy model and the proposals that drove the Bauhaus agenda, I now turn my attention to the details of the pedagogy. At the start of the school in 1919, the teaching method had not been developed, however the course programme at the school were divided into three levels not too dissimilar to the Beaux Arts one. These were the *Lehrlinge* for apprentice, the *Geselten* for the journeymen and the *Jungmeister* for the junior master as pointed out by Wicks (2000).

The pedagogy was underpinned on the idea that all students would learn a craft related to architecture. The workshops were used to build models of types of houses and all kinds of household utensils and there was collaborative work with other allied disciplines such as advertising arts, stage planning, photography and typography. The teaching of craft was integrated into the studio, as all students had to take arts. Local craftsmen gave instruction that politically allowed Gropius programmes of reforms to gain support from the local guilds. However, craft was taught very differently from the way Morris and company would have. Gropius saw handicraft as means to an end in that it was a solution for creating social groups or community of craftsmen working together. They would be the seed for a new more humane just arrangement of society based on ideas of harmony.

1919	1921
1. Study of elementary Materials	1. Study of elementary materials
2. Six (6) Workshops [sculpture, stone masonry, woodcarving, ceramics]	2. Study of Nature
	3. Instructions in design [(drawing, painting, modelling, building); elementary forms; design of planes; body; space; composition]
3. Metals workshop 4. Cabinet making 5. Painting and Decorating 6. Printing and Weaving 7. Drawing and Painting 8. Colour Theory	4. Technical drawings [(projection and construction); building of models of 30 structures of objects of daily use; furniture, rooms and building]
9. Basic business Studies 10. Art History	***Disappeared from the curriculum***

Table 1.3: Areas of Teaching at the Bauhaus.
Wicks (2000)

I: INSTRUCTIONS IN CRAFT (*WERKLEHRE*)						
Stone: Sculpture workshop	Wood Carpentry Workshop	Metal Metal Workshop	Clay Pottery Workshop	Glass Stained Glass Workshop	Colour Wall painting Workshop	Textiles Weaving Workshop
A: Instructions in materials and tools **B:** Instructions in elements of bookkeeping, estimating and contracting						

II: INSTRUCTIONS IN FORM PROBLEMS (*FORMLEHRE*)		
A. Observation • Study of Nature • Analysis of materials	**B.** Representation • Descriptive geometry • Technology of construction • Drawing of plans and building of models for all kinds of construction	**C.** Composition • Theory of Space • Theory of Colour • Theory of Design

Table 1.4: Bauhaus Curriculum.
Bayer et al (1959, p.23)

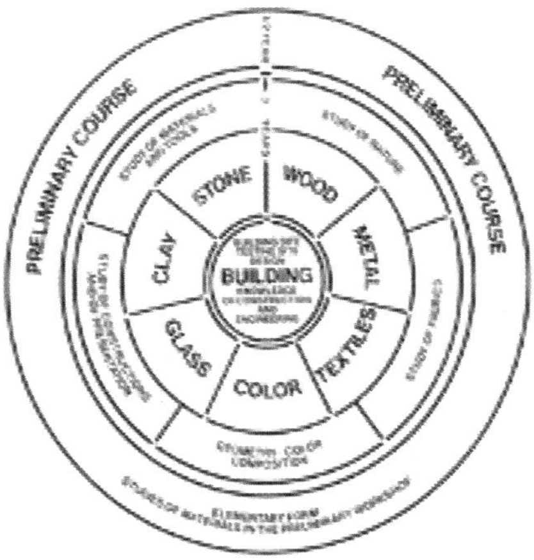

Figure 1.11: Areas of Teaching at the Bauhaus. Wicks (2000)

The programme at the start was very different from the academy one it trained students on crafts, drawing, paintings (ARTS); science & technology. Science included the natural science and technology through the understanding of the properties of materials, chemistry of colours, painting methods, art theory in the history of techniques and anatomy from living models rather than casts. It also included within the programme business skills to give the artists economic freedom in negotiating contracts (the Werkbund idea). By 1921, the programme had been well formed with instructions taking place in four rather than ten areas identified in 1919 (*Figure 1.11*).

Table 1.3 to the left of the curriculum reveal a shift from objectives in the foundation year to 1925. Its focus changed from crafts and social concerns to industry that interestingly had been blamed for the earlier social problems. It appears from the reorganization in 1921, that theoretical subjects like basic business studies colour theory had either disappeared or merged with the workshops. The workshops were reorganized to suit the leaders' interests that were aligned to the personality dynamics and staff changes that occurred.

Table 1.4 to the left is a reflection from Bayer et al. (1959). It is slightly different from one by Wicks in that has been broken in two groups. The upper portion of the table is from within as planned while the lower as viewed from the outsider years later, perhaps more objective. However, in essence they both summarize how the pedagogy was arranged around craft and skills related to it hence more practice based.

The workshops were built on the preliminary courses that provided training within specific skill areas. Even though architecture was the foundation of the courses at the Bauhaus, the programme was missing in the early years and it was not until 2 years after relocation of the school from Weimar to Dessau in 1927; almost 8 years after its inception that it was offered.

By 1923, the Bauhaus programme was criticised as being outdated (Barchardt-Hume, 2006) and in addition, the school came under enormous pressure to produce goods that were marketable. The criticism came from within modernism that had rejected the use of ornaments that lacked functions in design because form was seen as developed from design. Hence, when the school relocated from Weimar to Dessau, the glass workshop was abandoned and the curriculum revised accordingly.

1919	1921	1925 onwards
• To educate architects, painters and sculptors at all levels according to their capabilities • To become competent creative artists and to form working community of leading the future • To have knowledge to design harmonious buildings	• To educate ***gifted*** men and women to become creative designers of craft, sculptors, painters and architects	• To train artistically ***talented*** people to become creative designers of craft, ***industry,*** and architecture • To collaborate in building • To carry out ***practical research*** (experiments) in housing construction problems • To build and test prototypes for ***industry &*** crafts (mass production)

Table 1.5: Objectives of Bauhaus at various historical referenced points (1919; 1921 and 1925). Adopted from Wicks (2000, p.69).

It was not surprising to see the changes in the curriculum between 1919 and 1921 where some of the workshops disappeared. Moholy-Nagy and others at the Bauhaus held a positivist view that art contributed to the social reform of the society and technology and science were the tools or methods for organizing life. This continued the Bauhaus utopian dream of making the world a better place through good design. Another reason for the reorganization of the curriculum related to lack of co-ordination among the individual workshops contrary the initial ideals of collaborative work by a community of craftsmen working together (Wicks, 2000). One of the inherent problems I mentioned earlier was personality clash inevitable in the structure of pairing 2 talented leaders in each workshop.

The preliminary course was still compulsory for all the students in as much the same way as it was in the Beaux Arts academy system. It was taken for a period of half a year. Its pedagogical strengths ensured at completion all the students would have similar knowledge and skills in design for instructions in form and design that was to come in the years ahead. As pointed earlier even though architecture was the foundational base for the training activities at the Bauhaus, until after 1927, the workshops was used fundamentally to build objects related to buildings.

The *table 1.5* above reveals a shift from training all new students in *skills* for craft and creative arts to accepting *artistically gifted* persons. This goes against the original grain of argument that art could not be taught, only craft and techniques. By 1921 the focus was now on taking those already gifted to be trained as designers of craft. There are expected to use their gifts, but only trained in techniques essential for design, as was the basis of the *Werkbund* idea.

By 1925, the objectives are similar to the 1921, focus however a new element is emphasised; the collaboration between various craft workshops. It focused on the developments in technology coming from industry and on prototypes for mass production. The industry that was once blamed for causing social problems was now embraced if not actually allowed to drive the pedagogy at the Bauhaus.

In the period after 1925, the basic course was extended in length from 6 months to 1 year with pedagogical instructions now divided into two areas; basic design in form and practical design in the workshop building various artefacts and models. The subjects taken under each category was simplified, becoming more rigid, less experimental than initially planned. Wick points out that after Itten left in 1922 the "...plan very precisely represents the increasing instrumentalist and utilitarian pedagogical orientation of the Bauhaus..." (2000, p.70).

Bayer *et al* (1959) pointed out that instructions in architecture at the Bauhaus would be taken after one had become a journeyman. This means at a point when a student had been sufficiently trained and had experience in workshop practice and instructed in the study of form that enabled them to collaborate in the building. The learning was through doing in research, design and construction of actual buildings that the Bauhaus had been commissioned to do.

In America, the awareness of Bauhaus idea occurred "...after the great Bauhaus Exhibition of 1923..." According to Bayer *et al* (1959, p.5). The school was depicted as a place for collaborative workshops where expressionist painters, craftsmen and industrial designers worked together as a community. The dissolution of the school in 1933 on one hand brought an end the great experimentation idea, but on the other hand dispersed the students and their masters elsewhere in the world though predominantly to the USA.

1.7.2.3 The Wind in the Air?

The arising challenges caused fluidity in the educational policies of many academic institutions, creating opportunities for cross-disciplinary research as a means to an end. This enabled aesthetics, social, technical and political aspects to be considered in projects in almost the way the notable educationalist John Dewey had envisioned years earlier. The euphoria generated by the idealism, the urgency of the mission and hope for a new paradigm in knowledge building that was based on activism proved to be difficult to sustain. This is because it was anchored on the political challenges to the established technocratic authority, yet lacked the depth to deal with the philosophical and design challenges that were associated with the urban problems of 1960s and 1970s.

The new educational model required reflection on all actions carried out thus providing the 'reflection in action' in the Donald Schön way. The activism of the 1960s achieved a lot in the transformation of the built environment, but failed to rely on a holistic approach to social service and was therefore blind to existing class

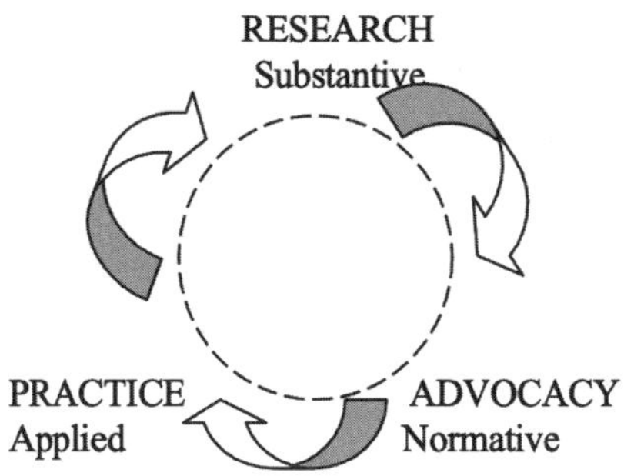

Figure 1.12: Knowledge Model of Urban Design. Author based on description of (Vernez-Moudon, 2008)

divisions. The activists failed to see their own lives and own spaces as being rooted in social injustice. The design professionals thus became blind to their ethical role in acting wilfully upon the environment and succumbing to the pressures of the market place (private sector). They thus relinquished their role of place-creation to the tyranny of the elite and private sector.

Vernez-Moudon (1992, p.54) argues that knowledge building is a loop that has three interrelated areas; practice carrying applied knowledge, advocacy carrying normative knowledge, and research with substantive knowledge (*Figure 1.12*). The typical loop works from academia where knowledge is built through research, interpreted and transformed in advocacy, it is tested in practice (*prototyped*) then goes back to academia as feedback for further development.

It has to be pointed out however, that knowledge building could start from any of the three areas in the loop. Knowledge is built by integrating and applying different *ways of thinking* and acting which makes urban design knowledge building complex because of the large number of allied professions, knowledge areas and actors involved. In urban design, knowledge building must as a matter of necessity keep reinventing itself, be inclusive, rooted in ideology (theory) and tested in reality through practice. There are challenges to dealing with this in education because of the difficulty of integrating the reality part within the short and structured academic curriculum.

The difficulty has always been how to fit the fundamental precepts of design education, and the universities' objectives within the community in the academic framework. This arises from the fact that historically architectural education has been studio- based and it does not provide the means to explore, to know, and to create the built environment that responds to the complex challenges of the real world, the community.

The structure of architectural education traditionally has had a narrow focus in the form of a prescribed canon of subject-object relations as pointed out by Harrison:

> "...The roles of the professional and client; of the process and the object or commodity; of the lived experience and theoretical projection and indeed of the place of education and the sites and subjects of investigation..." (1998, p.8).

The space between the theoretical and the real has been avoided by most academic disciplines. This is very much at odds with the model of knowledge- creation that Vernez-Moudon (1992, p.54) argues is a loop that has three interrelated areas; practice carrying applied knowledge, advocacy carrying normative knowledge and research with substantive knowledge.

The academic institutions have narrowed their focus to one that is self-referencing, exclusively using the vehicle of representation alone rather than in a dialogue with experience. The current studio approach to design studies produces sometimes really exquisite work, but raises the question of whether the students have *learned any skills of production or have they just merely acquired those skills? The former are useful in the exploration, experience and communication of the design objectives, goals and processes.*

The space between the theoretical and the real can be frightening because of the unknowns that may cause conflict and change the focus of the academic exercise, its tight regulated schedule and the anticipated products of the design studio, (Harrison, 1998). Instead of facing the unknowns, the pretext has always been the need for rigour and measurable outcomes as required by the academic canon of objectivism. Palmer argues that the "...objectivism separates the knower from the world for the purpose of keeping the knowledge from contamination by subjective prejudices and bias" (1987, p.107)

The process of intersection between desire and the experience of others to frame the ritual of community building, and students who have no opportunity to engage in the place of residence, are not able to act as members of that community, and therefore are denied the creative process. They therefore learn to disregard the significance of place either from their own or others' narratives. A growing number of educators have recognized the dis-juncture between the content of design education and context. Unfortunately, holistic and experiential experiments of issues of community and place have had awkward structures lacking the visual components that are the basic mode of presentation in traditional schools of design.

The educational framework has to be modified by redefining the audience to include what Harrison sees as:

> "...Non-academics; locating the investigation within real context as well as in the studio and the revision of the goals of pedagogy to include the phenomenon of culture, economics on the built form..." (1998, p.9).

The process of knowledge building should be done collaboratively with other academic disciplines. This enables the establishment of a link between the tower and the street that provides sustainable, informed and creative design thinking.

Place-creation and community issues have preoccupied the modern era, judging by the literature published. The challenge has been how to reconcile the humane scale of buildings with the industrial and technological advancements and massive urbanization. Within the body of knowledge of design of the built environment, one can trace a thread of radical desire for reform commonly known as 'social architecture' whose roots are Marxist and positivist.

The various movements such as the Utopian s, the Arts and Crafts Movement, etc., that have come and gone have all approached social reform through built environment. Historically, architecture has been a product of the elite authority as pointed out by Harrison (1998). The radical movements on the other hand have tried to distance themselves from the dominant elite, and thus failed to create a great impact on both the profession and the educational institutions.

The traditional approach of the Ecole des Arts in both Europe and USA has been concerned with the grandeur of public expression of the established elite power. Architecture as such was seen as high art that is dissociated from technological advancement, is above mere craft, evoking poetic ideas through imagery and associations. The core underpinning of this tradition is that the ideas, critiques and production generated are contained within the confines of the disciplines and institutions Harrison (1998).

The process of learning is more dependent on the master teacher handing down the problem to the student who then goes through a fairly prescribed design process that insulates the student from doubt, imprecision and the unruliness of lived experience. The whole process is idealized or relies on the type with the emphasis on individual achievements through beautiful completed products. The whole paradigm of learning is geared towards the product rather than the process. This model has been embedded in the academic environment for such a long time and is very much at odds with the radical tenets of social architecture.

1.8. An Alternative Approach: Urban Design Laboratory?

The roles taken by the designers in relationship to the clients and the projects have an impact on the place created. The methodologies used in the traditional practice of urban design translates into the educational realm and is aimed at meeting the brief set by the client rather than vision making, as pointed out by Francis (1992, p.62). Francis criticizes this approach because it is not a problem-solving exercise but rather one in which the client comes to the designer with a solution. This approach has infiltrated the educational system as criticized by the 1996 Boyer report entitled '*Building Communities: A New future for Architectural Education and Practice*'. The report is critical of the traditional model of design education for continually training students without inculcating a concern for larger social issues.

There is no doubt that an alternative approach to the education and practice of architecture and urban design is needed: one rooted in larger ethical and social values, which demands a proactive practitioner and is based on social architecture. The social architecture approach has since the 1960s been based on four groups

Stages/ author	Sanoff	Hamdi	Spinuzzi
EXPLORATORY Appreciating Context	Fact finding [material strengths, contextual forces] Gauging Attitudes [the interpretation of those facts, etc]	Problem identification Problem prioritizing [What are the problems]	Familiarization with context Understanding community assets and liabilities Morphological studies
DISCOVERY Creating Urban Structure & Making Connections	Co-discovery between experts and users Explore alternatives Design games	Strategies set Options looked at Trade-offs done [What approaches; what actions are suitable?]	Design process developed Objectives set Benchmark developed [**designers, community representatives**,]
PROTOTYPING/ EVENT Detailing Place	Design alternatives, Typologies Co-design Town hall meeting Negotiation/ consensus Reflection	Design for implementation Typologies [when, how, etc]	Typologies developed 3-D models Design games
FOLLOW-UP	What next? Where next? Future plans Evaluations etc.	Monitoring How is it working What can be learned from the exercise?	-

Table 1.6: Typical stages.
Author developed from sources above.

of participants; the private visionary; the public professional with a vision; the professional based at a non-profit organization and the activist university. The urban laboratory model is one such model housed in the activist university.

In this system, the conceptual growth in knowledge comes from sharing the various perspectives held by the various stakeholders and at the same time the simultaneously changing of our internal representations in response to the perspectives held by others during the dialogue and cumulative experience. There are three to four basic stages to participatory design thinking process as proposed by various renowned scholars (Hamdi, 1997; Sanoff, 2000; and Spinuzzi, 2005) as summarized in *table 1.6* above These are: the initial exploratory work, the discovery process; prototyping and implementation phases.

The first stage is exploratory in nature and involves meetings between the designers, clients, politicians and community to familiarize them with the context, and to begin to observe how the community works and discover the linkages. The system analysis is carried out on the economic health, social health and the physical morphology. The designers observe and listen to the community to gain the tacit knowledge about the community: they learn from the community. The interaction between the actors during this stage is not as exhaustive as in the second stage.

The second stage is the discovery process where there are interactions between the designers, the community stakeholders and other partners in a participatory mode. The goal is to make meaning out of the design process co-operatively. The key crucial issues are identified, objectives are set, benchmarks are determined and the relationships between the various policy frameworks are carried out.

The third stage is the prototyping or event phase, sometimes called the visioning stage. A variety of techniques are used to iteratively shape the urban design framework from the second stage, including the use of mock-ups (3D model and visualization), pictive (imagery) and paper mock-ups etc. The typologies explored further in detail and a detailed area of focus is used to create the critical mass.

There is a fourth stage, though not mentioned by Spinuzzi. This is what is done with the outcome of stage three processes, dissemination in various forms that the participants can understand and to the potential developers, and financiers of the potential projects to inspire continued investments. It has to be highlighted that there are other ways of communicating the developments as the process goes along. Spinuzzi (2005, p.168) points to contextual design practice throughout the process using walkthroughs of affinity diagrams and consolidated models with the participants, allowing the progress to be seen and checked. There is always opportunity to revisit issues deemed not resolved from other stages.

References

1. Babbie, E. (1992). *The practice of social research*, New York: Macmillan.

2. Carmona, M., Heath, T., Oc, T., and Tiesdell, S. (2003). Public Places, urban spaces: the dimensions of urban design. Oxford, England and Burlington, MA: Architectural Press.

3. Downe-Wamboldt, B. (1992). Content analysis: Method, applications, and issues. *Health Care for Women International*, Vol. 13(3), pp.313-321 [Online] available from http://www.tandfonline.com/doi/abs/10.1080/07399339209516006 [Accessed] April 18, 2012.

4. Dworkins, M., S. (1959) Dewey on Education. New York: Teachers College Press

5. Findeli, A. (1990). Moholy-Nagy's Design Pedagogy in Chicago (1937-46). *Design Issues* Vol. 7, No. 1, Educating the Designer (Autumn, 1990), pp. 4-19 [Online] from http://www.jstor.org.ezproxy.qub.ac.uk/stable/1511466 Accessed 1 September 2010.

6. Gans, H. (1969). Planning for people, not buildings. *Environment and Planning* 1(1) 33 – 46

7. Guillen, M., F. (1997). Scientific Management's Lost Aesthetics: Architecture, Organization and Taylorized Beauty of the Mechanical. *Administrative Science Quarterly.* Vol. 42(4) pp.682+ [Online] from www.questia.com accessed 9 September 2010

8. Hsieh, H. and Shannon, S. E. (2005). Three Approaches to Qualitative Content Analysis, *Journal of Qualitative Health Research,* Vol. 15, pp.1227-1288 [Online] available from http://qhr.sagepub.com/content/15/9/1277 [Accessed] April 18, 2012.

9. Illich, I. (1973). *Deschooling Society.* Middlesex, England: Penguin Books Ltd.

10. Johnston, R., J. (1982). The American Urban System: A Geographical Perspective. London: Longman Group, & St. Martin's Press (USA and Canada).

11. Krippendorff, K. (2003). *Content Analysis: An Introduction to Its Methodology,* Beverly Hills, CA: Sage Publications

12. Lincoln, Y. S., & Guba, E. G. (1985). *Naturalistic inquiry,* Beverly Hills, CA: Sage Publications.

13. Manning, K. (1997). Authenticity in constructivist inquiry: Methodological considerations without prescription. *Qualitative Inquiry,* Vol. 3(1), pp.93-115 [Online] available from http://qix.sagepub.com/10.1177/1077 80049700300105 [Accessed] April 18, 2012.

14. Mayring, P. (2000). Qualitative content analysis. *Forum: Qualitative Social Research,* Vo. 1(2). Art. 20, June 2000 [Online] available from http://www.qualitative-research.net/index.php/fqs/article/view/1089/2385UTH [Accessed] March 8, 2012,

15. Moholy-Nagy, L. (1947). Vision in motion. Eighth edition, Chicago: Theobald

16. Morgan D., L. (1993) Qualitative content analysis: a guide to paths not taken. *Qualitative Health Research* Vol. 1(3), pp.112-121

17. Potter, W. J., & Levine-Donnerstein, D. (1999). Rethinking validity and reliability in content analysis. *Journal of Applied Communication Research,* Vol. 27(3), pp. 258-284. [Online] from http://www.tandfonline.com/doi/abs/10.1080/00909 889909365539 [Accessed] April 18, 2012.

18. Rosengren, K. E. (1981). "Advances in Scandinavia content analysis: An introduction". In K. E. Rosengren (Ed.), *Advances in content analysis* (pp. 9-19). Beverly Hills, CA: Sage.

19. Taher, G. (1971). *University Urban Centers,* Washington, DC: The Urban Land Institute.

20. Tuan, Y., F. (1977). Space and Place: The Perspective of Experience. Minneapolis, MI: University of Minnesota Press.

21. Wallis, L. (2007). "Building the Studio Environment" In Salama, M., A.; & Wilkinson, N. eds. *Design Studio Pedagogy: Horizons for the Future,* Gateshead, UK: The Urban International Press.

22. Kaesler, D. (2004). Max Weber. Die Protestantische Ethik und und der Geist der Kapitalismus. Vollständige Ausgabe. Munich: C. H. Be

23. Parker, S. (2004) *Urban Theory and the Urban Experience: Encountering the City.* London: Routledge Martin, R. & Euchner, J. (2012) Design Thinking, *Research-Technology Management,* 55:3, 10-14, DOI: 10.5437/08956308X5503003

24. Tonkinwise, C. (2011) A taste for practices: Unrepressing style in design thinking, *Design Studies* 32 (2011) 533e545

25. Gobble, M., M. (2014) Design Thinking, *Research Technology Management,* 57:3, (May/Jun 2014): 59-61

26. Brown, T. (2008) Design Thinking, *Harvard Business Review,* June. http: hbr.org/2008/06/design-thing/ar/1

27. Martin, R. & Euchner, J. (2012) Design Thinking, *Research-Technology Management,* 55:3, 10-14, DOI: 10.5437/08956308X5503003

28. Katoppoa, M., L. & Sudradjat, I. 2015. Combining Participatory Action Research (PAR) and Design Thinking (DT) as an Alternative Research Method in Architecture, *Procedia - Social and Behavioral Sciences,* pp.118-125, [Online] from https://reader.elsevier.com/reader/sd/pii/S187704281503311X-?token=F8FF98CE-375A33896309309B1B-4961600C3F933AD01E7B14A4 1C83D053F6471C67649F7F5B-4DC8FBA0BE6CB127EEDB-1B&originRegion=us-east-1&originCreation=20230119161041, [Accessed] January 19th 2023.

29. Tepavčević, B. 2017. Design thinking models for architectural education, *The Journal of Public Space, Vol. 2(3),* pp. 67-72, [Online] from https://www.journalpublicspace.org DOI:10.5204/jps.v2i3.115, [Accessed] January 19th 2023.

CHAPTER 2

Urban Design Laboratory at Carnegie Mellon University, Pittsburgh

The previous chapter explored the historical contexts that framed the urban laboratory with reference to USA and Pittsburgh in particular. It made references to parallel circumstances that occurred in Barcelona and linked the deteriorations of the physical and environmental conditions to the demand for a new approach to urban developments. In addition, it examined the transformations in the social and economic conditions and the political realignments after the Second World War.

This chapter will examine the extent to which the historical context contributed to the methodological practices of the UL at Carnegie Mellon University in Pittsburgh. It starts by giving some background information on the Pittsburgh region where the UL projects were located, followed by a brief history of the laboratory and the founder David Lewis. The methodologies of UL are then described and how the strategies and tactics used correlate to the historical context are looked at by use of examples from case studies. These are taken from three different distinct UL phases. Each phase of the UL is investigated and linked to the sphere of influence that drives it. Three case studies are taken from the three periods of UL (UL1: 1963-1968; UL2: 1982-1992; UL3: 1992 to date), to see how the methods are used, and how they have changed over the years as outlined by Toker (2007).

2.1 Historical Context

In 1960 almost half of the dwelling units (238,000) in Alleghany County were built before 1920 and more than 90,000 before 1900. By implication most of the housing units were of old stock and a census report of 1960 indicated that at least almost a quarter (112,318) of them were deficient, as pointed out by Lubove (1995, 143). The matters were made worse by revelation that only 13 out of 80 municipalities were participating in the urban renewal program. This meant that most of the units were likely to be condemned under the Housing Act of 1949.

The arrival of German, Polish, Italian and Irish immigrants, and freed black migrants from the southern states contributed to the shortage of housing in Pittsburgh. This continued despite a report in 1957 by the Pennsylvania Economic league that explicitly linked the future of the renewal to the housing deadlock. It pointed out that "…the minority, the aged and the lower-middle income housing market had been neglected …" Lubove (1995, 144). The urban renewal efforts had been focused on providing housing for those able to access the financing, in other words both the middle income and the wealthy, yet was funded through the Federal government programs meant to befit all.

In 1936, the Pennsylvania Economy League (PEL) was incorporated aimed at cutting government spending through research. Cooke (1961) pointed out that it came to wield great influence over the making of public policy instead of being only a research agency. It was financed by big business, respected by politicians in both parties, commended by the press and cooperated with by groups that might be considered natural enemies.

In this sense it was a common vehicle to achieve business despite political differences. This was possible because, as Cooke argued "…the League has furnished from time to time men from its own staff for important public assignments…" (1961, p.69-70). It was therefore an inside-outside organization that allowed the business elite to run the city and county through the urban coalition regime. Decisions were made that suited their business interest as opposed to their initial objectives of merely cutting government spending on behalf of the citizens.

Because of the challenges faced by the minority groups pointed to earlier, the PEL "…recommended the formation of new non-profit agency the Allegheny Council to Improve Our Neighborhood-Housing (ACTION-Housing) which was established in 1957…" (Lobove ,1995, 145) ACTION-Housing however, was a non-profit organization; it operated in an efficient, business-like manner, acquired sites for development, and worked with professionals to experiment on the best way forward in the provision of housing. Between 1961 and 1966 it had erected and sold 187 townhouses.

In 1959 ACTION-Housing had attempted to approach the redevelopment differently by collaborating with owners and tenants of Windless Street. It had worked with "…architects and planners of the Amber Company's established home division and tenant group who had formed self-help group…" according to Lubove (1995, p.154). The efforts failed due to the lack of a master plan for the area available from the city. By 1966 ACTION-Housing was working with low-income residents in the Hill district to assist in providing capacities for self-improvements of the homes. This was enabled by the passing of the 1964 Employment Opportunity Act that allowed for expansion of the rehabilitation efforts.

According to Lubove, "…in 1958 ACTION-Housing participated in the organization of East Liberty Citizens Renewal Council, in 1959 the Bluff Area

Citizens Renewal Council and the Perry Hilltop Citizens Action Committee on North side, in 1961-63 worked intensely with the South side citizens groups…" (1995, p.161). One would therefore argue that Pittsburgh had by 1963 well-organized community action groups that fought for their rights. The Civil Rights Movements therefore dovetailed onto the existing community network.

The growth in citizen participation and neighborhood organizations in Pittsburgh was a result of the City Planning Department's programmes established in 1961 under the Community Revitalization Plan, CRP. The Mayor's office employed a liaison officer, James Cunningham as associate director to aid the formulation of the CRP and neighborhood programs that went beyond citizens' council and housing renewal.

He brought experience from Chicago from 1956 where he had successfully experimented on arresting the deterioration of neighborhoods. Lubove points to two important lessons he brought on board: "…an alternative and superior strategy to bulldozing was the use of conservation and rehabilitation and secondly acknowledging that renewal was a long-term process that depended on the establishment of machinery for widespread citizen participation in decision making…" (1995, p.162).

Cunningham's ideas and efforts brought a dilemma for ACTION-housing in that it had been established as an urban coalition of business interests and now had to mediate between the neighborhood interests it aroused and the business interests.

By 1964, ACTION-Housing had started to play an important role is shaping the anti-poverty programs in Pittsburgh through what Lubove pointed out were "…encouragement of the emergence of new neighborhood leaders that provided the other citizens with some voice in decisions affecting the physical and social environment…" (1995-174-175).

It is interesting to note that ACTION-housing was involved in neighborhood extension programs that relied on extension workers to "...alert and equip citizens so that they would be willing and able to take upon themselves much responsibility for developing their neighborhood..." (Lubove, 1976, p.233). It helped develop partnerships between the universities, school systems, and government departments into a working relationship with the neighborhood residents. The context, which David Lewis came to in 1963, was ripe for the experimentation of ideas. It was not unique in any way in that the framework had existed for at least five years as demonstrated by the projects ACTION-housing was involved with.

2.2. Urban Laboratory (UL) at Carnegie Mellon University

David Lewis, the founder of the UL came from England in 1963 to join the faculty at Carnegie Mellon University. He had previously moved from South Africa to England and joined a group of modern artists at St Ives in Cornwall in 1947. He was described as "…an inspiring young poet who met and married Wilhelmina Barnes-Graham…" (Hall, 2010). There is no record of his involvement in painting, though he curated and wrote on subjects related to art and architecture while in St Ives. David Lewis joined the University of Leeds School of Architecture in 1956 where he stayed till he moved to USA in 1963.

While still married to Barnes-Graham, Lewis met the modern artists of the day based there. These included Terry Frost, Peter Lanyon, Bryan Wynter, among others, according to Stephens (1997). As a contributor to *Archigram 2* in 1962, he met members of Team X such as Peter Cook and Shadrach Woods and collaborated with Peter Stead in 1962 on Houses built from Industrial Units in Huddersfield, as pointed out by Hall (2010). He contributed to a commentary on art and architecture in *Architectural Design*, an influential mouthpiece for Team X (Gathercole, 2006).

Lewis and Peter Stead were to later move together to Pittsburgh USA where they formed a practice, Urban Design Associates, and to join the faculty at the school of architecture at Carnegie Mellon University (Johnstone (n.d.)) Several things need highlighting from the above; firstly, when David Lewis had contact with artists and architects through the circles of artists residing at St Ives he was a writer and a poet.

Secondly, Stephen (1997) points out that artists such as Peter Lanyon at St Ives strove to underpin their work on the local context. He is however very critical of the writings of Lewis on the work, considering them as lacking in the fundamentals: "…in place of a historical narrative or analysis there is a personal memoir by David Lewis, a 'St Ives" protagonist between 1947 and 1955…" (1997, p.624). I suspect there is a bit of self-promotion going on here, the type talked of by Pierre Bourdieu. He argued that the elites could use art as a tool of power. He posited "…the cult of art is intensified by the discrepancy between *subjective* radicalism and *objective* wealth, but also by political disappointment…" (1984, p.366).

Despite the criticisms leveled at his writings and interests, it is acknowledged that "…St Ives was an *avant-garde* center in 1950s whose notional leaders had been subversives of the 1930s…" according to Garlake (1986, p.83). Having trained in architecture at Leeds he moved to USA as an architect rather than an urban designer. He was an architect who had been in contact with the new thinking coming out of Team X, considered rebels to the CIAM movement. However, he was still a strong believer in experimentation, of technological determinism, as revealed by his collaborative projects with Peter Stead at Huddersfield.

Having given some background information on David Lewis who founded the Urban Laboratory at Carnegie Mellon University, the research will next look at some background material about the UL followed by analysis of three projects to work out the methodological strategies adapted and their influences.

A review of universities that have urban design or architecture programs that engage communities, reveals that it was the first such program (see UL timeline *Table 3.1 in Chapter 3*). However, Paul Davidoff at the University of Pennsylvania had started the Advocacy Planning program in the 1950s. A review of the list of visitors to the school during the UL when Paul Schweikher (1956-1969) was the director of the school includes Jane Jacobs, Kevin Lynch, Sibyl Moholy-Nagy and Ludwig van de Rohe. There was therefore influence coming from other schools including writings by Dennis Scott Brown who was based at the University of Pennsylvania who wrote extensively on planning, urban design and the city during that period. Therefore UL as a process of students engaging the community was not the first, but as an architectural program that used community engagement within its urban design course, it was a leader.

David Lewis in his acceptance speech for the 2007 Athena Medal pointed out that the founding of the UL coincided with the activities of the Civil Rights Movements of the 1960s where citizens were demanding a platform for "... participation in the discussion and design of social and urban futures..." (2007). He thus acknowledged a link between the founding of the UL and the fight for social justice in USA and the Pittsburgh area in particular, where he lived and worked. Lawrence Glasco (2001), a notable Pittsburgh historian corroborates this view; however, the direct linkages seem difficult to establish.

The UL proponents argue that the principles of democracy articulated by President Thomas Jefferson are at the core of the UL program. Lipscomb and Bergh cite the following words:

> "I know of no safe depository of the ultimate powers of the society but the people themselves; and if we think them not enlightened enough to exercise their control with wholesome discretion, the remedy is not to take it from them, but to inform their discretion by education. This is the true corrective of abuses of constitutional power." (Quoted in Schuman, 2009).

Two aspects of the UL are reflected in the above statement; firstly, the process acknowledges that the *power of decision-making lies with the citizens* and is therefore a participative methodology. Secondly, it accepts that *not all citizens have the knowledge and skills that would give them the full capability to make that decision* and as such its methods are underpinned by ethical values. This requires the designers to have the moral responsibility of building the capacities of the community to enable them to participate fully in the decisions that affect them. How well they participate is investigated in the dissertation.

The course materials suggest that the UL program at CMU is mandatory for students in the final year of the Bachelor of Architecture undergraduate degree and those undertaking the Master of Urban Design postgraduate degree. In addition, it is also open to students from other disciplines interested in *urban issues* and *participatory* approaches that can be used to solve them. This openness introduces

PHASE	SYSTEM ANALYSIS PHASE	URBAN DESIGN FRAMEWORK PHASE	PLACE-MAKING & VISIONARY PROJECT PHASE
	This phase mines and analyses 1. Economic data 2. Social Data 3. Physical morphology	1. Identifies crucial issues 2. Sets objectives 3. Looks at bench marks [use of typologies] 4. Finds relationships [building framework] 5. Makes connections to success 6. Strengthens existing relationships between various area/ corridors	1. Details single area of focus 2. Explores typologies [how they can be applied appropriately] 3. 3D contents and representation 4. The area of focus must be at CRITICAL location of community 5. INSPIRES continued investments 6. Is the larger urban design goals for community investments
Skills acquired	1. Gain communication skills [students] 2. Leadership skills [students] 3. Capacity Building [community] 4. Analytical Skills [students] 5. Collaborative skills [community and stake holders] 6. Learn importance of INTERDISCIPLINARY nature of design process [students, community and professionals]	1. Learn team-work / collaboration 2. analytical skills 3. Leadership skills 4. Relationship between buildings and surrounding 5. Learn about typologies as urban building block to be varied and repeated 6. Use of community vision for building and revitalization	1. Learn about team-work/ collaboration 2. Acquire creation skills for outdoor urban areas 3. Role of landscape architecture in urban design 4. Learn about landscape typologies to creation of public space
Participatory Activity	**Community Meeting 1**	**Symposium** **Community Meeting 2**	**Community Meeting 3**
Products	1. Physical models [3 D large scale] 2. Maps [2 D] 3. Demographic data, diagrams 4. Photographic records 5. Publications/ Exhibitions	1. Strategic Vision 2. Creation of brief or programme for interventions 3. Typologies [building and urban] 4. Publications/ exhibitions/ symposium presentations	1. Typologies [building and landscape] 2. Detailed design [architecture, infrastructure and landscaping] 3. Reports 4. Publications [journal papers, conference outputs, exhibitions]
Theoretical Framework	1. Social-Usage Tradition [Chicago School]	1. Visual-Artistic 2. Social-Usage Tradition	1. Visual-Artistic Tradition 2. Place-Making Tradition
Beneficiaries	1. Students 2. Community	1. Students 2. Community 3. Community leaders 4. Practitioners	1. Students 2. Community 3. Practitioners

Table 2.1: Summary of Design Process of the UL at CMU

a multi-disciplinary approach without necessarily adding new courses to the curriculum.

The stated aim of the 2006-2009 UL design studio programs was to educate architects (*not community*) to be leaders with *a vision* at the level of neighborhood, city and region (Gatti, 2009). This was done by broadening students' training through the introduction of new skills in *community leadership* and *urban design* that other architecture and urban design programs lacked (*see the Realm of National Architectural Accrediting Board criteria discussed in the previous chapter*). The urban design methods used approached the integrated problems through a *participatory* design process. The students worked *directly with the community* to create visions for change [emphasis mine].

The ethos of the UL is that urban design created the physical structures for collective life: in other words, places that foster and support activities of the people (Gatti, 2009). This implies that the designers are responsible not only to the clients who commission them but to the collective city as a whole (users). The UL strives to train the architects and urban designers who make places for people that are also *beautiful, inspiring and open.*

The last section of the ethos of the UL points to both the visual artistic and social usage traditions of urban design as discussed in chapter 2. The visual artistic tradition is characterized by emphasis on the product rather than process involved in creating places. It focuses more on the visual qualities of urban design and the aesthetic experience (delight) of the spaces produced than other aspects. This tradition was very much influenced by the work of Gordon Cullen, *"The Concise Townscape"* (1961). David Lewis must have been aware of this publication, having lived in England for a while and having just arrived in Pittsburgh just two years later in 1963, as revealed by the reading list at the UL he led (*See Table 2.1*).

The UL studio focused on a particular kind of urban project to achieve the aims by creating a long-term vision. The success is measured by the existence of three key characteristics; a vision that is shared and supported by the community; one that is comprehensive yet detailed and finally is positive and inspiring. Hutzell and Rico-Gutierrez, argue that it requires that the process "....be interdisciplinary and hands-on and iteratively improves the quality of the design..." (2007, p.1-2). It is thus action-based and reflexive through the looped iterative and engagement process as illustrated (*Figure 2.1*).

2.2.1 The Design Process

The documents from the 2006-2009 UL reveal that the design process occurs in three key phases; the system analysis, the urban design framework and finally the place-making- visionary project phase (Gatti, 2009). The three phases are organized in such ways that not only are the school's curriculum objectives met, but also those of the community at large. These include enhancing skills in team-work and

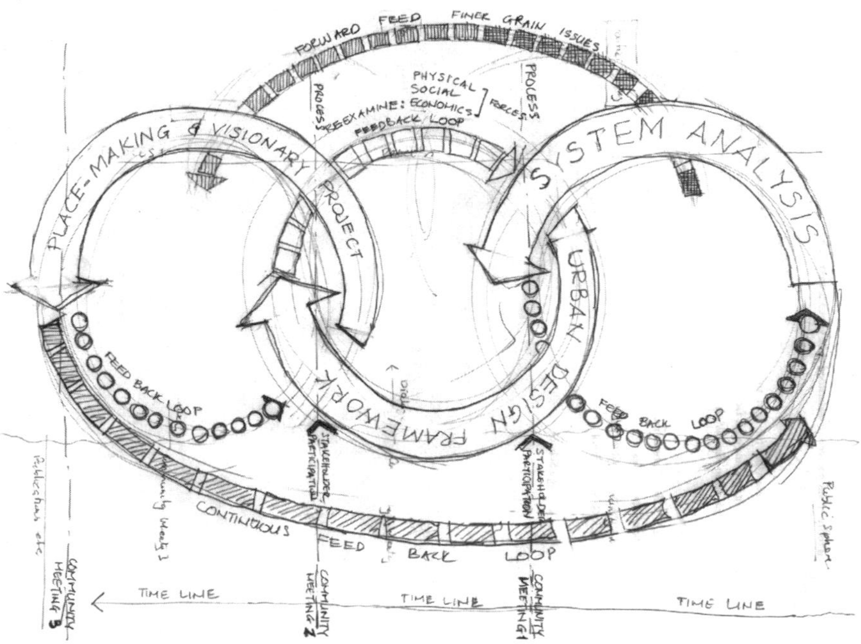

Figure 2.1: Diagram of Model Reflective Urban Laboratory Process

collaboration; analysis and communications. The process is summarized in *Table 2.1* and *Figure 2.1* and followed by detailed description. In the examination of the design process, several questions are examined: what is the UL process used at CMU? How well does the UL adhere to their aims and objectives; (used as a measure of their success?) How does the UL interact and relate to both the client and users? How do they achieve the right balance without compromising the other visions?

The first diagram (*Table 2.1*) was built from the description given in the student's handouts and the Remaking Cities publication. It is used in this research to identify the skills that the professional urban designer needs (Kumar, 2009) and locates the different phases when community participation occurs. Also, it indicates the products expected and who the beneficiaries are. The first row with the phases suggests to the student's issues that they need to focus on in discussions with the community at a later date. The community even though it is argued it is at the center of the process, is actually engaged later within each phase as discussed elsewhere within the chapter.

Even though the UL syllabus indicates that there are no predominant theoretical underpinnings, an analysis of the reading list and documents provided reveal that two schools of thought dominate. These are the social-usage and visual artistic traditions.

The diagram, (*Figure 2.1*) is the author's model of a reflective urban design model and has been developed from the materials provided and literature review on learning methods. The key text used to draw the diagram is Schön (1983) *"reflective practitioner"*. The diagram reveals emphasis on an open-ended design process that has feedback loops embedded within it at every stage. The process is a linear iterative loop. How much reflection is allowed will be revealed from interviews with former faculty at the school and published texts. I will now describe the various phases and what occurs in them.

2.2.2 Phase 1: Systems Analysis

The first phase is used as the stage for the students and the participants to understand the community, to discover the weaknesses, strengths, opportunities, and perceived and real threats to its existence and growth. The phase uses several methods for discovering the common interests within the community and the subsequent induction of convergence (agreement, see more discussion on methods by Sanoff, 2008; and Till, 2005) of interests from what initially appeared as sticking points, which are explored below.

The whole process is constrained by the typical short sixteen-week academic semester schedule, in addition to the limitations on the capabilities of the institutional partners involved and the nature of their political agendas and processes. It changes the perception of the roles and responsibilities of the designers from provision of services to enabling and empowering the stakeholders, the community.

The phase starts with the interrogation of the question of what a place is, through the use of a think piece. It is an opportunity for individual perceived interpretation of what defines the community where they are working. It is also used as an aid to developing personal observation, and documentation of what has been seen. This is in reference to the linkages between different points, one within the study site, and the other which could be either within or outside. They are especially encouraged to look at connections to the other areas of the community. The students finally interpolate the character of the connections between the points, (*Figures 2.2 and 2.3*) by creating compelling representations of what the connections are.

Figure 2.2 in the following page is my interpretation of what connections between two different points under study might look like. This is developed from literature reviews of the forces that impact place making/ quality of place (Bianchini and Parkinson (1993); Danson and Mooney (1997); Landry (2000), CABE (2005) and others). It relies on identification of two distinct locations and a mapping of linkages between them. These could be a physical link (road, river etc); economic (e.g. residences and shops); social/ cultural (residences and say community building like a church or library) and so on.

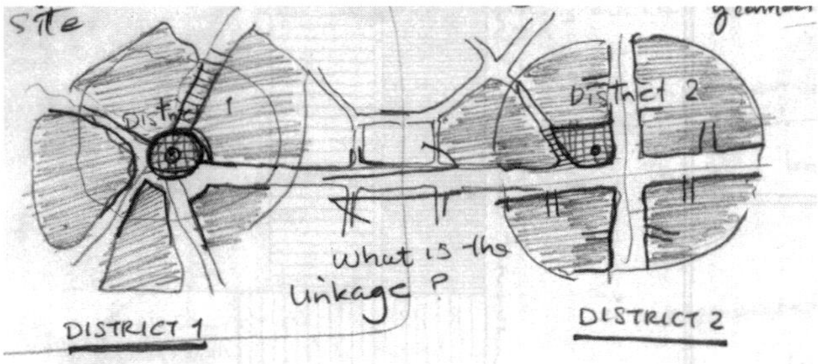

Figure 2.2: Connections
Source: Author

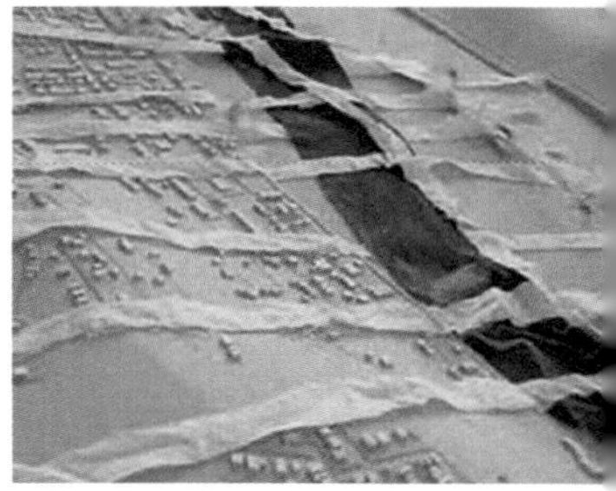

Figure 2.3: Think Piece Representation
Source: RCI, (2008, p.124)

The process of drawing the diagram encourages investigations of what the possible relations could be, very much in line with the work of the Surrealists discussed later in the section. Figure 2.3 above brings to mind works of Surrealist artists. Between 1947 and 1962 David Lewis was very much involved with the artists at St Ives in Cornwall: some such as Peter Lanyon were Surrealists. Their style and methods of work must have influenced not only his work, but also his methods. For example, Andre Breton (1924) wrote about the surreal in the first manifesto explaining that the

> "...Visual hallucination of the image of a man cut into two by a window is the product of the exploration of the relationship between the unconscious thought and the poetic production..." Williams (1981, p.10).

This he saw as an important means to express the content and process of the unconscious. The technique involved the use of games where random objects are placed out of context to research on the irrational knowledge of the object. Williams argues that the "...Surrealist artistic images only pretended to create illusions of real spaces, no matter how meticulously drawn or photographed the object might be..." (1981, p.12).

In the think piece above, the ribbons flowing across the model are separated from their customary surrounding and combined with other objects of wood to create illusion of the new context. The ribbons are used to elucidate the connections between the two sides of the model, I assume the community to be divided yet united by the wider ribbon of the river. One sees in the methods, the techniques of the Bauhaus period, a new way of thinking about space and objects within it. This was different from the traditional methods used in architectural schools where the

Figure 2.4: August 1956 (Val d'Orcia) Ben Nicholson. Source: Tate Exhibition St. Ives exhibition Scratching the surface

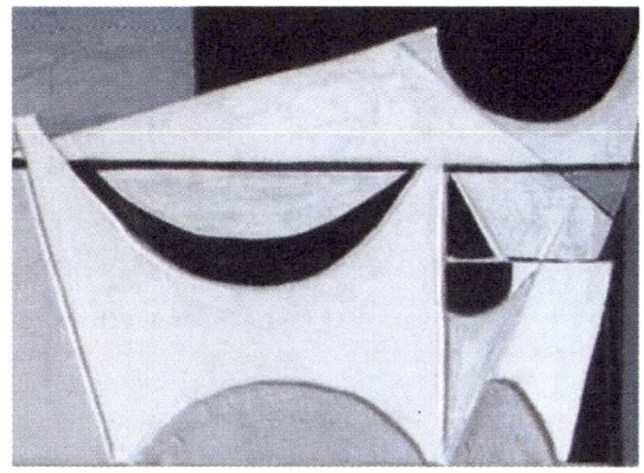

Figure 2.5: White Relief on Black and Grey - 1954 - acrylic on board by Barns-Graham (1954). Source: Wilhelmina Barns-Graham Trust

representations had to be more realistic as opposed to wacky and personal. It raises questions on how well the community was involved in the creation of the image used in the think piece.

In addition, David Lewis spent time with Ben Nicholson (whom he was very fond of) and wrote an article on the 'Scratching the Surface' exhibition of 2009 at Tate St. Ives. Ben Nicholson was a constructivist artist and surrealist. His work was abstract and he argued that:

> "...A good idea is exactly as good as it can be universally applied, that no idea can have universal application which is not solved in its own terms and if any extraneous elements are introduced the application ceases to be universal. Realism has been abandoned in search for reality: the principle objective of abstract art is precisely this reality" (1971, p.75).

The abstract representation of the landscape at Val d'Orcia depicted by Nicholson (*Figure 2.4*) and Wilhelmina Barns-Graham (*Figure 2.5*) are similar in style to those used by students in the think piece (*Figure 2.3*). The influence of abstract and constructive art is inherent perhaps from the time Lewis spent at St Ives and encouraged the students to look at.

The process interrogates the connections by looking at what the economic interrelationships are; what the social interrelationships are and finally what the physical interrelationships or the connectivity are. The process also considers the scale of the linkages, be they local, regional, national or global. At the end of the UL process, a compelling representation of the chosen place under study has to be constructed illustrating the character of the place in use, its scale, and the morphological relationships as observed and documented.

The term 'compelling representation' suggests the idea of marketing or use of power of persuasion. It brings to mind two important writers of the period, Breton (1969) who pointed out that Surrealism could not be defined solely from constructive or destructive points but from the events in life of the period. The second is Sert who used the persuasion of photo-montage developed by Moholy-Nagy to portray the state of the city (*Figure 2.6*). Mumford asserts:

> "...The images suggest how the modernizing processes are inevitably producing the constituent elements of the functional city underscoring that the CIAM polemic was indeed a scientific response to these forces..." (2000, p.136-7)

In addition, the compelling representations seem to borrow from the works of the Situationist International artist methodology of psycho-geography. Coverley (2006) suggests that psycho-geography is the interaction between psychology and geography and the emotional and behavioral response of the environment. The assignment could be interpreted as examination through navigation between the two points. The design would thus be reflections of the response in derive as individuals (think piece) and as a collective (community visioning). The process allows for a critical awareness of the potential of the urban spaces they live in and a response by modifying to improve it .

This first phase of work is carried out in groups within the studio to lighten the task at hand as well as to impart communication, collaborative and negotiation skills in the students. The three-value system of the place is represented in three different ways; as perception of the place, as evaluation, and as the understanding of the place. The term value-system is used here to refer to the factors that determine the meaning of a place. Tuan posited that "...a place is the center of meaning constructed by experience..." (1975, p.152).

The representation of the place is evaluated against the data collected during the walk through of the site, their own preconceived notions, and checked with the community during the first meeting. Later during the second phase, the work is checked against the benchmark set up and agreed with the community.

The success of places is measured by their usage by people and therefore the creation of places is linked to the understanding of how people interact with each other in the place, how they use and modify the environment they use, and how universal the place is in accepting all people regardless of gender, age, or ability. It also looks at the various layers of the community that exist; and the politics of the community organization suggesting ownership to the process is thus critical for its success.

The documents of the laboratory state that there is no sole theoretical framework that underpins the design process at the UL, but it draws from all the

Figure 2.6: Representation of Future means of Communications. Source: Mumford, (2000, p.137)

three well-known existing frameworks (Hutzell and Rico-Gutierrez, 2007). The reading list reveals that the study of the social value system is underpinned by the social-usage tradition. (See literature review on the traditions and *Figure 2.7 & Table 2.2 following pages*).

The Figure 2.7 is a representation of the theoretical frameworks based on an analysis of the reading lists provided to the students. According to Jarvis, (quoted in Carmona *et al* 2003, p.6) they are the visual-artistic, the social-usage and place-making traditions. The figure is a reflection of the percentage breakdown of the reading in the course handed out at UL2. The books were then categorized by the main emphasis the authors were aligned to *Table 2.2.* The list is compared with those at other schools contemporary to the UL at CMU in the discussion section.

It reveals that although the program claims that there is no single dominant theoretical direction, almost half of the books can be categorized as underpinned by the social-usage tradition. I therefore argue that the methodologies are likely to be influenced by this.

If we are to go back to the place-making process, we find that space (Euclidian) is transformed into place by the meanings attributed to it by the users, and, I would argue, the community. The meanings are attributed for various reasons and this is what gives it the sense of ownership and responsibility to the place. Therefore, we may argue place creation demands willing user-participation in what happens to their community so that they can have a sense of shared responsibility to the space so created.

There is a gap that exists because of the competing interests between the client, the users or community, and the designers who are typically aligned with the clients. The gap is an ethical one because it relates to the competing interests in the built environment as realized, against one where the desires and needs of the users are ignored or interpreted by one group over the other. This is the conventional way of designing and developing the built environment. The participation as a process of place-creation provides the space to address the difference if the parties with inherent interests are engaged early in the production of the place they live in.

There are very many methods that can be adopted and used in the participatory design and planning process. Sanoff (2000) gives three purposes for participation as, firstly, involvement of the people in the design decision making

Required reading (main author)	Urban Design Tradition
1. Haussmann (1809–1891 civil planner)	1. Traditional Beaux Arts
2. Summerson, J. (1963) The Classical Language of Architecture) Historian and critic)	2. Traditional Beaux Arts
3. Le Corbusier	
4. Theo Crosby/ Team 10/ Smithson	3. Modernists CIAM .
5. Camillo Sitte	4. CIAM
6. Rodrigues Perez de Arce	5. Traditional Beaux Arts
7. German, Dutch and Viennese Socialists	6. (no fixed leanings)
8. Bruno Taut	7. Modernist CIAM rebels
9. W. H. Whyte	8. ?
10. Aldo Rossi	9. Social- usage tradition
	10. Social-usage tradition/ visual artistic
11. Maurice Culot	11. Social-usage tradition/ visual artistic
	12. Garden city-functionalism
12. Ebenezer Howard	13. Visual artistic tradition
13. Kevin Lynch	14. Post modernist?
14. Rem Koolhaus	15. Visual artistic
15. Collage City	

Table 2.2: Representation of Future means of Communications. Source: Mumford, (2000, p.137)

THEORETICAL URBAN DESIGN FRAMEWORK

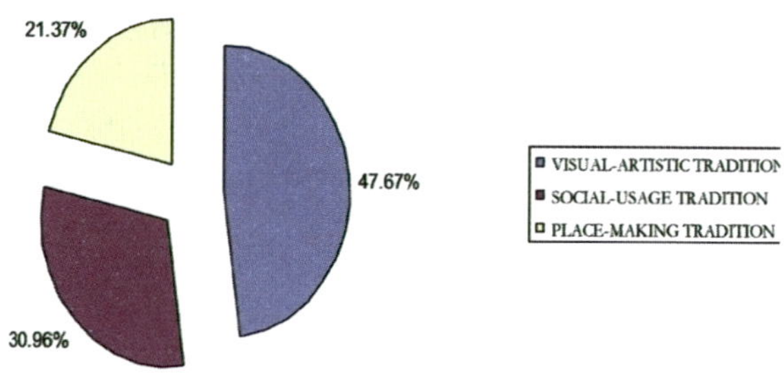

Figure 2.7: Reading list. Source: Onyango (2011)

processes; secondly, giving a voice in the process; and finally, the promotion of community cohesion and a sense of pride.

The use of interactive methods serves the purpose well and there are different formats to meet those. There are five methods used singularly or in combination to enable participation. They are: "awareness, indirect, group interactions, open-ended and brainstorming methods" as pointed out by Sanoff (2000, p.68).

A review and analysis of the 2006-2007 UL studio programs reveal three main methods used in the first phase of the UL process; awareness, indirect, and group interaction methods.

2.2.3 Systems Analysis: Methods and Influences

The first, the awareness method, involves finding out perceived meaning that the site of study in relation to other areas and factors has to the community and the student designers. It has to be pointed out here that the students tour the site with community leaders or representatives. Hence the meanings may not be the true reflection of how the community understands and perceive the place. The information gathered is specific to the locality, hence driven by context, and allows for later discussion at the first community meeting on the differences in perception of the issues the community see as assets or threats, and the view point held by the students and other stakeholders, such as developers.

For example, at the 1991 UL worked on a proposal for the South side Community on behalf of the South side Local Development Company (SSLDC), according to Faassen, Fredrickson and Temkin (1991). The site in question was owned by Ling- Temco-Vought (LTV) and was to be developed over a period through the Urban Redevelopment Authority of Pittsburgh. The briefing documents had a condition requiring the designers to work with the community through a liaison (SSLDC). The final study was presented to the South side Planning forum at completion. At no point in the process were the community involved directly except at the end to be given the final proposal (*Figure 2.8*). The feedback loops that would have embedded the process were lacking. The community were therefore surrogates to the process.

There are three basic ways that the community's awareness can be raised, the order depending on the organization. These are: use of media, holding of exhibitions or rallies, and walking tours of the community to see the current contextual state of their built environment. In UL the community awareness is raised through friendly media like the *Post-gazette and the Pittsburgh Courier.* I call them friendly here since I could hardly find critical reports from any of their commentaries on the works of the laboratory (See captions *Figure 2.9*) at the following page.

The *Post-gazette* was first established in 1786 and as such is a historical paper for Pittsburgh. They claim to have had a reputation for fighting for the public good, and campaigned vigorously for the urban renaissance in 1950s that unfortunately led

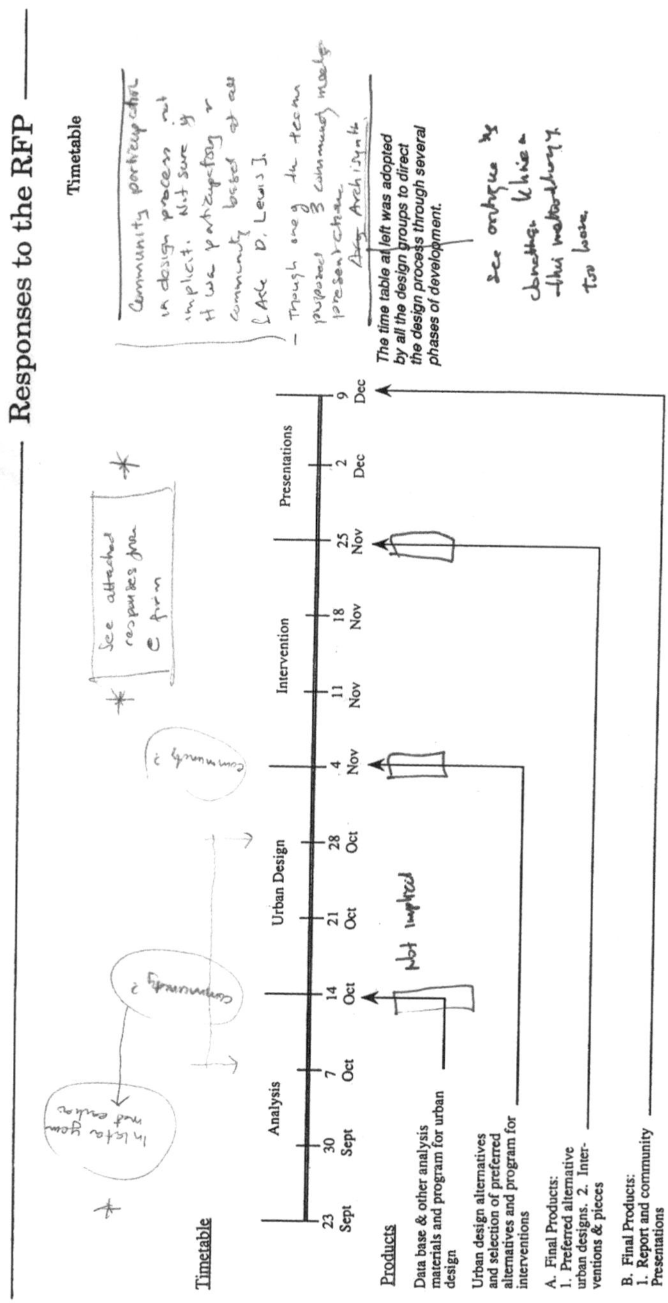

Figure 2.8: 1991 The Southside Time Table.
Source: Faassen, Fredrickson and Temkin (1991).

'Urban lab' meeting set

Saturday, November 26, 2005
Pittsburgh Post-Gazette

A third and last community meeting for North Siders to contribute to a Carnegie Mellon University "urban lab" study will be held Wednesday from 6:30 to 9 p.m. at the Children's Museum.

CMU architecture students are proposing ways to "mend disconnects within the neighborhood," said Flora Bao, one of the students.

CMU architecture students plan for Downtown of the future

Monday, December 13, 2010
By Diana Nelson Jones, Pittsburgh Post-Gazette

The Urban Lab's plan for Downtown Pittsburgh promotes a pedestrian friendly environment that connects Downtown.

Imagine a Downtown with an iconic part of the Civic Arena as a scenic overlook, a cable car connecting the Hill to the Convention Center, a looping midtown tram, river buses, and pedestrian alleys connecting river to river, and small greenspaces dotting the path from the Point to Uptown like breadcrumbs.

Figure 2.9: Press Reports
Source: Post-Gazette Archives

to the destruction of many communities. They promise to continue to highlight, in their commentaries and reporting, what they perceive as public good, the community collective.

The Pittsburgh Courier on the other hand, is a much younger paper established in 1907 and has had an established history of calling for improvements in housing, health and the education of black people. The paper also had a very large circulation among black people in the pre-civil rights movements and therefore historically the local black community have associated with it.

The Audit Bureau of Circulations (2005) report on reader profiles of the Post-Gazette newspaper reveals that 92% are white, 63% are in full time employment. Of these over a fifth of them are in professional jobs and also own their residences and over 50% are educated to university level. The first paper, the Post Gazette, is likely to appeal to a conservative audience, while the second, the

Figure 2.10: Lorimer Studio 3D model
Source: Remaking Cities Institute (2008, p.10)

Pittsburgh Courier, is likely to appeal to the minorities in the Pittsburgh area.

It thus appears that the selection of the two papers is strategically based on historical facts about Pittsburgh and the complex racial relationships that have always existed (*See Section 2.1*). The local political context thus was a driver to choose of the awareness methods. One could therefore argue that the method used for creating awareness responds to the historical context of the place.

The second technique used in the awareness method is "the walk-about" where both the students and the community leaders take a walk in the community to jointly discover what is actually happening on the ground rather than relying on the perceptions of what is on the ground. At the end of the walk-about the students are able to examine the value system of the community such as; what does the ownership of land and property in the area look like? Who works there? Where do they come from? Where are the perceived edges to the locality, what historical changes over time, etc? A 3D physical model of the site is built up to assist the discussion of the context later during the first community meeting (*Figure 2.10*).

This method has an academic history in the rebels to rationalism of CIAM like Bakema, Allison and Peter Smithson, Woods, Candilis, De Carlo, etc, who advocated for the return to contextual "critical regionalism". The situation or context was important to them and hence was aligned to the ideas of the Situationist International. They were driven by the "...totalistic will for change..." As indicated by the founder Debord (quoted in Sadler, p.2). The will for change created the new consciousness, new thinking completely different from the functionalism of CIAM.

John McKean (2004) in his monogram *"Giancarlo De Carlo: Layered Places"* points out that for people like De Carlo, it is the design process which is dependent on the identification of the layers of the context; reading these layers then designing a response to the contextual forces.

An examination of the minutes of the first community meeting during the 2008 Wilkinsburg UL held on 17th September reveal that the model was used in discussion around the physical environment; the social activities, economic activities and to identify problem areas that needed addressing.

The residents were able to identify misrepresentations of vacant lots within the model and had extensive discussions concerning the dilapidated buildings and vacant lots. One resident commented:

> "There needs to be single family homeowner- occupied houses. The Pittsburgh History and Landmarks Foundation, (PHLF) has done that. Single family homeowner- occupied homes raised the tax base and provide relief for other taxpaying community members." "There's a lot of kid activity on Whitney. All of Whitney Ave. is inundated with kids. The activity has both positive and negative influences on the neighborhood." "Wanted to replace them with community gardens. ? * Centre / Holland could become a neighborhood grocery store. The vacancies could become children play spaces" (Urban Lab-Wilkinsburg (2008))

Suggestions also came from the community in response to prompting by the facilitators on ways to improve the areas. And possible areas of catalytic projects that might help develop the community economically.

The third technique adopted by the UL is the indirect method. It is used to develop the understanding of the value system of the community through direct observation, surveys and questionnaires. The data can be easily quantitatively analyzed and most researchers and some design professionals prefer it as it avoids the feared pitfalls of confrontation that direct participative methods may bring.

A sample of the questionnaire that was used in conjunction with the School of Social Policy and Management is included (*appendix B*). The questionnaire collected the profiles of the residents, how frequently they used communal facilities, positive and negative aspects of the existing facilities, activities they enjoyed and whether they intended to purchase property in the area.

It may be perceived as a weak method because the information obtained will be based on the questions asked by the researcher and as such may not reflect the true voice of the community. Also, the sampling procedures assumed a homogeneous population which may not reflect true social-cultural and political forces that shape that community.

For the city of Pittsburgh, this could probably not reflect the true picture in a context that has had a history of racial tension. However as indicated above, it still is a robust technique to yield data, especially ones based on co-observation and discussions on perceptions held by both the community members and the students.

The forces that affect the physical, social and economic systems of a community are complex and require research to understand the local context. The local knowledge base provides the materials for research which can be untapped using the skills of expert students from outside the community acting as catalysts to unpack the intricacies. Community participation is used as a process where co-design and co-discovery of issues occur on equal footing.

Most architects and schools of architecture approach design as consisting of instrumental problems as Till points out:

> "...In education, the architectural studio is held up as an exemplar of problem-based learning, the space where students are set a problem and through creative and reflective act of design come to a solution..." (2005, p.35)

The approach is negative because it ignores the assets that already exist in the community in which the design is situated, and crushes the hope of the community with the only hope being transforming places from being bad to less bad. The process of seeking the solution is separated from the one of forming or framing the problem to be solved.

The participative process becomes an asset as the citizen-experts (resident) come together in a shared negotiation with expert-citizens (professional) to reach consensus on what the problem to be solved really is. The definition of the problem is not the preserve and privilege of the experts, but of all who experience the forces that shape that community. John Forester (1985, p.119) introduced a new way of seeing design not as a "...search for solution but for sense-making". I would argue it is not only sense- making, but design becomes place-making; place-creation because in the process of the co-design, a community is built.

It comes from the trans-formative approach of participation and empowers the users, it builds consensus and community, creates cohesion among the participants and a sense of belonging. This is underpinned by the desire of the will of the participants to achieve mutual understanding; thereby also developing new ways of communicating to be able to reach this consensus.

The images above (*Figures 2.11A and 2.11B*) are an illustration of how co-design methods are used at the UL at CMU. An examination of the images reveals that the power of decision making still resides with the design-expert rather than the expert-citizen as the designers rather than the residents/ community are in control of the drawings.

Success in the participative process requires good communication between the designers and the other stakeholders. In traditional processes the predominant method is almost always a one-way communication system with those holding power informing or simply telling the users what decision have been made. Thus, even though it will affect their lives, no one really seems to care. The main language of communication used by architects is drawings, which as reduction representation are not always clearly understood by lay persons. Furthermore, the main hurdle with the method of representation is that it resides in the mind of the designer and as such is not "available for mutual understanding with other participants" Jill (2005, p.37).

There are several possible reasons for this; firstly, the community's capacity to express views may not have been built to the level required prior to the meeting. Secondly, the pedagogical agenda drives the process and methods. The students

Figure 2.11A: Co-Design at Community Meeting?. Source: Remaking Cities Institute (2009)

Figure 2.11B: Co-Design at Community Meeting?. Source: Remaking Cities Institute (2009)

have to present their finding in a particular manner to meet their submission requirements.

The choice of the two methods mentioned above have a historical background that is rooted in the local context both socially and politically. Whether they make a difference to the outcome is open to debate. In both methods, the pedagogical needs seem to be the driver rather than the community who are used mainly to gather data required for the students' design.

The level of participation by the community residents in decision making is secondary because they are asked during the meetings to respond to what the students have prepared outside the scene in the design studio. However, there seems to be an attempt to get them involved through the use of focus group discussions. I will now look at some of the social and political layers that fostered circumstances where such methods could succeed.

Participation in design processes by any community required the existence of strong community organizations and networks that start to build the desire to participate beyond protesting stages. Laurence Glasco points to the existence of "... interracial coalitions that provided the Civil Rights Movements in Pittsburgh with additional momentum..." (2001, p.5).

The coalitions included the all-white member Urban League, the Pittsburgh Presbytery, National Association for the Advancement of Coloured People (NAACP), etc, who tackled various important issues that would have divided the community on race: examples include housing, and employment. Collins argued that:

> "...Segregated schools led to unequal education... and in Pittsburgh in 1959 an overwhelming majority of the city's classes for "slow learning" and "retarded" children were located in schools with 80 percent or higher black enrollment. At the same time, 85 percent and 69 percent of the classes for "mentally superior" children at the elementary and secondary levels, respectively, were in schools that were at least 75 percent white..." (2003, p.124).

This multi-racial coalition, Glasco (2001) further points out, helped change public perceptions of the Civil Rights Movement from one that fought only for the exclusive benefits of blacks to one that fights for social justice and the rights of all Americans, as enshrined in the constitution and promoted by Jefferson.

The group interaction method was thus adopted in the UL in the form of a participatory community meeting. The method responded to the political context in Pittsburgh where the minority groups were demanding to be heard and to stop the demolition of their communities. David Lewis (1978) attributes the methods adopted in response, to understanding the community better.

This argument is based on the premise that the citizens have a better view and understanding of the local needs, with greater clarity and wholeness than the bureaucrats and the technocrats looking in. This came from the "...help offered by people coming out, public officials and citizens' working together to identify and resolve problems..." And in addition through the meetings with the community leadership; the result was that "...many local issues of the community were identified because of citizen participation..." (1979, p.28). There is thus a claim to collaboration between not only students of architecture but also from other disciplines such as Social Policy and Management.

However as pointed out earlier, the minutes of the Wilkinsburg Community meeting in 2008 reveal that just over a third of the participants were students or faculty members of the UL. In addition, the minutes reveal a muted response from the community as previously pointed out by David Lewis, the participation is not as overwhelming.

In Pittsburgh, a different approach to renewal was used even though underpinned by the Housing Acts of 1949. Mayor Lawrence in his speech at the first Harvard University Conference in 1956 argued that redevelopment of Pittsburgh was taken with the view that:

> "...It was a city worth saving; that a successful organism in the plan of nature must have a head and nerve center; that the people of a city can take pride and glory in it in our own times as the Athenians did under Pericles or the Florentines under Lorenzo..." as posited by Kreiger and Saunders (2009, p.200)

This highlights important aspects to a community's redevelopment; firstly, the belief by all involved that it is worth saving. Unfortunately, in the case of Pittsburgh during the first urban renaissance of the 1950's-1960's, it was the belief not of the community but the elite business people, politicians who thought they knew what was best for the city. The second aspect it highlights is the importance of visionary leadership, in this case Mayor Lawrence and wealthy patron Richard King Mellon both usurping the opportunity for community participation, thus negating their importance. It was a top-down decision making process that was bound to cause problems as it did.

The third important aspect to the approach in Pittsburgh's redevelopment was the reliance on building a coalition between politicians, developers, bankers and influential wealthy patrons. This approach is what one may call the urban regime coalition, as pointed out by the seminal work by Floyd Hunter in 1950s.

Hunter used "a power matrix to describe a network of top financiers and corporate executives that had the ability to influence the local policy agenda" (quoted in Crawley; 2005, p.9). He examined the decisions by a panel of fourteen highly knowledgeable people in the community to select the top ten leaders from four categories of leaders in business, government, the non-profit sector and social circles.

His findings revealed a high correlation between the panels on which the top leaders or movers and shakers sat that revealed the existence of a closed group mostly from the corporate world that influenced the policy making before it was brought to the public agenda. This basically pushes the community interest to the bottom of the rung of decision-making; they are merely surrogates. It was the feeling of not being involved in decisions that affected their lives that partly contributed to the rise in the Civil Rights Movement, the formation of community advocacy groups and the involvement by institutions in the provision of service to these communities.

Most active participants in place-creation are property investors, developers, estate financiers and users. The interest of the first three groups is purely economic gain. It is not therefore surprising that the key stake holders will come from this group rather than the consumers and users of the place created, whose contribution is always on the margins.

In Pittsburgh as early as the 1940s, the ruling elites controlling development worked through the Allegheny Conference on Community Development (ACCD), a private sector leadership organization dedicated to economic development and quality of life.

The ACCD coordinated the partnership of the private and public sectors in dealing with issues of redevelopment in Pittsburgh even before the Federal government had provided the funding for most of the redevelopment efforts. This placed Pittsburgh on top of the nation's cities as a model for urban renaissance.

The ACCD started in the early 1940s with projects to improve transportation links within the region and to tackle environmental pollution that was typical of Pittsburgh from the coal industries. The coalition consisted of the wealthy Richard King Mellon who also was the president of Pittsburgh Regional Planning Association; the Carnegie Institute of Technology president (perhaps from influence of Andrew Mellon), the mayor David Lawrence and other local leaders. The process was top down in that the community views were not solicited, yet decisions to redevelop were taken that affected their lives completely. They lost homes, businesses, schools and social relations through the demolition and renewal efforts as discussed elsewhere in the dissertation.

In Pittsburgh, the renewal of the Point district has been cited as one of the successes of the private-public partnership. Teaford posits that the renewal was the result of:

> "...Product of state, local, and private effort...example is the park development on which Equity Life Assurance Society constructed a complex of office towers...triggering further private office construction" (2000, p.457).

The idea of the rebuilding of Pittsburgh was driven by the leadership of Richard King Mellon who chose to rebuild the city rather than abandon it, as pointed out by Lubove. He argued that ACCD was effective because

> "Mellon's leadership and the recruitment of the corporate elite provided it with the extraordinary potential power to be exercised through person deliberation as individuals rather than as representatives of their companies..." (1996, p.109).

This effectively interjected "moral and ethical responsibility" to the individual who was a member of the ACCD committee on a voluntary basis without being influenced by parent company. One wonders whose ethics they were underpinned on. I argue they paid allegiance to their parent company.

The process of urban regime coalition is different from the typical voting system as pointed out by Crawley who suggests:

> "...Widely shared political interests often fail to organize effectively because the constituents have rational incentives to free ride on the effects of others while the small group of elites on the other hand do not suffer the same organizational problems and will normally defeat their many, less well-organized opponents" (2005, p.12).

This further explains the reasons why in place-making, the power still resides with the few elites rather than the community it is supposed to serve. However, the advantages of such a coalition is that once a consensus is reached, the actions could be quick and significant but carry the risk that the actions would likely be based on satisfying the needs of the business community and thus alienating the rest of the community.

The uniqueness of the ACCD was the collaborative approach where not only key movers and shakers of development were involved but also, they relied on:

> "...Technical and professional assistance of the leading planning and research agencies such as the Pittsburgh Regional Planning Association..." Lubove (1996, p.110).

Also, Richard King Mellon was a wealthy Republican businessman who had never met or spoken to David Lawrence, a Democrat mayor of Pittsburgh, but they were able to work across party lines in collaborative ventures.

It is thus not surprising that the UL at CMU used similar methods and techniques that were already well established historically within Pittsburgh. They however modified the approach by ACCD in that they involved the community in minor aspects of decision making. The collaboration was between the key stakeholders such as the developers/ landowners and financial institutions with the community involvement coming in when the decision to develop the area has been taken. The minutes of the UL at Wilkinsburg in September 2008 reveal that out of the 44 participants, only 2 are recorded as either resident or neighbor.

The UL relied on the existing grassroots network through the Community Design Centre of Pittsburgh, CDCP and the delegated leadership that already existed within the community, to learn about the community issues. The majority of the community had surrogate roles. It is not clear why they did not participate in large numbers despite the public announcements. The clue perhaps comes from the comment by Prof. John Nolan of CMU:

> "A lot of Wilkinsburg residents are suffering from 'plan fatigue,'" he says. "They've heard a lot of ideas, but their outcomes are not readily apparent. We are going to come up with an idea, one concrete thing, and we will leave something behind." (2008, p.1).

However, the urban regime coalition approach enabled them to identify and formulate the vision statements and "community" objectives, and the partnerships with the local politicians and businesses to ensure success of the proposals.

Hutzell & Rico-Gutierrez in their conference paper presented at the 43rd ISOCARP Congress point out that:

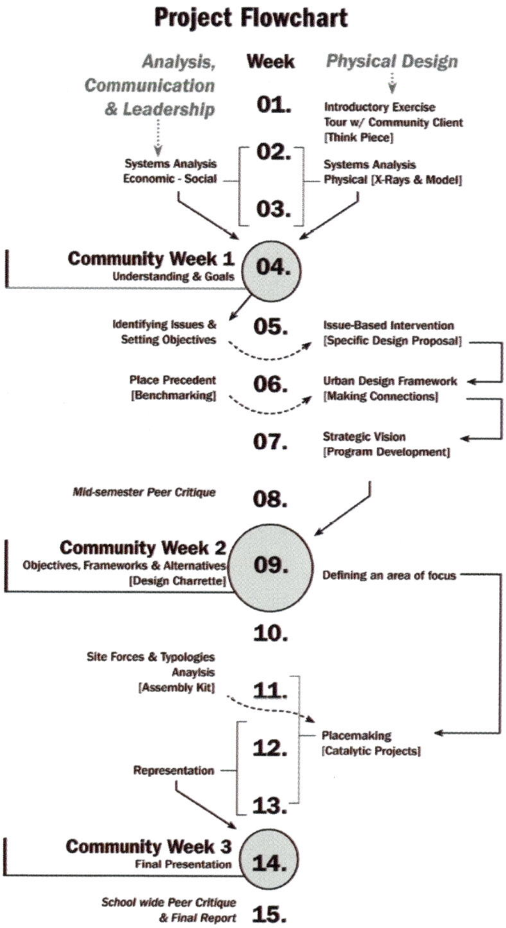

Figure 2.12 (Left): UL Process Flow Chart
Source: Gatti (2009, p.14)

Figure 2.13 (Below): UL Process Flow Chart
Source: Rico-Gutierrez & Hutzell (2006, p.xiii)

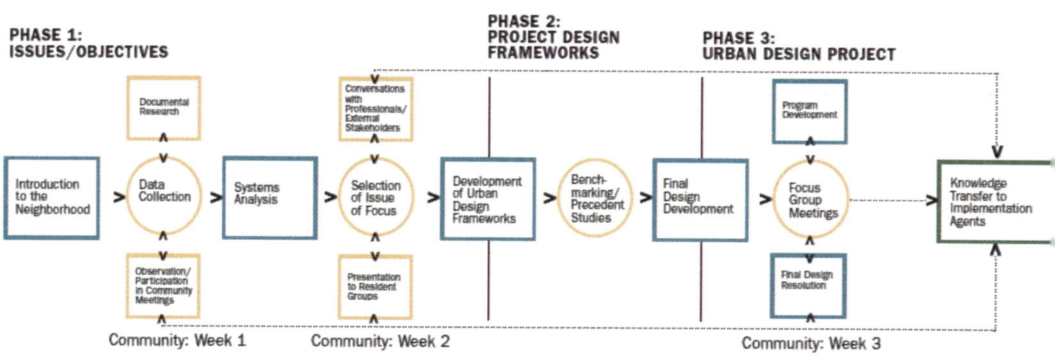

> "...The students and community have developed several visionary designs and have left behind a community group trained on participatory design process..." (2007, p.2).

The university has therefore provided a long-term partnership with the community without necessarily being providers of direct technical assistance. The methodology of group interaction where partnership is formed is cognizant of the already existing history of a community working together, rising out of the civil rights movement in 1960s. This view is supported by comments from Don Carter of Urban Design Associates and the current director of Remaking Cities Institute in an interview in April 2009.

A community meeting is held at the end of the systems analysis phase as discussed above. It provided the opportunity for reflection on what had been done so far and also for the students to check with the community if they had understood what the issues were. The use of the community meeting served as space for reflection and as part of what Hutzell & Rico-Gutierrez point out is "...a sequence of cumulative feedback loops that lead to a detailed and nuanced urban vision..." (2007, p.4). However, the flow diagram of the process (*Figures 2.12 and 2.13*) does not reveal the presence of continuous feedback loops. It is a linear telescopic process rather than a cyclic and reflective process. The direct interaction method thus responds to the community's needs and demands to be heard.

2.2.4 Urban Design Framework Phase: Methods and Influences

During the urban design framework (UDF), three main techniques emerge as preferred ways of working; indirect, group interaction and brainstorming methods. The first has been discussed but the second and third are discussed below. In the group discussions and brainstorming methods, participative processes really come to the forefront. I will first give a summary of the methods used in this phase then discuss how the techniques arose from the circumstances.

The UDF is one of the most important phases of the Urban Design process of the laboratory. It could potentially break the whole of the UL's work as pointed by Hutzell & Rico-Gutierrez (2007, p.5). It is developed through five stages; issue-based intervention, precedent study, making connections, strategic visions and definition of an area of focus.

The systems analysis findings from the first phase are presented to the local community meeting and discussed. It provides opportunity for the residents to express their views on the walk-about, and also for the setting up of the objectives as pointed out in the previous section. The feedback is recorded to summarize the issues, goals, and objectives for the area and in addition to amend the initial goals set after the meeting with community leaders during the systems analysis phase when awareness methods were used (*See minutes in Appendix B*).

The community meeting is a participative process even though the agenda seems to be run by the outsiders (students) acting as facilitators. Sanoff (2000, p.13) argues that the "appropriate or good decisions are not a preserve of the expert professional designer" hence even the non-professional designer has the capability and ability to examine alternatives and make decisions given the facts. It is from this basis that the student designer as an expert takes on the role of a facilitator to guide the community in identifying, discussing the various options and consequences and stating an opinion.

It involves a lot of listening, which allows the community to draw (representing thoughts visually), build models, modify, and analyze maps together with the students to come out with a problem statement (*Figures 2.11A & 2.11B*). The issues identified as problems are discussed and mapped with correlating community objectives. This becomes the brief or basis for generating and evolving the design idea. The methodology therefore responds to the local contexts in that it evolves from local issues.

2.2.5 Issue Based Intervention

In the first stage of the UDF, the UL work is carried out through focused intervention that is based on one objective. The objective is selected from a summary list that came out of the first community meeting. In this sense, the community has contributed to the definition of what is at the heart of the community. A review of the minutes of the 2008 Wilkinsburg UL reveal consensus on the need to tackle the vacant properties on the site. One suggestion was:

> "...To replace them with community gardens; a neighborhood grocery store or children play spaces..." (Urban Lab -Wilkinsburg (2008))

The scope of intervention is limited in scale, but is on the urban scale, not limited to a small building. These could be used as areas for catalytic projects that might help develop the community economically.

This echoes Solà-Morales' argument where he tells his students:

> "...Always to distinguish size from scale, in other words to say that being urban does not mean to be big, and that the question of urban scale, which is certainly large, does not mean it has to be expressed in huge elements or in huge buildings. Sometimes small elements, small buildings, small spaces are charged with urban meaning with larger implications than huge interventions or large combinations of it" (cited in Klebanow; 1998, p.5).

The proposed intervention must be clearly communicated to the audience and the changes proposed must be physically visible. This method seems to be heavily leaning on the visual-artistic tradition theoretical framework that follows on from works of Lynch (1960) and Rowe and Koetter (1978).

A method used by the UL to address issue based intervention is that of participative community meetings. The process can be quite tense as pointed out by Lewis that:

> "...Something good could come out of the fights that occur during participation as it allows for dialogue that would lead to a healing process..." (1979, p.27).

It is claimed that the community meeting resulted in two important things; firstly, healing began as the resident participants started to see the assets of their neighborhood and started talking of their visions and inspirations, where they would like to see the community go. It is claimed that their capacity to listen to one another was enhanced through the process and their public speaking skills developed leading to the capacity for civic responsibility. Would this process lead to the development of a new consciousness, a new way of thinking of place creation process?

Secondly the new participative process brought forth the realization that architecture is an act of intervention informed by the social, political and physical forces of that particular moment, time and place and therefore responds well to the local context. The help offered by the local people dropping in and out of the venue where the design *charrette* was taking place allowed the stakeholders in students and the citizens to work together to resolve the common problems. The desire to participate is driven by the importance of the issues at stake and their wish to resolve those issues. This allowed for the formation of collaborative joint ventures that are focused the issues. However, it seems contradictory in that the documents of the UL reveal that joint ventures had existed prior to the engagement with the community.

It is difficult to ascertain otherwise all processes would be underpinned on this methodology. What might emerge as crucial in the abilities and charisma of the facilitator? It appears that the facilitation process relied on methods coming from psychotherapy of the 1960s. The benefits are suggested by Frank who argued that the

> "...Primary function of all psychotherapies is to combat demoralization which aggravates and is aggravated psychiatric symptoms through restoring the patient's sense of mastery..." (1974, p.271).

The aggrieved community are given a forum to vent their feelings freely in order to break the boundaries that separate them. Frank further argued that "psychotherapy was an influencing process and that we may learn about what accounts for change by looking at other influencing processes" (quoted in Arkowitz 1997, p.242).

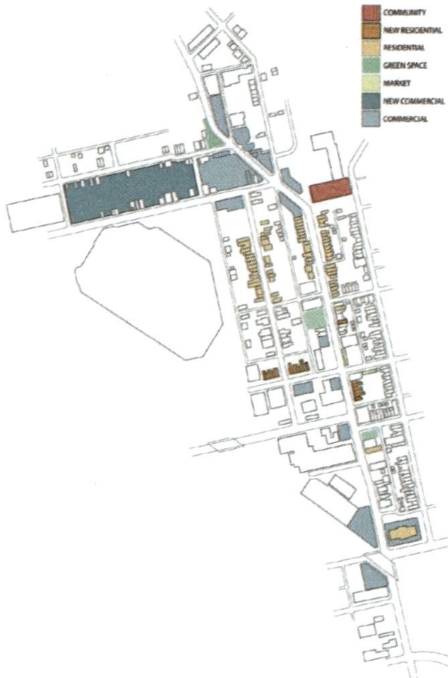

Figure 2.14: Brighton Road UL Proposal
Source: Rico-Gutierrez & Hutzell (2006, p.105)

Figure 2.15: Santa Catarina Market, Barcelona (designed by Enric Miralles). Source: Onyango (2008)

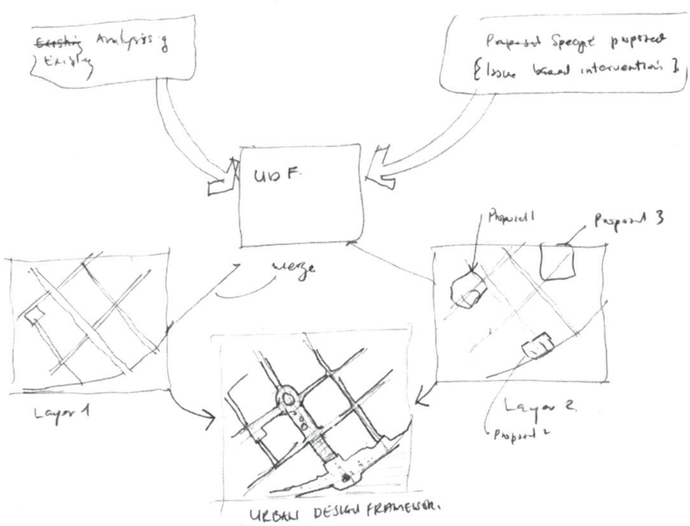

Figure 2.16: Urban Design Framework diagram. Source: Onyango (2008)

Faber (2006) noted that the sharing typically occurs after difficulties such as antagonistic fights over decision making, resources etc. He identifies the origins of use of psychotherapy methods to the:

> "...Political sensibilities of the 1960s such as civil rights, women's rights, sexual openness offered and at times demanded, new ways of accepting and understanding others that emphasized learning about and sharing of ourselves with others..." (2006, p.8).

Therefore, one would argue that the objectives of a good facilitator are to persuade to align the community's objectives with those of the designer who normally is paid by the elite. Here we see the use of palliative cure as a process of engaging the community.

2.2.6 Precedent Study

The second stage of the UDF is called benchmarking, that is, setting the standards that drive the framework. It starts with the identification of relevant place precedents that relate to the selected objectives. The precedent must be a completed and "successful" project hence its use as a benchmark. It is not clear what is meant by "successful", however. The choice of the precedent is important to demonstrate relevance. The precedents are represented in graphics; photos, diagrams, etc.

Figure 2.14 illustrates how the proposal relies on the traditional urban morphology of the area. The infill typology echoes the urban block of Brighton road prior to deterioration. For the market proposal, the students looked at two precedents; Santa Catarina Market in Barcelona by Miralles (*Figure 2.15*) which is within residential neighborhood and the markets in Istanbul.

2.2.7 Making Connections

The third stage of the Urban Design Framework is focused on linking the various strategic single projects by making connections between them. This is done through the analysis of existing linkages (phase 1), corridors, districts, nodes then recommendation of areas of intervention and what the new connections will be.

The Figure 2.16 (precedent page) is my interpretation of what an urban design framework might look like. It highlights that the methodology chosen is in response to the recognition that the place-creation process is the result of a mesh of layers. This is underpinned by the situationist methods of Italy, France and UK where the Team X rebels were going back to regional criticisms, as previously pointed out.

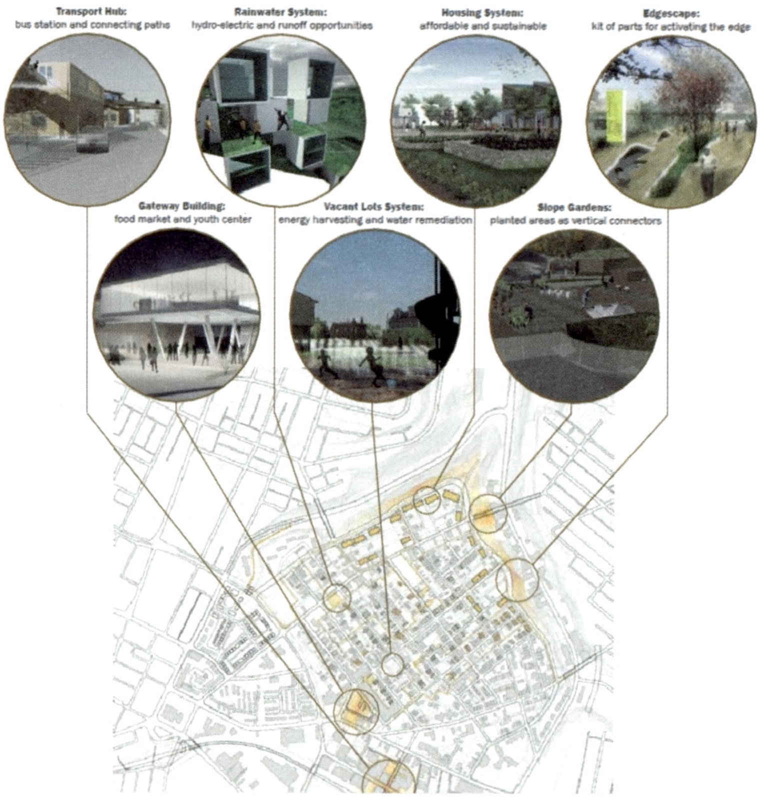

Figure 2.17: Strategic Vision: The Urban Lab: Larimer Studio-Visual Artistic tradition?. Source: El Samahy and Kline (2008, p.5)

2.3 Strategic Vision: Program Development

The fourth stage of the UDF is aimed at producing a guide of *where* and *how* the intervention will be required to address the issues that meet community objectives. The concrete intervention is informed by and checked against the issues the system analysis revealed. Alternative proposals are produced, not just a single idea and are used as tools for generating and evaluating the proposals.

The key word in this stage is *strategic*, not everything everywhere, but an intervention that is limited in scale and number. It should not be a rebuilding program that will disrupt and disperse the community. The strategic vision is seen as the catalyst that positively transforms the community, tackling questions such as which comes first, where and why. It should be flexible and not prescribed, and as such it is not a comprehensive plan.

This stage is presented and communicated in the form of perspective sketches, modified photographs, sections, plans and precedent studies. It leans heavily on the visual artistic traditional framework of Urban Design (*Figure 2.17*). Note that ten proposed projects are located in specific areas within the site as agreed in the community meeting number 2. This strategy allows for focus that would be catalytic to the renewal of the area

2.3.1. Defining an Area of Focus

This is the last stage in the UDF and is used as community feedback. The use of a single focus allows for depth of the intervention and a catalyst for community renewal. However, the project selected must be complex enough for further development for the rest of the semester (design process) to meet the pedagogical requirements of the course. The area of focus is selected through a mini- *charrette* at the community workshop where work done to date is presented to a group and discussed.

The student groups then work with the affected neighborhood to refine and develop the area of focus during the second community meeting. The methodology used relies on a series of questions to gather feedback from the community (*see minutes of Wilkinsburg UL in appendix B*). This is how dialogue is introduced into the process since it is the community that should drive the area of focus and not the designers. However, the minutes reveal that the designers prompted the community to respond in a particular manner as reported by Nolan:

> "Could the Park and Ride facility be used as weekend gathering space while it is vacant? What areas shown on the model are often traveled for pedestrians and cars?" (2008, p.1).

The UDF is seen as the guideline for the future growth and change of neighborhood over time. It looks at; strengthening existing corridors (filling up empty sites, nodes, re-aligning blocks, introducing pedestrian areas etc); interrogating the potential for new nodes; connections of activities. To do this it uses multiple scales, not just one.

During the UDF phase, the potential for change is identified and analyzed and the areas that are stable are highlighted, as are the areas that are changing in land-use, economics, and social and physical value systems. For example, in the Larimer Studio, some of the opportunities identified for action by the community included; "...greening of vacant lots, new green business start-ups, new charter School, more local shops, vacant lots to gardens, pedestrian routes..." El Samahy and Kline (2008, p.10). The UDF is used to demonstrate how the proposed interventions tie into the changes identified above.

The proposal is presented in graphical form based on community objectives and is an outline spatial guide for the physical form of change (*Figure 2.18*). The

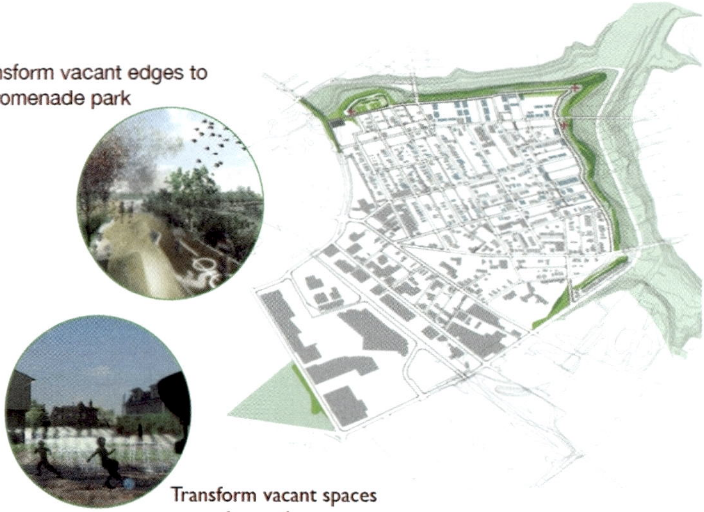

Figure 2.18: Larimer UL Studio: Example of UDF response to objectives. Source: El Samahy and Kline (2008, p.48)

image illustrates the interpretation of the vision from the community objective to provide more green space and to transform some of the empty lots into activity areas These are represented as bike path and river walkway and urban garden that includes children's play area. The UDF is the conceptual guideline for the next phase of design, but still accepts changes or refinement as the specific design develops.

2.3.2 Strategies and tactics of the processes at the CMU laboratory

The three methods that are predominant in this phase are indirect, group interaction and brainstorming methods. The indirect method is used during the community meeting to gather information about urban problems. This is done through the use c surveys and questionnaires that are sent out to the community earlier in first phase.

The data is analyzed and presented to the community for discussion in graphic forms. Its drawback is that the information obtained is based on the questions asked by the researcher and as such might not reflect the true voice of the community. The student designer who facilitates the conversation has the power to direct the conversation in ways that suite the pedagogical objectives of the studio requirements. Also, the sampling procedure assumes a homogeneous population, which may not reflect the true social-cultural and political forces that shape that community.

2.3.3 Indirect Method

The indirect method arises out of the historical circumstances of injustices of the new deal of 1950s and 1960s. Communities red lined for renewal efforts through demolitions had not been involved in the proposals. The understanding of how communities were formed and what actually makes them work had been ignored by most professionals involved with the renewal efforts despite good work coming out of academia in that period led by the Chicago School of Sociology.

Within academia there had also been research work coming from the Chicago School over the previous half-century. This impacted the research into urban problems through their new methodology which used the city as both the laboratory and truth spot. (Gieryn, 2006). The appreciation of the complexity of the problems increased and the use of the traditional top-down regulatory and re-distributive techniques for seeking solutions were waning. A bottom-up approach or a mixture of both seems to be a way forward.

Not far from Pittsburgh, at University of Pennsylvania, (UPenn) a sociologist Herbert Gans, who had studied at University of Chicago, was critical of the renewal efforts. His work was based on the study of a diverse neighborhood in Boston occupied mainly by an Italian community targeted and red lined as a slum. Gans, along with many other professionals like Davidoff and Denise Scott-Brown at UPenn, was willing to challenge the accepted common wisdom of the time.

Of interest perhaps is the possible link between David Lewis and Denise Scott Brown who were both born in South Africa and were aware of the disparities in economic and social justice that existed there. She pens: "...no child in South Africa could be unaware of the agonized issues of justice and equity among the races there..." (2004, p.107). Denise Scott-Brown had studied in England where she met Peter Smithson during the 1956 CIAM summer school in Venice who encouraged her to study at UPenn under Louis Kahn if possible.

At UPenn, Denise Scott-Brown met David Crane and Herbert Gans who were among the first to criticize the urban renewal for ignoring the '*is*' and focusing on the '*ought*'. Gans saw the *ought* as a top-down approach to renewal that ignores the context and people in it as it was and suggest that the

> "...Social thinkers at Penn set the kinetic notion of city building that focused on sequence and the roles of many players, against the traditional view of architect-controlled master planning, action and reaction..." as pointed out by Scott-Brown and Venturi (2004, p.114).

In parallel there was the work of William F Whyte on urban society that studied the social organization of an Italian Slum in Boston published in 1943 as *Street Corner Society* where he illustrated that "...the urban underclass relied on its participation in dense social networks, albeit visibly different from those of middle-class Anglo-American society..." as pointed out by Haumann (2009, p.36). This work not only dispelled the core idea of the renewal efforts through redlining by making the argument that the poor were not living in conditions at the peripheries of social decay that needed intervention.

Herbert Gans like Whyte followed up on the work, publishing findings on another Italian community in Boston where he was critical of the approaches used by the designers then that:

> "...The professionals' evaluation of the behavior of slum residents is based on class-based standards that often confuse behavior which is only culturally different with pathological or antisocial acts..." (quoted in Haumann; 2009, p.36).

He argued for a change in approach to one that considered the values and opinions of the communities affected by the renewal efforts if legitimization and acceptance were to occur.

By 1962, Davidoff and Scott-Brown were teaching their students at the School of Design radical approaches that questioned the role of the professional within the society. Scott-Brown had as early as 1950 researched on "...Gesalt psychology's notion that meaning is derived from context..." (2004, p.8). Her work contributed to the revolutionary reactions to the failings that were coming out of the CIAM's ideology of functional purity and minimalisms.

In the late 1950s and early 1960s, Scott-Brown and others at UPenn were working on the evolving ideas that connected politics and planning through democratic community participation. She points to the work of David Crane emphasizing the importance of understanding the change within a city in order to design for it. The efforts at UPenn contributed to the adoption of the new methodologies of understanding community formation, the communities themselves and also the development of participatory methods by planners and architects.

2.3.4 Group Interaction Method

The second technique, the group interaction method, relies on a smaller number of participants, of about six to ten, working with a facilitator to discuss relevant issues as pointed out by Sanoff (2000). It is interactive and takes the form of workshops where ideas, recommendations and decisions are made. It is a hands-on approach using all available materials in the discussions such as photographs and models to explore alternatives (*Figures 2.19A, 2.19B & 2.19C*).

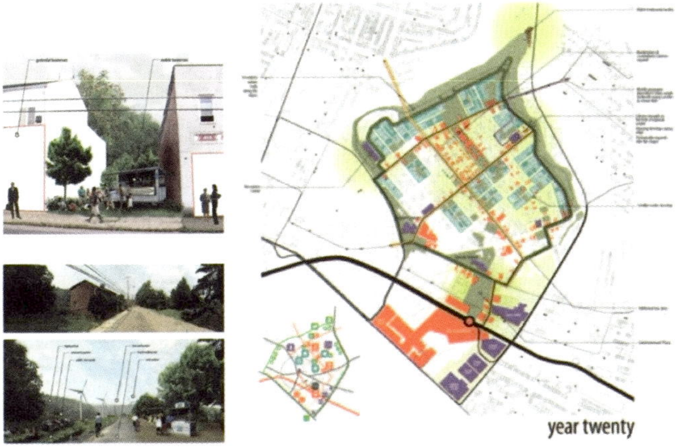

Figure 2.19A: Larimer UL Studio. Example of UDF Alternative 1. Source: El Samahy and Kline (2008, p.42)

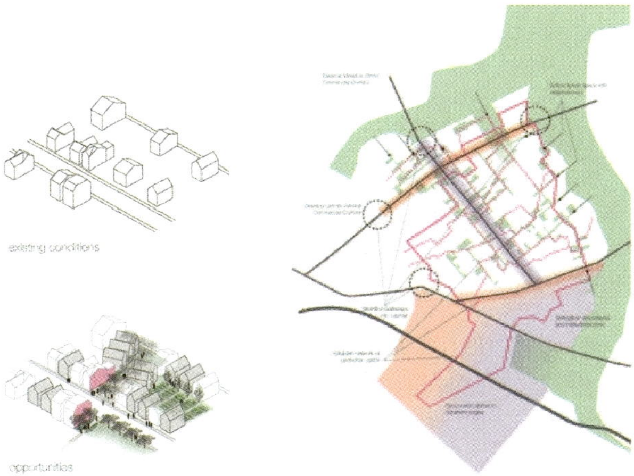

Figure 2.19B: Larimer UL Studio. Example of UDF Alternative 2. Source: El Samahy and Kline (2008, p.43)

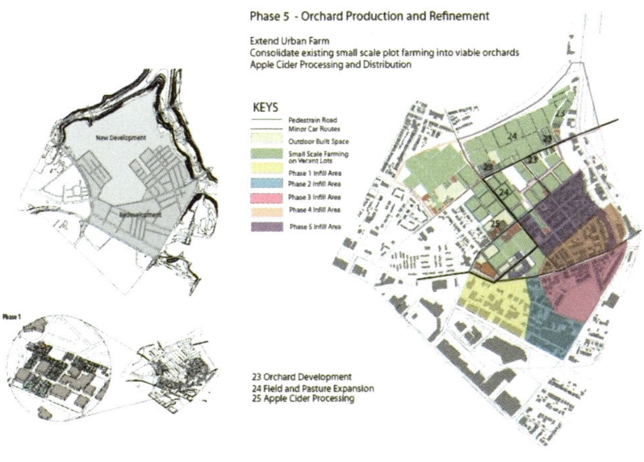

Figure 2.19C: Larimer UL Studio. Example of UDF Alternative 3. Source: El Samahy and Kline (2008, p.44)

The Larimer Studio demonstrates how the group interaction technique was used to come up with three UDFs or alternatives. The image above illustrates three alternatives, Figures 2.19A/B/C. Figure 2.19A, and is one proposal that deal with vacant land by firstly tackling the smaller spaces between the existing building stocks. These are catalytic projects with a mobile kiosk, which becomes the gathering space. At a later stage this can be moved elsewhere when the decision to infill the gap is carried out. The next two images illustrate the before and after intervention of a lonely block on a stretch of road at the edge of a steep cliff. The proposal is to demolish the block, build a bike/ footpath and create a picnic area overlooking the rest of the city. The strategy responds to the community objective of greening the area and in addition, a wind farm is proposed.

Figure 2.19B has two images illustrating infill-housing blocks. Note how the immediate work is provision of canvas for community artists or public use to enhance the area. Secondly the infill blocks are placed in such a way as to create square/ open spaces for local gathering. The area at the back of the blocks is proposed for urban farm/ allotments to provide employment as well as locally produced fresh vegetables and flowers. The gables are to be used as a canvas for painting murals by local artists or young persons.

Figure 2.19C proposes targeted redevelopment starting with areas with the most building stock. The areas with most vacant lots were used as apple orchard linked to cider processing plant that both meet community objectives of provision of employment. The areas used for the orchard were earmarked for expansion later should the community grow.

The interactive group meeting at the end of the UDF phase and the first community meeting takes the form of a *charrette*. The community is broken down into small groups working to facilitate students to explore issues and design. It also relies on the third method, the brainstorming.

The brainstorming technique is very good for the generation of many ideas by a group working rapidly, relying on producing as many ideas as possible without criticism. Sanoff (2000, p.71) identifies six ways in which brainstorming is carried out: gallery, pin card, nominal group techniques, Cranford Slip Writing, the *ring ii* process and the Delphi method.

UL uses the pin card techniques where cards are passed around the table and facilitators ask the community participants to write down ideas within a limited time. After the time has elapsed the cards are passed around and ideas shared; additional discussion is encouraged in the process. These cards are then evaluated by another group and ranked according to perceived priority. The groups then reconvene and discuss the ideas from each group and consensus is reached.

As previously pointed out (*Section 2.2*), David Lewis' time at St Ives must have exposed him to the Surrealists like Peter Lanyon and their methods that were common at that time that relied on what Breton calls:

> "...Psychic automatism in its pure state, by which one proposes to express verbally, by means of the written word, or in any other manner, the actual functioning of thought. Dictated by thought, in absence of any control exercised by reason, exempt from any aesthetic or moral concern..."
> (1969, p.26)

Many design professionals and even institutions have avoided direct community participative techniques because of the risks of unpredictability and hostility, a fear that perhaps stems from Saul Alinsky's (1909-1972) radicalism where he argued in '*Rules for Radicals: A Pragmatic Primer for Realistic Radicals*' that "...moral rationalization is indispensable at all times of action whether to justify the selection or the use of ends or means" (1971, p.43)."

He saw the immediate interest of the community as the driver for rallying to its defense and hence he organized people around sensible ideas and identified opponents to fight. In his view the power must always lie with the community to hire and fire the organizer or ask him to leave once the objectives were met. The role of the organizer was facilitation and capacity building through education in an effort of self-help.

Alinsky's approach has been criticized for its antagonistic and confrontational approach towards the established institutions and authority. David Lewis agrees that because of this antagonism "...most architects are afraid of citizen activists..." (1979, p.27). The idea that the designer would use participative methods to work with the community is therefore shunned out of fear of the activist, an empowered citizenry.

In Alinsky's model, according to Bailey, "the organizer is a consultant from outside the community whose job is to get people to adopt a delegitimizing frame to break the power structure that holds them." (1971, p.137 in Stoecker and Stall, 1996). One may argue that the architect's role traditionally has not included organization. It is therefore a different approach to design that has been adopted at the UL which tries to meet some of the criticism of the Boyer report (see chapter 1). His model called for trained and experienced people.

In the 1960s Paul Davidoff challenged planners to promote participatory democracy and positive social change. He argued for advocacy as a method of achieving these goals by enabling all groups of society, especially those representing low-income families, to have a voice in the transformations of their built environment.

In the UL, the methodology responded to Alinsky's model by providing opportunities for training the designers to be facilitators, leaders who collaborate and work with the community for social and environmental justice. In addition, it responding to Davidoff's model of advocacy for the poor.

In the 1960s and continuing into the 1970s there was a decline in industrial activity from the steel mills, resulting in a decline in the city's population, rising unemployment, an increase in empty sites, abandoned buildings and the general blighting of the physical built environment of Pittsburgh. Several areas were affected by the so-called urban renewals that destroyed inner city neighborhoods.

The physical morphology of the city of Pittsburgh revealed an extensive network of vacant lots from aggressive demolitions by the city authority contributing to further blighting of the city. In areas such as the Hill district the areas considered blighted and eligible for redlining increased from 22 percent in 1950 to 66 percent in 1960 according to McIntyre (quoted in Hays; 1989, p.106). The vacant lots and destructions have caused a physical disconnect and isolation between various destinations of Pittsburgh that actually have great historic assets.

The poor communities saw their neighborhood destroyed or earmarked for destruction and the proposals that were on the table did not represent their views or way of life. The new development had no meaning to them. For the redevelopment to be meaningful, the *process* of its creation; the *involvement* of the citizens in its creation and the *sharing* in its creation process is what will give it value.

When the communities rejected the proposals for urban renewals in the Hill district, David Lewis saw the opportunity coming from an alternative view. In his article "*Listening and Hearing*" he attributes one of the UL methodologies to the

> "...New consciousness having been born out of situations like the students' riots and citizen activities..." of the 1960's (1979, p.27).

He points out that this called for a new way in which architects looked at urban problems, how they engaged the users not as subjects, but as co-designers to the solutions that affected their lives. The architects had to start responding by acquiring skills that were sensitive and responsive to the local contexts in order to create the right form.

The community participates at various levels and times in the design process. This responds to several forces, including political ones, in the context of the Civil Rights Movement. Firstly, the political context that surrounded the USA, and Pittsburgh in particular, including during the 1960s several legislations that were enacted to deal with poverty, racial problems, social, economic and environmental injustices. The landmark legislations were the Voters Act of 1964, which gave minority black communities the right to participate in the democratic voting process and therefore, determination of their built environment. The Employment Act of 1967 also enabled the pursuit of employment that was previously inaccessible due to discrimination.

Prior to the passage of legislations in the 1960s the US government through Community Action Programs had placed emphasis on resident participation in key decision making, budget controls and risk analysis in all improvement programs that involved outside consultants. Today this has been transformed to what Kingsley, McNeely and Gibson (1997, quoted in Sanoff 2000, p.6) see as community-driven initiatives that place the community at the center of both the planning and implementation of the projects.

In the academic field, Paul Davidoff challenged planners to promote participatory democracy and positive social change. He argued for advocacy as a method of achieving these goals by enabling all groups of society, especially those representing low-income families, to have a voice in the transformations of their built environment. Attempts were made to relate design to social as well as its physical contexts through the setting up of the joint inter-agency and citizens' review processes such as R/UDAT (*see section 3.31*).

The UL methodology was also driven by the ideas that were based on Team X especially in the US where Perceval and Bakema were teaching at Columbia, and Lewis Mumford at UPenn, as pointed out by Van den Heuvel and Risselada (2005). The approach heralded a new thinking in designing cities that emphasized sociological cluster formation as a method of creating human associations and also collaborations with other professionals and users/ participants.

Denise Scott-Brown points out that "Herbert Gans rocked their functionalist ideas asking the question, functional for whom and was critical of modernist experts who set norms for others without awareness of their own biases..." (2009, p.30). The essential political questions underpinned by social and environmental justice were thus information on who participates, who decides, who benefits.

The Civil Rights Movements and the riots of late 1960s fostered "citizen groups who were engaging or using professional architects and planners as advocates [vehicles] for confronting the insensitive official policies" and to plead the citizen's case by demanding a hearing, as pointed out by Lewis (1979, p.27). The environment in government offices created bureaucrats at all levels that made decisions on behalf of the citizens without reference to those whose lives were affected by those decisions.

But then one could argue that the citizens have a better view and understanding of the local needs, with greater clarity and wholeness than the bureaucrats and the technocrats looking in. This necessitated a need for a different approach to designing communities, cities, neighborhoods, underpinned on consensus building.

Jeremy Till (2005) in his article "*The negotiation of hope*" illustrates how the transactions in the new deal for communities are reached through the statutory mandated process that embeds consultation and participation. I have in mind here the Fair Housing Act 1968 that was to be a remedy to discriminatory practices in renewals and mandated participation of the affected communities in the process.

Unfortunately, forced participation by legal means not only leads to fatigue and numbness because of this reminder to the participants of the history of failed promises. The failure is in the methodology that does not transfer power of decisions from the designer professionals to the community as Till (2005) explicitly pointed out there is barely discussions that take place about the merits of the schemes during the meetings yet a consensus must be reached to conclude and move forward.

The problem here lies in how the whole process takes place; the community has not been party to the creation process, neither were they party to the decision to have the community hall, but yet they have to decide on one choice, the drawing presented and the drawing presented! The alternative is missing; the very idea of their vision of what makes their community is also missing.

The statutory requirements must be met by a vote; preferably a positive vote, and any attempts at absentia are coaxed into a positive vote through manipulation...

> "...The facilitator is concerned about the hands that have not gone up and gently coaxes a response out of two old ladies sitting at the back of the hall...'couldn't hear a word you said' to which they shout, 'but it is a lovely building'..." Till (2005, p.23)

The mismatch between ideal participation and real participation has the undercurrents of power play that lead to manipulations, and disenfranchisements. In most of the cases where participative processes are used, the level of control given to the citizens is minimized for various reasons. One of the oft-cited statements is that the:

> "...Open design process and meetings become stages for confrontations..." between the various contending and competing interests which "...result in verbal abuse, violence and even arrests of one or two of the participants..." Lewis (1979, p.27).

This may be the case because, for peaceful participation, the political context has to be right; in other words, the capacity of the citizens to participate has to be built to accept divergence of opinions and views.

Jeremy Till rightly points out that participative architecture is fraught with challenges and it is probably not the first time such views have been expressed [see S. Arnstein, "The ladder of citizen participation" *Journal of the Institute of American Planners*. The range of participation in the place-creation process is wide, starting from barely any involvement to complete control of the decisions. The seminal paper by Sherry Arnstein (1967) identified the various levels of participation that she called "the ladder of participation" (*Figure 2.20*).

The top of the ladder represents a participative process in which the citizens have complete control of the process from the ignition of the idea to the transformation of their community. This is done through the identification of the problems, formulation of the problem, designing a solution to the problem,

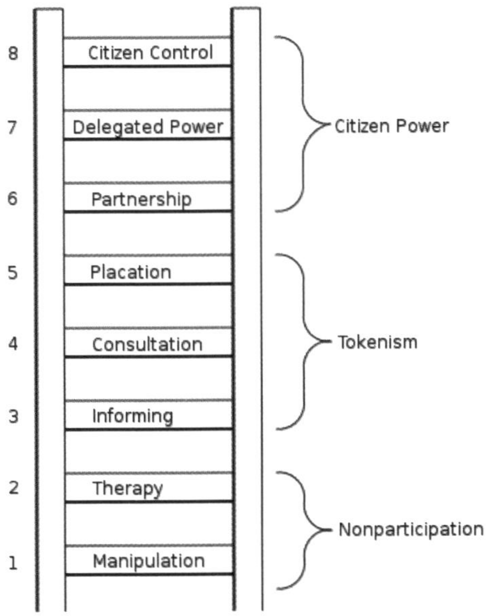

Figure 2.20. Levels of participation
Source: Arnstein (1969, p.2)

implementing the solution and finally reviewing or monitoring the transformed place. The middle part of the ladder, placation, is what is problematic because "...it is effectively deemed as an acceptable outcome of participation" Till (2005, p.25).

Literature reviews of participation and democracy reveal that in reality participation does not in itself shift the locus of power in decision-making hence "defeating the expectations of the participant citizens in actually gaining anything from the real process of spatial production". Till (2005, p.24). Despite the critiques, a participative process in place creation is definitely a better way of doing things because it does foster engagement of all stake holders in the decision process, if done properly and taken beyond the simple dialectic of 'you against us', inclusive versus exclusive; democratic versus authoritarian; bottom up versus top down.

But the politics of participation is complex, yet it lies at the core of the Western democratic ideal in that it:

> "...Serves as part of an educative process through which an individual will eventually come to feel little or no conflict between the demands of the public and private sphere..." Pateman (quoted in Till, 2005 p.25).

One may argue from the above that participation is likely to create the sense of belonging to a community, however; in contrast, its power to transform could threaten the existing democratic political systems, as can be seen in the health-care debates in the USA today. For this reason, there exists a power matrix where the maintenance of the status quo is to be desired and as such it leads to the acceptability of a placebo in the participation process.

In architectural participation, there is no difference from the model by Pateman in that in most cases the process is often used as a means to legitimize the decision by getting the support of the citizen user to decisions already taken and acted upon through a government's agent, the professional designer! This is supported by authoritative writer in the field, Sanoff, who argues that:

"...Participants have a sense of influencing the design process...it is not so much the degree to which they have their individual needs met, but the feeling of having influenced the decisions...". (1985, p.178-234)

This is further confirmed by Watts and Hirst (1982) and Lozano (1990) both advocating and accepting that their use of participative process is not only to increase acceptability of the designer but also to see the designer's role as steering the decision process to the desired goals. This raises questions on who does the designer work for as pointed earlier by Scott-Brown (2009).

The UL uses a *charrette* technique at the end of the urban design framework phase as part of the direct participation and brainstorming method. This is a forum where an interdisciplinary team, typically consisting of the community, elected officials, designers (students), developers, business owners and other stakeholders, work together to create a plan that could be implemented within a time frame. The key element of a typical c*harrette* is the compression of the process in time to an average of between four to seven days, participants working together through a series of feedback loops in brainstorming sessions, and sketching workshops.

The UL *charrette* however, is carried out on a community evening. One would thus be tempted to argue that the time frame may be too short for it to qualify as one. The mismatch between the ideal participation and real participation has the undercurrents of power play that lead to manipulations, and disfranchisements. In most of the cases where participative processes are used, the level of control given to the citizens is minimized for various reasons. However, in the UL, the short time is a response to the time constraints imposed by the rigid and short academic semester.

The meetings take place in the evenings at a community site which allows for the community to feel empowered by having control of the venue of the meeting and also having meetings occur at a time that suits them. The entire community, however, participates whenever it suits them without the need to take several days off, as there are at least three community meetings held over the entire semester. However, most other stakeholders such as developers, architects, business owners, transportation authorities and local leaders participate through scheduled meetings. This may raise questions of whether there is an urban regime coalition going on. (*See chapter on literature review*).

A review of the minutes of the UL available reveals that the time available for community participation is limited to the one given on the notice. The community do not in actuality have the opportunity to give feedback. However, a blog was set up in the Larimer Studio, but it is not certain if this alienates most members of the community who are in need as they may not be adept at using digital communication systems and may not even have access to a computer. In addition, only eighteen out of the forty-four attendees at the meeting were not either affiliated to CMU or an interested empowered stakeholder body such as consultant, owners of the building or the developer. The environment could easily have been intimidating to say the least.

The success of the *charrette* as a method is very much dependent on having a good facilitator who can read the group mood, and deal with participants who try to stall the process. They need to have certain personal characteristics that encourage participation by all, be patient, generous and humble. Not all these are available to all persons hence a question that arises is whether the UL process would produce good facilitators at the end of their education. I argue that it is not the case as these are personal characteristics of charismatic persons.

Therefore, it may not be a good method to use where mandated by legislation. It is very intense and as such is effective when the problems have been identified. Even though the students arranged and led the community meetings, the experienced teaching staffs were always at hand to assist in steering the discussion should it stall because of difficult participants with hidden agendas. The record of the meetings reveals that the community meeting ended with concluding remarks by the faculty leading the Studio thanking the participants and asking them to spread the word. There is no evidence of agreements on what to take forward or promissory notes that the views had been heard and would be considered.

The *charrette* process has typically been adapted to fit different projects using the same basic strategy with the planners as the catalysts; involving as many stakeholders as possible in a series of short, intensive design sessions. During the *charrette* there are times when collaborative hands-on sessions are used where the participants help root out potential problems, identify and debate possible solutions.

The forums are not merely to be used for informing the community about the development but they are in addition encouraged to be actively engaged in the shaping of the development and the building of confidence and community. The method could be successful as an approach to setting goals, where collaborative dialogue is needed, and for solving problems that cross different disciplines like those encountered in architecture and urban design. It can also be used in combination with other techniques during the participative process.

There are four types of *charrettes* as identified by Zuker (1995); educational, leadership forums/ retreats/ focus groups, traditional problem-solving and interdisciplinary teams all depending on how well the problems are defined. The first category of *charrette* is carried out by university students and their faculty members as facilitators/ guides and are geared toward service provision to the local community.

The students are not yet professionals, but the process is used as a training ground for their future career in urban design. As such the problems must be well defined for it to be a success and the faculty members must be available to take over the process dynamics if it is stalling. Just as urban design is difficult to define, the handouts given to the students in the various laboratories are not precise on what the task at hand was other than to develop a vision for the community. The pedagogy seems underpinned on enhancing students' experience in leadership and communication skills as pointed out by Gatti (2009).

Because of being rooted in the community and neighborhood, the various forces affect them in a way that the traditional method would not have dealt with. The choice is crucial in that it is the appropriate scale where the community can find meaning and be empowered.

The *charrette* has a fast pace in the participation and problem-solving process. Because all the stakeholders are in the same room willing to participate, the process allows for consideration of the individual's interest placed for discussion which is then modified by others through the discussion. The modification is important to the process; reflection of decisions made earlier is carried out to eventually arrive at a consensus.

The consensus itself is not a loss to the original idea that the individual came to the meeting with, but rather again as Avery (1981) commented:

> "...Consensus is not a compromise where one gives up something they want, something assumed fixed, but is rather a profoundly different event, allowing for reformulation such that what you had wanted changes with new information and a better vision is generated..." quoted in Sanoff (2000, p.52).

The UL methodology at CMU emerged in response to the need for reflection if the citizens are to be empowered. It should allow for reflective feedback loops that occur at various levels (*see Figure 2.1*) to constantly echo the citizens' views and iteratively correct the design to achieve an acceptable outcome. However, it is not explicitly clear from the flow charts of the process that feedback loops exist (*Figures 2.12 & 2.13*). From the minutes, though,one may suggest that feedback did occur, the purpose and effectiveness is debatable. The key to the process is the ability to respectfully listen to the ideas and constraints from each side and the results achieved through negotiations.

The urban environmental development required flexibility and collaborations at both the individual and community levels, necessitating the civic innovations that involve community dispute resolutions, good neighborhood agreements and institutional collaborations. Empowering strategies that went beyond the dominant newer, elite-directing mode of participation began to form, such as the public interest groups that permitted greater precision and details in the representation of the individual and the group. It is not surprising that of late the UL has been transformed to concentrate on research on the local context.

The UL is now under the Remaking Cities Institute (RCI), which is an urban design research center in the School of Architecture. The Institute's objectives include real time capturing and evaluation of the conditions of neighborhoods and regions. The reports of the laboratory became documents that are aimed at policy changes, as frameworks that the community could use to hire professionals who would work in changes that affect them.

The products include the requirement to have a poster presentation for the community. The UL therefore becomes a resource for the community by going beyond a mere academic program. It becomes a university-community partnership building infrastructure of shops and schools. This positions the university as an affiliate to the community to carry out research on the local community in a practical oriented way.

The UL curriculum process also addresses the leadership skills of the students and, by engaging city leaders in the process of participation, the capacity building takes place. The students are trained through the support of partners like the Community Design Centre of Pittsburgh (CDCP), on the value of being a neutral facilitator who comes to the community without a hidden agenda.

The partnerships with Urban Regional Authority of Pittsburgh support the process by fostering the client's ability to have a design developed. CDCP empowers the communities to be able to choose the right designer through the lobbying process and hence acts as an urban design advisor. Heinz Foundation supports the process by providing funding for the studies through CMU's UL.

2.4 Methods and Influences: Place-Making Phase

The final phase of the urban laboratory is the place-making phase and has three stages: "the analysis of site forces, the identification of typologies and the use of catalytic interventions to address the objectives" as indicated by Hutzell and Rico-Gutierrez (2006, pxii). Two main techniques emerge as the preferred way of working; the group interaction methods and the brainstorming methods. The first and second have been discussed but the third is discussed below. But first I will describe the methods based on content analysis of the 2007 UL.

The content analysis is "a research technique for making replicable and valid inferences from texts to the contexts of their use…" as pointed out by Krippendorff (2004, p.18). It is used to find meanings hidden within a body of work in textual form through breaking them into meaningful units developed from grounded theory. The categories in this context arise from the literature review related to the research on urban design, place making and participatory processes.

In it the data analysis is iterative or cyclic in a process that continues until time runs out or the questions are understood. The analysis was carried out on the data that has been transcribed from the interviews, and the published material on the UL process. The content analysis started with line-by-line reading to break it into units of analysis called categories by either inductive or reductive reasoning. These categories or themes emerged from the data through careful examination and constant comparison between the various forms of data. There are three approaches

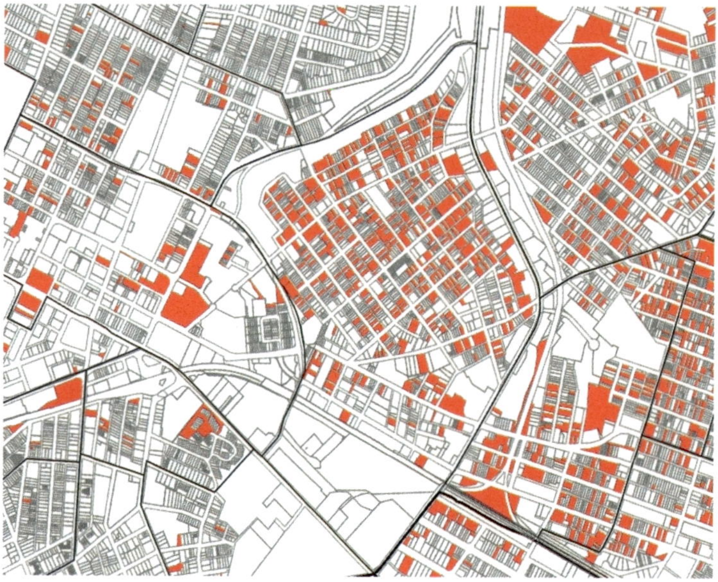

Figure 2.21A: Larimer UL Studio.Example of Site Force analysis identifying problem of vacant land. Source: El Samahy and Kline (2008, p.9

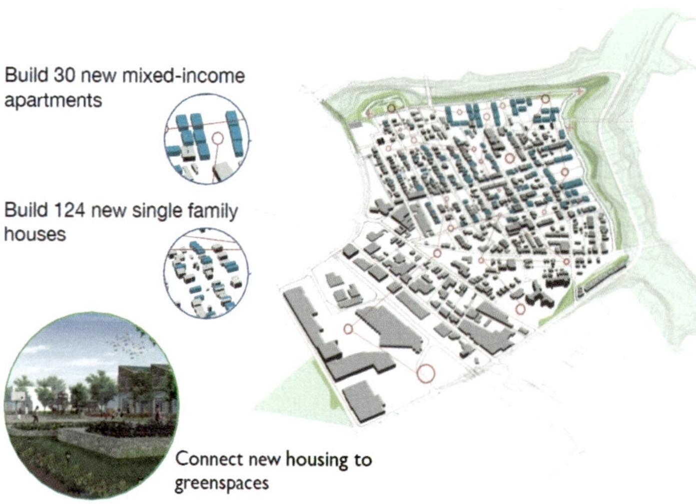

Figure 2.21B: Larimer UL Studio. Example of Response provision of housing and green space Source: El Samahy and Kline (2008, p.49)

to content analysis according to Hsiech and Shannon (2005); conventional content analysis, direct content analysis and summative content analysis. The coded texts, code book and analysis are available in *Appendix A*.

2.4.1 Methods and Influences: Site Forces Analysis

The first stage starts with further detailed analysis to extract the specific cues and sources for architecture, development and place-creation. It is underpinned by two theoretical frameworks; the visual artistic and place-making traditions. The stage involves the re-examination of analysis from phase one with specific areas of focus in relation to the value systems acting on the community.

Examples of the use of site forces is illustrated on *Figure 2.21A* which reveals that the high percentage of vacant land is a problem for the community, causing blight and reduction in both people and tax revenue. The response is found from within, transforming vacant lots into greenery as well as adding more housing units. The analysis was followed by the identification of key site forces and layers impacting the place specifically as identified and confirmed during the first community meeting. These included a radically reduced population that meant a lower tax base; a high proportion of vacant lots concentrated in the area; and the edge conditions unclear with a resultant lack of identity etc as pointed out by El Samahy and Kline (2008). It is important to correlate the specific local issues with the global ones. A massing model is required at this stage to illustrate the impact of the proposed development. The design tool included the use of several drawings representing the various alternative proposals.

2.4.2 Methods and Influences: Identifying Typologies

UL teaches and emphasizes the importance of type as abstractions, which is a methodological tool in urban design guides and does not determine the future form. Colquhoun in discussion on typology suggests that it is the part given to the problem of "design methodology, and to the process of design as a branch of the wider process of problem solving." (1969, 71).

He pointed to arguments against type on the basis of being a vestige of an age of craft. But craft in itself as a vocation has been considered dying because of the developments in the sciences and technology. However, in history, the craftsman used the type as a model resource for creating the new objects or artifacts. The object then became a signifier of a culture with value. Fundamental to Colquhoun's thinking is that the "creation of the socio-spatial schemata is endowed with meaning that is not measurable…" (1969, 71) and thus is a representation.

Quetremere on the other hand argued that "…the type is the original reason of a thing…" (quoted in Westfall, 1991; p.148). In other words, it is vague rather than precise. In this sense the type when used in architecture provides the symbolic value to the building yet its character is contingent on the contextual timescale.

Figure 2.22A: Larimer UL Studio: Example of Block typology at urban level. Source: El Samahy and Kline (2008, p.98)

Figure 2.22B: Larimer. UL Studio: Example of Response detail of building (apartment)? Source: El Samahy and Kline (2008, p.99)

The importance of the type in this sense is related to the finding an architectural form that would provide the pragmatic solution to the activities. Although in modern architecture of 1950s and 1960s there was a denial of the use of imitation as a method through which artifacts including buildings were made. Colquhoun suggests that the:

> "...Intuition must be based on knowledge of past solutions to related problems, and that creation is a process of adapting forms derived either from past needs or on past aesthetic ideologies to the need of the present..." (1969, p.73).

Therefore, the typology as used at the UL is mere representation of the forms of possible solutions to architectural programs that respond to the objectives. The detail of the immediate however is left to the individual student designers when working out the catalytic project (*Figure 2.22A & 2.22B*).

The typologies are manipulated and are used to help to understand and reveal connection before the urban place-making, architecture and developments that would occur. The various typologies are identified, the urban types, building types and landscape types, chosen on the basis that they would dictate the future direction of the development. It is therefore critical that the appropriate typologies for the specific area of focus are found, as the vision of the community would be dependent upon it.

The UL clarifies and emphasizes that even though urban typologies are related to use they are not always dependent on use. Typologies are not about *styles*. One example is the use of row typology in, say, a place like Nairobi: this does not mean it has to be Victorian even though the row house has its history in the Victorian era.

This stage places emphasis on the visual-artistic traditional framework with the outcome being a series of axonometric, perspective images to propose the types to be used. The details that include the stylistic issues or otherwise should be kept out and the massing models and images should clearly suggest the locations of parking, courtyards, entrances etc. In the earlier studio, the outside and Felicity studios, the stylistic details seem to have crept in either by design or default. I suggest this was by design based on criticism raised by Kline (2009) during an interview on the UL process prior to the modifications to the curriculum as discussed later. The proposed uses for the projects must be visually clear without the use of texts (colour coding).

2.4.3 Methods and Influences: Catalytic Intervention

This stage contains the use of detailed elemental design to propose catalytic interventions that include all aspects of architecture, infrastructure and landscaping (*Figures 2.21B and 2.23*). The making or creation of the public realm or space

Figure 2.23: Hazelwood UL. Studio: Example of Four. typologies.
Source: Hutzell, and Rico-Gutierrez, (2008, p.149)

has been made clear because the threshold or interface between the space and the buildings are well delineated. Emphasis was placed on a 3D expression of architectural ideas to create the vision for an urban space. The recurring themes are what the appropriate typologies for the site are, and how they can be used to create an urban place.

The key to the exercise is the *modification* and *definition* of the urban space. It is a summary of the response to the system analysis. This includes the linked public spaces, a significant public space and a mixture of old (as is and as modified) and new (as proposed) that creates a catalyst and defines the urban space. The idea of the use of a catalyst to regenerate an area is a reductionist method. It operates on the premise that the wider problems of the community could be divided into smaller sub-problems identified as site forces. These could then be solved through targeted surgery and when several of these are put back together, the whole community's problems would be solved.

Emphasis is placed on the connections between the strategies developed earlier and the community objectives and the interventions. The result of this stage should NOT be a re-creation or reproduction of an existing city even if one used a precedent. The outcome is presented in a way that clearly shows the ground floor plan relationship with the exterior landscape. It should also show what the private/ public relation is with the other floor plan but with emphasis on how the spaces proposed relate and contribute to the creation on the public realm.

The next section takes three examples of Urban Laboratory projects at Carnegie Mellon University to examine how the methods were applied in specific cases and how the methods were transformed over time to respond to changing circumstances.

2.5 Examined cases of Urban Laboratories Projects 1

The first laboratory sessions ran between 1963 and 1968; the second laboratory period I have categorized as 1982-2000 while the third as 2000 to the present. The breakdown of the period was selected to correspond to the active periods of the UL. The gap between 1968 and 1982 represents the period when both David and Ray were away teaching at Yale University School of architecture and also to spend time building their newly formed firm UDA.

The period 1982-2000 represents when both David and Ray returned to teach urban design at CMU even though the UL in the current form had not been founded until 1992. The period 2000 to date marks the start of changes to curriculum and process carried out by Jonathan Kline in 2002.

It was difficult to access records of process, or programs of the first laboratory as unfortunately no records were kept at the UL archives. There were however some files containing correspondences and notes left by the former deans of the schools over the years. These were looked at in detail and the reconstruction of the start of the UL discussed at the beginning of the chapter come from them. It is therefore difficult to examine the period in detail other than from publications by David Lewis and Ray Gindroz and also from information gathered during an interview with Don Carter and Ray Gindroz.

The founder, David Lewis was kind enough to introduce me to both Don Carter and Ray Gindroz who provided valuable information about the firm, the processes and their work at CMU. Raymond L. Gindroz, a co-founder with David Lewis in 1964 and principal emeritus of Urban Design Associates Ray earned both Bachelor and Master of Architecture degrees from Carnegie Mellon University in 1963 and 1965 respectively. He taught urban design at the School of Architecture at Yale University.

Donald K. Carter graduated with Bachelor of Architecture from Carnegie Mellon University in 1967 and did postgraduate work at the University of Edinburgh. He is a consulting principal at the Urban Design Associates (UDA) and also the current director of the UL. His biographical sketch suggests that he has been a:

> "...Consultant to General Motors, Heinz, and Alcoa regarding the reuse of excess industrial land parcels, including their potential for mixed-use and residential developments..." (UDA, 2011).

This is interesting in that it reveals interests and influences in the organizations that have financed the UL projects over the years. Both Don and Ray were studies architecture under David Lewis and share same ideas which they have practiced at the firm since its founding in 1964.

2.5.1 Felicity City Urban Laboratory 1982

Professor David Lewis and Ray Gindroz, both practicing architects and urban designers from the local firm Urban Design Associates, led the Urban Laboratory project. This session of the urban laboratory started from a theoretical perspective taken from the Vitruvius Ideal: commodity, firmness and delight, i.e., structural stability, appropriate spatial accommodation, and attractive appearance. The argument Lewis and Gindroz posited in this laboratory project was that:

> "...Citizens of a *good* city are happy because of their relationship to the environment and other members of the society. The relations are firmly based on tradition yet evolving continuously and as a consequence civic pride is inherent..." (1982, p.2).

The implication of the argument is that good urbanism must of necessity be rooted in the tradition and the local context and it is this that makes it acceptable to the citizens and therefore makes them happy.

Figure 2.24: Felicity UL Studio: Source: Lewis & Gindroz (1982)

As previously discussed in chapter 1, four main categories used in the content analysis emerged from literature review. These are: the historical context framing the founding of the laboratories; the interrelationships between force fields such as actors, community issues, and organizations; the strategies or tactics applied and, the final category, the consequences of those actions.

I used the suggestions of Ryan and Bernard (2003b) to discover the codes based on important themes related to design pedagogy, and grounded theory that emerged from the texts. I coded individual words and phrases that conveyed meanings related to the research questions *(Table 1.5 in Chapter 1)*.

The content analysis carried out on the report of the laboratory revealed that even though the Vitruvius Ideal was the starting point, the emphasis seemed rooted on the contextual issues and less on other themes such as interrelationships between various parts or stakeholders essential for the place-creation process. The drawings produced by the students were evidence of the emphasis on visual qualities tied to the traditional typology and historical values of the neighborhoods.

The reading list (*Figure 2.6 and Table 2.2*) reveals a strong leaning towards the social-visual artistic traditions from both Europe and North America. Most of the books in the required reading list confirm the theoretical leanings of the studio. A quote by Aldo Rossi: "...Social realism in architecture was seen as strongly linked to social order and political problems..." Points to the rationalist approach that the studio had taken. The rationalist saw the merging of functionalism of the modern movement with humanism. Lobsinger (2002) argues that Aldo Rossi approached architecture from a reductionist point of view in that "rationalist building assemblies determined the type to be the best form suited for it..." (2002, p.51). The list reveals that about half of the books had social-usage traditions as the theoretical leaning.

2.5.1.1 Strategy

The strategy of the seminar was linked to the understanding that place-making of a happy city was based on evolutionary processes that created episodes in the city. They were evolutionary in that the changes occurred in the city because of the systemic forces of economics, culture, politics and social relations. The designers are therefore required to observe, analyze and understand the processes and propose a design response that would support such a happy city. The methodology was based on a study of examples of perceived happy urban spaces from Europe and North America from a list provided by the tutors. These were Piazza Navona in Rome, Piazza del Campo in Sienna, Covent Garden in London; Post Office Square in Boston among others.

This methodology is not so dissimilar to Jan Gehl's approach used in Copenhagen where observation of activities in the public places of the city is used to decide which spaces are happy, based on the intensity of activities especially optional ones. This approach of design has its strengths and weakness. It may reveal locations where activities occur but unless the users are involved by revealing reasons for being in those spaces at those particular times, it will all be guess-work by the designer.

A lot of work had been going on in parallel during this period under the user participation; a notable one by William Whyte (1980): *Social Life of Small Urban Spaces*. His work described the substance of urban public life in an objective and measurable way. Whyte's starting point was how plazas are used. Whyte's methods involved use of time-lapse photography overlooking the plazas and recording daily patterns. The users were interviewed to reveal where they came from, where they worked, how frequently they used the spaces (under study). The main data collection method was observation of the people to see what they did.

The urban form was explored in three ways: firstly, from a theoretical perspective from a prescribed list of architects (*See Table 2.2, page 72*). Secondly, it was explored through the analysis by drawing on three kinds of urban spaces, historical, contemporary and infrastructural road systems. The final method was contextual in location, but was a similar task to the previous one except that the spaces are a local neighborhood street and urban space. The outcomes of the exercise were not clear as I have been unable to find examples of the work by students.

2.5.1.2 Consequences

The *Figure 2.23* reveals that the emphasis of the UL was on the use of traditional building. The approach would result in buildings that are deemed to create happiness, a reductionist ideal that "good" environment equals socially, economically and culturally satisfied people.

2.5.2 The South side Community: Urban Laboratory project 1991

This is a significant project in that it was formally the restart of the urban laboratory after having been folded in 1968 when Professor David Lewis returned as a full time staff member at the school. It involved the South side community and was undertaken under the leadership of both Professors David Lewis and Robert Coles.

2.5.2.1 Physical Context

According to the media report in the Pittsburgh Courier and other local dailies,

> "...Students will show primarily through illustrations, possible river treatments of the South side from the 9th Street to end of LTV property..."

Faassen, Fredrickson and Temkin (1991). This implied that the aim of the project as portrayed to the public was vision-making. The brief confirmed that the project was to show the relationships between the north and south sides of the river and also the impact of urban design study especially on the South side Community.

The south side riverfront area had a diverse community in the 1870s from eastern and southern Europe. Its location by the river made it attractive for industrial developments and nearby there were also coal mines that were used to fire the industries. The main activity was industrial but the fall of the steel industry severely impacted the community.

2.5.2.2 Historical Context

The content analysis revealed that the project proposals placed emphasis on the economic impact of the collapse of the heavy steel industries, social rights and justice through the availability of rental or multi-family accommodation. Properties were generally sold in a closed market through word of mouth or through the strong social networks in the community. The community lacked essential amenities close to the projects such as parks, yards and schools.

These were symptoms of a divided community where discrimination was likely. The community also had a declining population that could not support any local stores thus making it less attractive for businesses to stay. Young families were moving out as well and as a result more vacancies in properties were prevalent. The community had a strong network that the students would be able to tap into to obtain tacit knowledge.

Arnstein (1969, p.2)			Till (2005)
8	Citizen Control	Citizen Power	Genuine Participation
7	Delegated Power		
6	Partnership		
5	Placation	Tokenism	Pseudo- Participation
4	Consultation		
3	Informing		
2	Therapy	Nonparticipation	
1	Manipulation		

Table 2.3: Level of participation
Source: Onyango (2011)

Figure 2.25: Southside UL Studio: Source: Faassen, Fredrickson and Temkin (1991)

2.5.2.3 Interrelationship

The content analysis revealed that the proposals by the students were carried out using collaborative efforts, partnerships between the South side Local Development Company, South side Community Council, the South side Chamber of Commerce and South side Planning Community. The project involved partnership with the South side local development Company who prepared the Request for Qualification, (RFQ), and the Request for Qualification Information (RFI) document that the students used as a brief.

The students formed imaginary architectural firms with four consultants each to simulate reality for the purpose of responding to the RFI. They worked in collaboration with other student teams to collect the baseline data needed for the project then developed urban design framework as individual firms. Individual students then did the detailed work from portions of the urban design framework. What however is not clear other than placed within the brief is how the students interacted with the community. There is no record of the interaction or the events of the day.

2.5.2.4 Strategies

There were two underlying strategies used in the process: the participative process and reliance on catalytic projects to spur growth, even though the participation of the local community is mentioned several times in the report. Using Till's (2005) analysis, I would place the process as pseudo-participation. In Arnstein's Ladder, (*Table 2.3*) the community did have some power at level 2 or 3. The report is not explicit on what transpired.

2.5.2.5 Consequences

The content analysis reveals that the Urban Design lab project targeted a shared community vision and also looked at empowering the community in decision making. Even though the Charm Bracelet project is a follow up that came fifteen years later it is difficult to judge the progress those communities have made since the laboratory projects were initiated. The time span between the two could be attributed to two things; firstly, that initial plans had a time span of 15-20 years; secondly, perhaps are return to the community when most people have forgotten the promises from the first meeting fifteen years later.

The image on the left (*Figure 2.25*) is a representation of what the urban vision developed for the community was. It looks like a romantic memory recaptured, a call for a return to a nostalgic past perhaps. It is difficult to tell either what the interventions are or what it looked like prior to the proposal. It is also difficult, reading from the report, to see what the community objectives to be met were other than being a project aimed at meeting the academic requirements.

2.6 Transformations in Methods over the Years

The next Urban Laboratory comes after the curriculum changes had been implemented and as such follows a modified program and structure. In an interview conducted with Jonathan Kline (2009), he was critical of the approach used at both the Urban Design Associates (UDA) offices and UL at CMU that was based on Neo-traditional urbanism and lacked what he saw as experimentation and innovation. UDA's methodology is based on the *charrette* model, which he criticizes as being very formulaic; tick the boxes to meet the requirements. It is subject to manipulation and exposes the community to therapeutic participation. He points out that it is adopted because of its efficiency from a business perspective but in reality, is used as a control mechanism of who participates. In some schemes the participation was elaborate while in others there was none at all. This is very much in line with the thoughts expressed by Till (2005) who argued that there exists a mismatch between the ideal participation and the real participation because of the undercurrents of power play that lead to manipulations, and disenfranchisements (*see discussion on participation in chapter 2*).

The pedagogy of UL was "open-ended" prior to 2005 according to Kline and, furthermore, was without clear outcomes and objectives: not even the methodology to be followed was written down. The praxis was based on the social process of new-urbanism that was driven by traditional issues and form. As a result, some students were not happy to be forced to learn neo-traditional architecture neither were they enthused with the participatory methodologies. It is based on a reductionist fallacy that Harvey criticizes as "...trying to perpetuate the idea that the shaping of spatial order is or can be the foundation for a new moral and aesthetic order..." (1997, p1) He sees it failing due to its communitarian ideals that avoid confrontation with the economy of power.

Jonathan Kline, after discussions with Prof David Lewis, was given an opportunity to explore ways to introduce a more deliberate process over 3 years. He was granted an award that enabled the curriculum development review to happen and in 2005 Kelly Hutzell and Rami el Samahy joined the UL while Jonathan Kline took time off to pursue an interest in painting. Kelly and Samahy modified the curriculum, streamlining and consolidating the process, making it more focused.

In the previous years of UL under David Lewis three assignments were used; the first carried out through a Request for Pre qualification (RFP) given to the students. It was up to the students to Figure out how to address the problems and invent the program and turned out to be a challenge to weaker students, as it was not clearly structured with well-outlined objectives. They then presented this to the community in one meeting and spent the rest of the time working at details according to the academic program.

The class was divided into small groups of 2-3 student teams to work on models (GIS analysis); others would start community outreach to identify leaders and understand community dynamics and arrange community meetings. The students were responsible for running the community meetings. The result was a large number of teams (26) that was a burden for the community because of the 26 different ideas being presented that might not be very different.

In the modified curriculum, the class formed fewer teams but with more students (8-10) to improve the structure and generate only 3 urban design frameworks. This allowed the work to be more detailed than previously as the larger team structure contributes more through collaboration and co-design. The new team structure, however, has the weakness that some students who are used to working alone have disliked it. However, for purposes of pedagogy and curriculum it meets the needs and requirement of teaching leadership, collaborative and participative and communication skills.

The modification allowed for the presentation of 3 specific alternatives that could be discussed in depth and consolidated to show community actions. In the previous UL the community was bombarded with 30 different ideas! This was quite a task for them and it was difficult to get them engaged throughout; they got fatigued. The community are reported to have been very positive about the changes.

The changes to the methodologies of UL, according to Jonathan Kline, were: firstly, in terms of serving the community it was more effective in meeting their objectives and therefore the proposals were very likely to be adopted by the community. For the students, it allowed for a greater interaction and collaboration which fostered peer evaluation and learning within the larger group.

Secondly, the new methodological process was more deliberate in identifying the communities to work with through collaboration with the Community Design Centre of Pittsburgh, (CDCP). CDCP have been working with the communities for much longer and earlier than CMU urban laboratory and hence are able to suggest those communities that are ripe for working with. They would commission studies to map and identify the areas that have potential of suffering pressure or stress soon, due to the various system forces.

In an interview in April 2009, Anne Lubenau, the president of CDCP pointed out that it had been involved with the community, firstly through the use of education in helping people understand the value of good design (capacity building); secondly through the provision of a design fund for core programs, and thirdly through supporting, hosting and promoting events that help achieve the aims of the organizations.

In the period prior to the start of UL, the communities had received funding from the city and CDCP to carry out the planning process through the federal Housing and Urban Department. Unfortunately, the results were more talk between stakeholders rather than the creation of a community vision. The

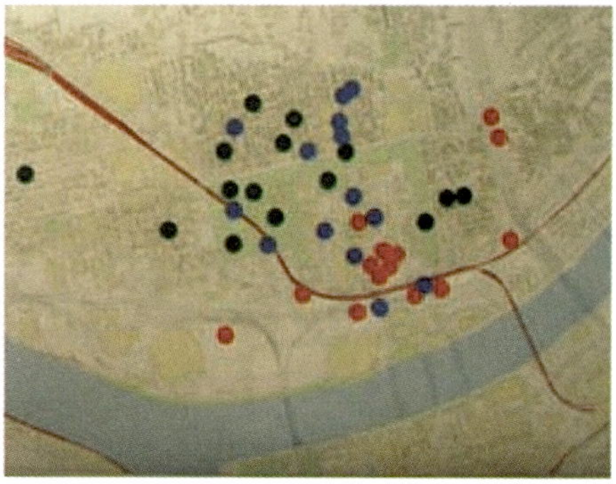

Figure 2.27: North side UL Studio: SWOT Analysis
Source: Urban Lab (2005)

community would then have applied for a grant to hire planners to create a vision. The studio was therefore inserted at the right place and time for the community. Even though the students are not professionals, their energy and innovations allow for a burst of creativity hardly seen in working with professionals.

The process of inserting UL in the community allows for the educational and empowering process to occur. This builds their capacity to be able to work with professionals later after the visioning process has occurred. The result of the studio is a report that allows for the community to prepare RFP to proceed to next stage. The flip side to working for a long period in any community is participative fatigue and frustration because of the slow progress in transformations.
The new curriculum is effective in that it allows for the partnership between city planners, the Urban Regional Authority of Pittsburgh and CDCP to collaborate in identifying which communities are in most need and which would be able to make most use of the technical support. In previous UL, the collaboration took the form of an Urban Regime Coalition that seems to have been set up to serve the elite through the organization network purporting to meet community needs. For instant, Don Carter who has been heavily involved with running the UL at CMU has also been a consultant advisor to Heinz Foundation among others that have controlling interests in the landholdings in areas where the UL has worked. It is reported that the students found the new proposal more diverse and rigorous and it has become very popular, judging by the increase in the number of students taking the course as an elective.

2.6.1 Community Meeting 1

The new curriculum allows for fewer schemes than previous UL processes where lots of proposals were carried out and the second community meeting was used as a critical review time. It was thus seen more as a critique than a meeting for dialogging as David Lewis had invited peer jurors. The community did not really get engaged, as they did not have space to give feedback, therefore the process lacked not only reflection, but also collaboration. It was a controlled process in the manner previously exemplified by Jonathan Kline. In the new UL process the community meeting is used for discussion and co-design and a separate critique is arranged back at school a week later for the students.

The community meeting is wholly student led and is held in a venue within the community. It starts with the students presenting systems analysis using Power Point slides to show maps and models. They then present the three urban design frameworks as exemplars but open to discussion and modification by the community at a *charrette* to follow shortly afterwards. A large model with x-rays of the community is available for understanding the context. The term x-ray refers to the systems analysis beyond what is visible on the surface. For example, the presence of a high percentage of vacant lots could be an indicator of racial flight from the area, and crime problems, which in turn impact the economic tax base.

The community members are invited to give an oral history of the place, to make the students and the community understand what the place meant to them in the past and what it means to them now. The use of flags or dots on the models for SWOT analysis [strength, weaknesses, opportunities and threats] has been found to engage the community more than using maps only. The objectives are identified and the potential uses explored together in small workshops of about 10 community members using design games. They would then vote against issues placed on the table for discussion. The use of the community location makes the process productive, as they are not intimidated.

2.6.2 Community Meeting 2

At this meeting the three student groups had developed the work in detail. The teaching faculty introduced work of the students and explained the differences and moves by three different groups of students. The students then take over and lead the discussion, mainly using models with objects that could be moved in the process of co-design. The changes are photographed to keep record of the process and this can be pulled back onto the screen for reflection using Power Point presentation techniques.

2.6.3 Community Meeting 3

At the third community meeting, the teaching faculty makes the presentation just like in the second meeting. The faculty's role is supposedly limited to introducing the key ideas and summary, but the students who designed the project answer questions by the community.

The next section will look at the Charm Bracelet project, which was carried out under the new curriculum, to see if there was any perceivable difference to the outcome.

2.7 Examined Case of Urban Laboratory Project: Charm Bracelet 2006

This was a project carried out after the changes to the curriculum and overhaul of the UL methodologies. It was located on the North side of Pittsburgh and was a collaborative project in partnership with Pittsburgh North side Community, Pittsburgh Children's Museum and the Urban Laboratory at CMU. The National Endowment for the Arts funded the project and they received a Heinz Endowment grant for an International Idea Design competition.

Two studios were run in this particular urban laboratory; the Charm Bracelet and the Brighton Road and Herron Avenue projects. The Charm Bracelet project, according to the studio leaders Hutzell and Rico-Gutierrez, was a catalyst aimed at "Creating linkages among the varied cultural, educational and entertainment destinations spread across the North side..." (2007, p.6).

This project had been improved in comparison to the previous ones in that it added a dialogue process between the community, the students and four international teams of designers.

The second of the studios collaborated with the Pittsburgh Urban Regional Authority, the Urban Land Institute and the Community groups, and was funded using Urban Land Institute grants. The aim was to integrate the blighted urban corridor in the north with Pittsburgh city center.

2.7.1. Contextual Issue

The content analysis of the urban laboratory report reveals that there was more emphasis on addressing the pressing economic context, social rights and political opportunities. This perhaps relates to the booming economic conditions that existed in the mid 2000s and the economic disparities that were apparent between the North side communities and even the destinations or charms as they were refereed to that existed.

The students carried out the baseline survey work which they shared with the international design teams that had been invited to participate in a competition. The students also participated alongside these teams in the competition. The local community were also engaged earlier in the process to identify and define the problem that the community faced, and to assess their existing assets.

This marked a change in the procedure in that previously the community were not involved in the identification and definition of the problems. The first community meeting was used to "check and confirm" whether the designers got it right! David Lewis concurs when he pointed out that:

> "...Conflicts over community design issues between the advocacy groups and the bureaucratic officials and technical specialists are caused by their different viewpoints..." (1979, p.28)

The perspective from which the scenario is viewed determined its understanding. As such one could argue that the citizens perhaps have a better view and understanding of their local needs, have greater clarity of the issues than the experts from outside.

This has necessitated a need for a different approach to designing communities, cities, and neighborhoods, based on the local contexts, by collaborating with, and allowing the participation of, the local community. The proposals in this UL were very innovative perhaps as a result of the higher degree of

Figure 2.28: Charm Bracelet Project (2007 Urban Laboratory). Source: Hutzell and Rico-Gutierrez (2007)

community involvement and also from the fact that the problems were jointly framed and therefore represented their vision (Figure 2.28). This is perhaps due to the fact that for the first time there was a real project on board, and four professional teams were invited and the students had opportunity to not only proved the baseline data but to participate alongside them.

The four teams were: Suisman Urban Design (collaboration between office from Santa Monica, California and Pittsburgh; Colab Architecture (collaboration between teams from New York and Pittsburgh); Muf Architecture/ art and Objectif (teams from London and San Francisco) and Pentagram from New York.

2.7.2 Interrelationships

The project was carried out using the collaborative model not only between the stakeholders and the students, but also with the students co-designing alongside the multi-disciplinary professional teams from both the US and abroad. This simulated real life project scenarios, enriching their learning. The laboratory used a mixture of methods to address the issues, beginning with a top-down approach where community leaders and professionals led in identifying the key issues. This was followed by a bottoms-up approach involving the community in not only framing the questions and clarifying them (week 1 and 4) but also in the *charrete* working out possible solutions (week 9).

2.7.3 Strategy / Tactics

The content analysis reveals that the strategies or tactics category had the highest scores of all the other categories as well as the other laboratory projects. There was great emphasis on community participation either directly or at some stage through the delegated power of the community leaders during the various forums. The engagement, unlike in the previous lab, began at the outset of the process and continued through to the last community meeting where the final framework and detailed proposals were presented and celebrated.

The x-rays of students' work showed the community before and after the intervention proposals, the 3D models and drawings; all showed understanding of the contextual issues, respect for typology and innovation through the use of light as the theme to connect the charms. The use of lighting as a feature has surely proven to be an innovative solution drawing communities out in the evening to use the new public places created and has spurred other activities along the routes. It has been catalytic indeed judging by the continued investments in the area and its growth. The Children's Museum has continued to invite the community to participate in annual projects to improve its vision and outlook based on adverts in 2011:

> **Urban Garden Art + Design Project**
> The Children's Museum of Pittsburgh and Team Laminates Co. (TLC) invite architects, artists, gardeners and designers to propose artistic / design solutions for a new community garden at the corner of Vinial Street and Spring Garden Avenue on the North side. (2011, Children's Museum of Pittsburgh)

2.7.4 Consequences

The consequence of the project was a shared community vision that has developed legs and grown into the community events lasting years now since the Children's Museum got a new building as a part of the process. The reviews in Post-Gazette, Pittsburgh Courier, MetropolisMags were positive. For instance:

> "Most design competitions pit one group against another to generate the best design for eventual construction. Here, however, Children's Museum Assistant Director Chris Siefert worked with architect Paul Rosenblatt, of Springboard Design, to select and work with teams whose variety of skills and perspectives would enrich the project in a more collective fashion." (Pittsburgh City Paper; February 22, 2007).

"Siefert cites light installations, projects for an underpass, and museum/school partnerships as noteworthy proposals. "There are things that stand out--a strong idea for a public art program which would look at specific sites and curate events and installations over time," says Siefert. "One exciting idea is an annual treasure hunt across the whole district." (PopCity Media)

The project has not only connected the community icons, but by strategic placing of the active functions and activities there has been increased surveillance, new places created, enhanced cohesion and businesses started along the paths connecting the charms.

Phase	Methods	Influence/ cause
Systems Analysis	1. Awareness methods 2. Indirect methods	1. Rationalist approach: (Lynch, Rossi, Rowe, Team X) 2. Civil Rights Movement 3. Advocacy (Davidoff)
Urban Design Framework	1. Indirect methods 2. Group interaction methods 3. Brainstorming	1. Rationalist (Whyte, Rossi, Team X) 2. Advocacy 3. Civil Rights Movement
Place-Making	1. Group interaction methods 2, Brainstorming	1. Rationalist (Team X) 2. Civil Rights Movement

Table 2.4: Summary of phase, methods and influences

2.8 Summary

This section will summarize the UL model at CMU by type of organization and the methodologies adapted with their roots to contexts. The work is based on the material provided from the websites, interviews with staff at the school, and commentary by partner organizations that have worked with them.

The table on the next page (*Table 2.4*) is a summary of the activities, the technique used to carry the activity and the influence or cause of the choice of the method. It is claimed that the work of UL at CMU is characterized by its interdisciplinary approach, public participation, collaboration and partnership with professionals, political leaders and private stakeholders as well as community. The UL seems to fit within the community as a provider of services through their long-term public engagement processes in design issues as well as in building the capacity of the communities they work with to participate. It is however doubtful how effective the participation by the community is and how representative the sample of participants is as discussed further below.

This is as opposed to many other labs such as the University of Cincinnati that provides cheap technical assistance in competition with professional practice. This is important in that the choice of methodology allows for the professionals not only to be co-designers with the students, but also to act on the opportunity to train them in community work. However this was only used in one occasion during the Charm Bracelet project of 2006. Most of the UL did not have co-design involvement of professional designers and as such the design methodology is no different to the traditional design studio process. It is expert-tutor led with the student learning to mimic the work of the expert.

The analysis also revealed that the UL process occurs in three key stages or phases as illustrated above (*Table 2.4*)**.** The theoretical leanings of the UL are the Social-

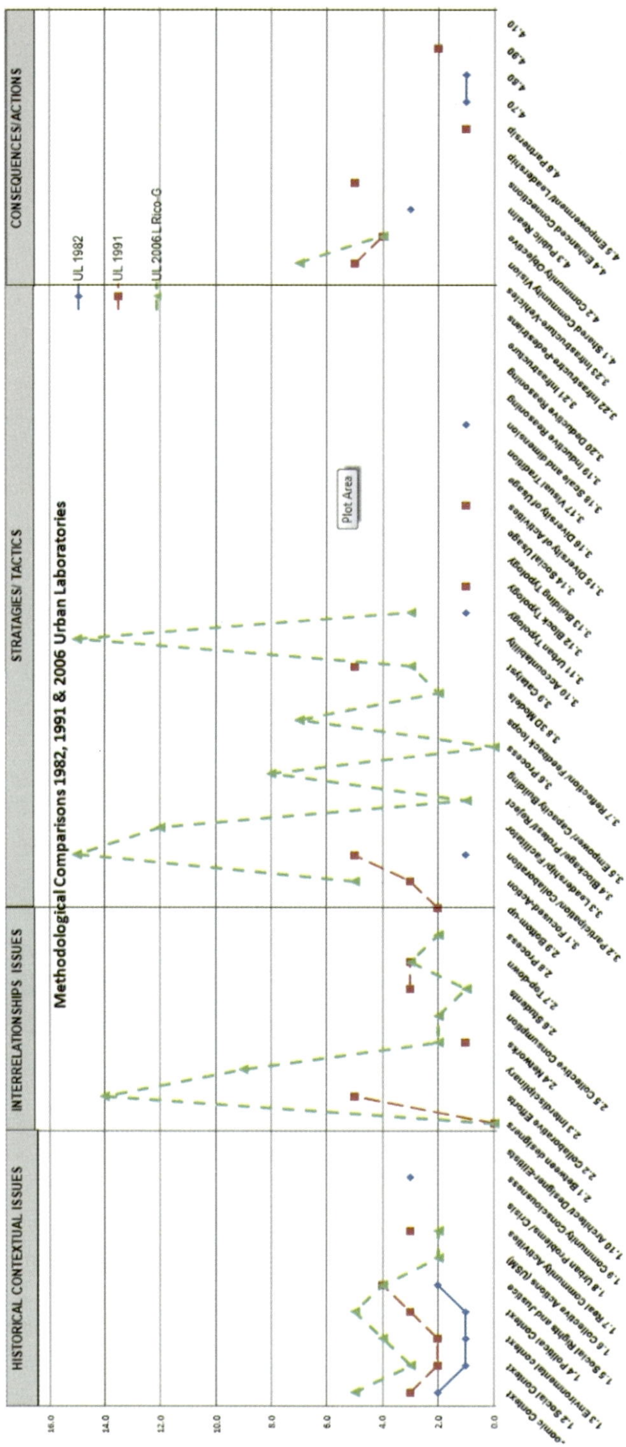

Table 2.5: Content Analysis: Comparison between 1982 UL and 2006 UL Source: Onyango (2011)

Usage tradition even though from their documents and in interviews they continue to argue that no single theoretical tradition dominates. Four methods are used that could have arisen out of the circumstances in the political history of the place, the social and environmental histories and the academic traditions of the time. These are the awareness method, the indirect method, the group interaction method and brainstorming methods.

Content Analysis was carried out on the reports of the 1982 and 2006 UL that was then checked against data from interviews with Anna Lubna, Jonathan Kline, Luis Rico-Gutierez and Jared Friedman (CMU Alumni). It revealed the transformation on what was emphasized in comparison to the previous urban laboratories, as illustrated precedent page (*Table 2.5)*. There is a marked difference between the two ULs in 1982 when David Lewis had just returned to CMU and in 2006 after curriculum changes.

In 1982, the emphasis appears to have been on contextual issues with other categories barely being mentioned. Even within the contextual categories that are supposedly the cause for the founding of the laboratory, only the social right and justice is mentioned twice. One would have expected that this category would be mentioned continuously on the documents handed to students and papers written describing the process. In addition, the collaborative efforts between the designers, students and community are hardly mentioned. The tactics used that would have underpinned the methodology selected are unclear as are the consequences of those actions, which is not surprising. This perhaps reflects the critiques identified by Jonathan Kline that the "…curriculum was open ended without clear objectives or community benefits…" (2009).

On the other hand, by 2006, the curriculum had changed significantly, as reflected in the location of the emphasis. The context as driving force is still important, however the interrelationship between the various stakeholders seems to have become the most important element. The use of collaboration in forms of coalition arrangements, and reliance on existing networks has become critical. The tactics or strategies used are now clear with emphasis placed on community participation and reflection is embedded in the process. However, the interviews reveal that the form of reflection and participation by the community is reactive with the designer listening, whether they respond to these or not is debatable.

In comparing the various periods of the UL; 1982, 1991 and 2006, content analyses reveals that the context is considered important. The main things that are highlighted as exerting the greatest spheres of influence are economics, political and social rights and justice (*Figure 2.29*). The difference between the periods is the level of emphasis within the texts. Historically there are no significant events that would account for the difference in the increase in score between the 1982, 1991 and 2006 ULs except a choice by the lab to change the focus.

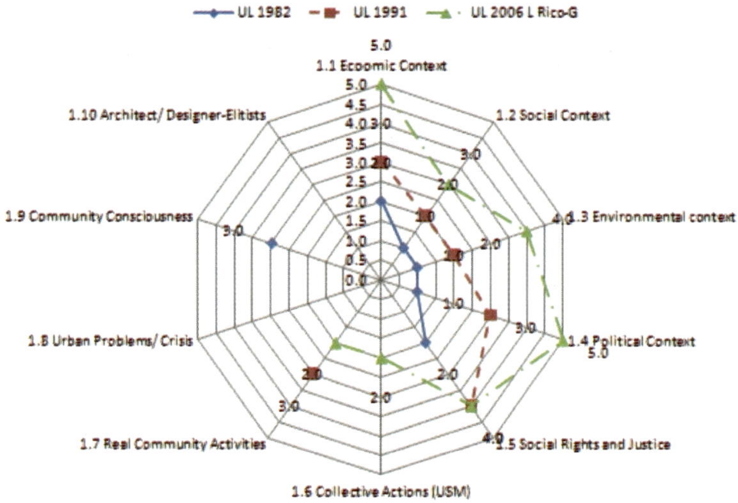

Figure 2.29: Comparison: Historical Context
Source: Onyango

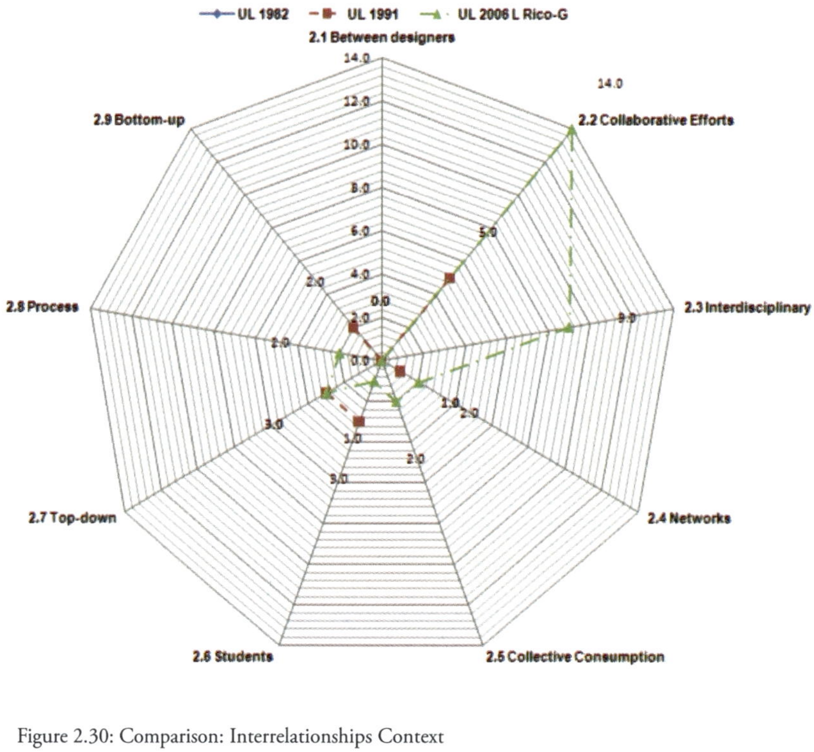

Figure 2.30: Comparison: Interrelationships Context
Source: Onyango

The content analysis of the data on interrelationships reveals that even though the objectives of the UL have been to train student designers to have ethical values and engage the community, this was hardly mentioned in the reports and handouts (*Figure 2.30*). However, there is a marked change in the level of emphasis by 2006 when the UL operated under a different director, Luis Rico-Gutierrez, and also used the revised curriculum. The emphasis is now on collaboration, reliance on an interdisciplinary approach and the building on existing networks of the community. The community's role in the design process was increased from mere listening to co-design as previously illustrated (*Figures 2.9A & 2.9B*). In addition, the partner organizations still have a much greater influence in the decision-making process than the local community.

The minutes of the Wilkinsburg UL reveal that the local community represented less than 41% of the participants. In addition, interviews with students who participated reveal that they were disappointed by the low level of participation by the majority of the socially, economically deprived residents. Perhaps the location of the meetings, and the manner of invitation made it less inviting to the local marginalized residents.

The citizen's power for self-decision making has been the foundation of the participatory process. It has taken different forms over the years, as seen from the literature on participatory design processes from the 1960s to the present. Wulz (quoted in Toker and Toker 2006, p.157) conducted a study that revealed a shift from the advocacy approach of the 1960s to the continuum approach in the 1980s. In the latter, the power relations of the citizens in the decision-making ladder are reduced from one condition to another without abrupt changes being noticed.

Citizens′ power is reduced from one of "maximum say to a minimum say" starting from self-decision, to co-decision between the participating stakeholders and the designers. In the latter the alternative solutions are offered either by the designers or representatives of any of the stakeholder groups and not the community participants directly; it is a delegated authority or perhaps manipulated delegation. The next stage represents a shift to regionalism, where regional solutions are pushed for as the best alternative while in the final stage of the transformation the solutions are achieved through dialogue.

The urban laboratory marked the transformation from activist model to entrepreneurial model through a shift of emphasis; it being placed more on consensus building and less on advocacy. This transformation unfortunately shifts the focus away from citizen's participation.

There is a marked difference in the level of emphasis on participative collaboration, reflections and accountability between the UL prior to 2006 (*Figure 2.31*). These terms were hardly mentioned in the 1982 or the 1991 UL, it was probably 'business as usual', picking from where they had left in 1968. The tactics or strategies barely changed between 1982 when David Lewis and Roy Gindroz came

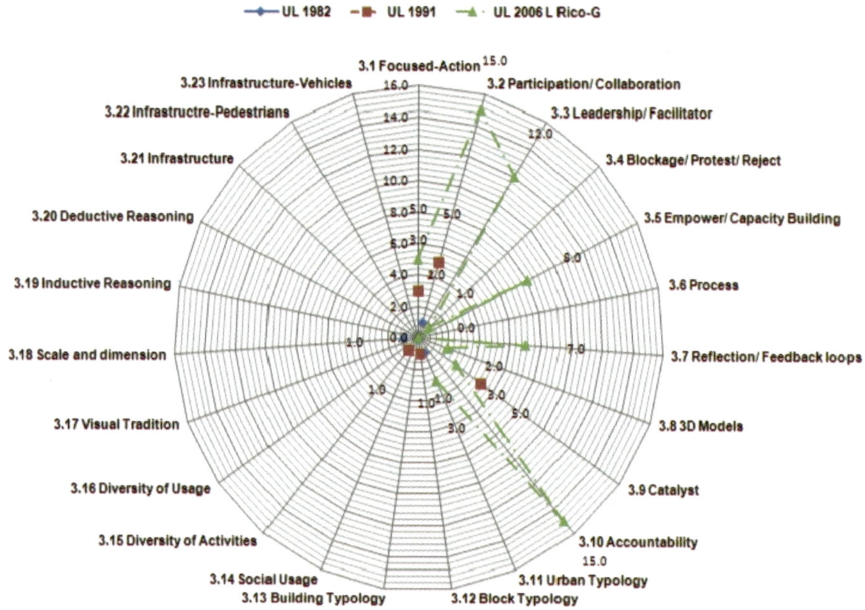

Figure 2.32: Comparison: Tactics / Strategies. Source: Onyango

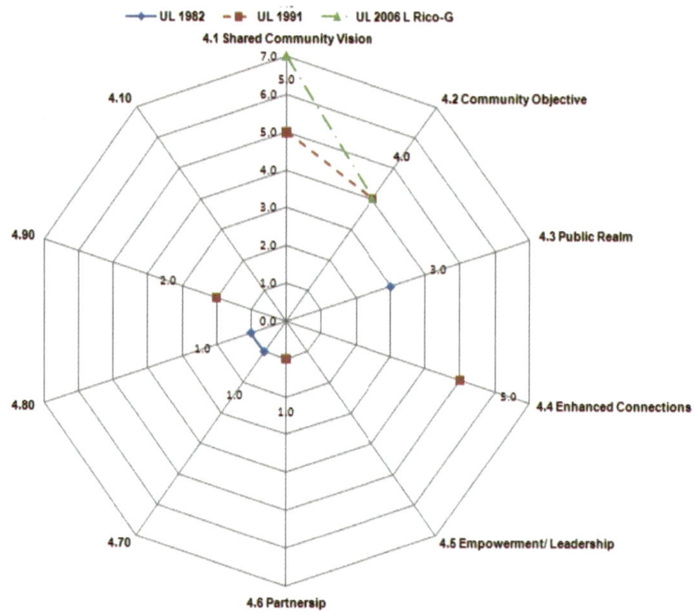

Figure 2.33: Comparison: Consequences Context. Source: Onyango

back to CMU and 1991 when the UL was re-launched. Little evidence is available to indicate that the methodologies adopted were driven by the local context as these were completely different between 1960s and 1980s. However, the training of students to be facilitators is now (in 2006) much clearer in comparison to the previous UL.

Content analysis of the UL reveals that the expected consequences of the UL were vague in 1982, and by 1991 onwards it had been clarified to look at a shared community vision and objectives (*Figure 2.32*). The other issues such as enhanced connections; empowered leaders, partnerships and creation of a public realm are hardly mentioned as a consequence. The community are not likely to be more empowered coming out of the process than they were before participating. Leadership skills have been geared towards the student designers, which I would say is no different to any traditional process. In the old system, the power resided with the elite (professionals, land owners, wealthy persons, the educated etc).

There have been transformations in how the UL has operated over the periods (*Table 2.6, next page*). These are responses to the changes in the political climate and in the availability of funding as the federal government's funds dried out in the 1980's. The UL looked elsewhere and developed working relationships with the Heinz and Carnegie Foundations, which have contributed funds to keep the UL working on community projects. Also, the partnership with URA and CDCP has ensured that they have a network of community organizations to dovetail into at the right moment when the community is ready and in need.

The curriculum has also been reorganized to make the program more versatile and less dependent on a central Figure, unlike before. A research institute (RCI) was established, which has become a platform for increasing its reach of influence beyond the local borders to national, and global. The Master of Urban Design program also provides opportunity for more research to be developed and built into the process.

The next chapter will look at Laboratori d'Urbanisme de Barcelona at Universitat de Politècnica Catalunya. It will examine the extent to which the historical context contributed to the methodological practices of the UL. It starts by giving some background information on Barcelona and Catalunya in the Spanish context, followed by a brief history of the laboratory and the founder Manuel Solà Morales. The methodologies of UL are then described and how the strategies and tactics used correlate to the historical context looked at, by use of examples from case studies. These are taken from three different distinct exercises published in the monogram "*Las formas de crecimiento urbano*" (1997).

Table 2. 5: Comparisons between different UL Periods

Type/ Period	UL 1963-1968	1982-1992	1992-
Focus	Studio and Community Advocacy Centre	Community Advocacy Centre	Research Centre
Characteristics	Dependent on a key figure who founded the lab (David Lewis) Ideas of central figure drove the studio Justice in social equity, inclusion and built environment were important Used participatory techniques [pseudo-participation, see Till (2005)] *Emphasis was on free or inexpensive practice* *Work on early stage of design-visioning.*	Geared towards helping the disadvantaged Provided crucial catalyst to community changes Raised awareness of dealing with ethical issues of social, economic and environmental justice	Changes to key figure position or responsibilities affect the lab. David Lewis left in 1968 to go to Yale ad the UL folded. Seen to gloss over the existing urban problems (being to deterministic) Could waste participants' time Curriculum objectives were not clear to the students. The project choice dependent of
Strengths	Dependent on a key figure (David Lewis) Run as an elective but driven by projects from own office. Ideas of central figure drove the studio Justice in social equity, inclusion and built environment Used participatory techniques Work on early stage of design-visioning.	Have a clear focus on what they want to do and do normally achieve them. Good reviews from local press Inspires loyalty on staff-translates to catalytic effect on design	Has been criticized for being too dependent on the key figure. Any changes to key figure, disagreements bring fall out. Could stifle alternative viewpoints (see critiques by Kline) Lacked research focus hence work not seeding outside beyond Pittsburgh. Changes to curriculum in next phase
Weakness	Remaking Cities Institute established in 2006 (UL placed under it) Network at to expand impact of the UL regionally and globally Position / policy papers Centre-identified research in urban design related issues Systematically investigates and answers questions (embedded in methodology) The Master of Urban Design programme will	Connected to university hence contributes to knowledge. Attract active researchers to faculty, Interdisciplinary approach to problem solving enhanced through attachment to RCI. Curriculum change made it more attractive to students and also mandatory for 5th year of B.Arch. Partnership with other organizations and politicians attracted more funds and ability to	At times seen to be cut off from the real world (critique by Jonathan Kline; 2009) Teaching is typically low in priority At the moment UL work is not peer reviewed. Use of 5th year reduces innovations, as they want to play it safe for their degree.

References

1. Alinsky, S., 1971. *Rules for Radicals: A Pragmatic Primer for Realistic Radicals.* New York: Vintage

2. Amy E. Hillier, A., 2003. "Redlining and the Homeowners' Loan Corporation" *Departmental Papers (City and Regional Planning)* (2003). *Journal of Urban History,* 29(4) 394-420. [Online] Available at: http://works.bepress.com/amy_hillier/3 [Accessed on 1 November 2009]

3. Arkowitz, H. (1997) "Psychotherapy Integration" in Wachtel, P., L. & Messer, S., B. (eds) *Theories of Psychotherapy: Origins and Evolution,* Washington, DC & London, England: American Psychological Association

4. Arnstein, S. R., 1971. A ladder of citizen participation. *Journal of the Royal Town Planning Institute.* April 1971. [Online] Available at: www.*ntru.aiatsis.gov.au/ifamp/practice/pdfs/Arnstein_1971.pdf* [Accessed 26 November 2008].

5. Audit Bureau of Circulations, 2005. *ABC reader profile service: PITTSBURGH POST-GAZETTE.* [Online] Available at: http://abcas3.accessabc.com/readerprofile/expired.asp#PA [Accessed on 1 November 2009].

6. Baron, J., 2007. A Children's Museum design competition proposes remaking the North Side as a "Charm Bracelet." *Pop City,* [Internet] 22 February, Available at: http://www.popcitymedia.com/devnews/48charm.aspx [Accessed 25 October 2009]

7. Bourdieu, P. (1984) *Distinction: A Social Critique of the Judgement of Taste.* London: Routledge

8. Breton, A. (1969) *Manifestos of Surrealism,* Seaver, R., and Lane, H., R. (tr). Ann Arbor: The University of Michigan Press. (The book was originally published in 1924)

9. Carnegie Library of Pittsburgh, 2008. *The Point: Mayor Lawrence on Urban Design.* [Online] Available at: http://www.clpgh.org/exhibit/neighborhoods/point/point_n102.html [Accessed 1 November 2009].

10. Children's Museum of Pittsburgh (2011). *The Charm Bracelet Project.* [Online] from http://www.pittsburghkids.org/Templates/CMP_Level3_List.aspx?CID=565&SECID=2&MENUID=338#The%20Charms [Accessed] 10 January 2011.

11. Collins, J. (2003). Taking the Lead: Dorothy Williams, NAACP Youth Councils, and Civil Rights Protests in Pittsburgh, 1961-1964. *The Journal of African American History.* Vol. 88 (2) pp. 126+

12. Coverley, M. (2006) *Psychogeography.* Herts, England: Pocket Essentials.

13. Crowley, G.J., 2005. *The Politics of Place: Contentious Urban Redevelopment in Pittsburgh.* Pittsburgh: University of Pittsburgh Press.

14. El Samahy, R. and Kline, J. (2008) Larimer Urban Laboratory Studio. [Online] from http://www.cmu.edu/rci/urban-laboratory/2008-urban-lab.html/ [Accessed] 10 January 2011.

15. Faassen, L.; Fredrickson, D. and Temkin, A. (Eds.) (1991). *An Urban Analysis and Design Portfolio for Southside Community in Pittsburgh, Pennsylvania.* Pittsburgh: Fifth year Architecture Students, Carnegie Mellon University.

16. Farber, B., A. (2006) *Self-Disclosure in Psychotherapy.* New York: The Gilford Press.

17. Folan, J. (2010) Constructing Community. In *Proceedings of the 10th annual symposium, SyracuseCoE Symposium 2010 titled 'Restoring Sustainable, Healthy Communities', University of Syracuse September 27-28th 2010*

18. Frank, J., D. (1974) Psychotherapy: The Restoration of Morale. *Journal of American Psychiatric Association.* Vol. 131 March 1974, pp. 271-274.

19. Garlake, M. (1986) Review Untitled. *Oxford Art Journal,* Vol. 9(1) pp.81-85 [Online] from http://www.jstor.org/sTable/1360378 [accessed] 10 January 2011.

20. Gathercole, S. (2006) Art and Construction in Britain in the 1950s. *Art History.* Vol. 29(5) November 2006, pp. 887-925.

21. Gatti, E. (2009). *Remaking Hazelwood, Remaking Pittsburgh: Urban Design Recommendation for Pittsburgh's Next Big Urban Project,* Pittsburgh, PA: Remaking Cities Institute.

22. Gindroz, R. &, Lewis, D., 1982. *Felicity City Urban Laboratory.* Pittsburgh: Carnegie Mellon University.

23. Glasco, L., 2001. *The Civil Rights Movement in Pittsburgh: To Make This City "Some Place Special.* [Online] Available at www.freedomcorner.org/downloads/glasco.pdf [Accessed 10 August 2008].

24. Hall, D. (2010) Wilhelmina Barns-Graham [online] from http://www.artcornwall.org/profiles/Wilhelmina_Barnes_Graham.htm [accessed] 10 January 2011.

25. Harvey, D. (1997) The New Urbanism and the Communitarian Trap: social problems and the false hope of design. *Harvard Design Magazine*, Winter/Spring 1997, Number 1 pp.1-3 [Online] from http://mitpress.mit.edu/HDM [Accessed] 10 January 2011.

26. Haumann, S. (2009) Vernacular Architecture as Self-Determination: Venturi, Scott Brown and the Controversy over Philadelphia's Crosstown Expressway, 1967-1973 in "Agency in Architecture: Reframing Criticality in Theory and Practice", *Footprint: Delft School of Design Journal* Spring 2009, pp. 35-48 [Online] from http://www.footprintjournal.org/issues/show/agency-in-architecture-reframing-criticality-in-theory-and-practice [Accessed] 20 January 2011.

27. Hirst, M. & Watts, J., 1982. User participation in the early stages of building design. *Design Studies*, 1982, Vol 3, No 1, pp.11-18. [Online] Available at: Elsevier B.V. doi:10.1016/0142-694X(82)90074-6 [Accessed 28 November 2008].

28. Hsieh, H. and Shannon, S. E. (2005). Three Approaches to Qualitative Content Analysis, *Journal of Qualitative Health Research,* Vol. 15, pp.1227-1288 [Online] available from http://qhr.sagepub.com/content/15/9/1277 [Accessed] April 18, 2012. http://www.exedes.com/Jefferson-on-information-and-choice.htm [Accessed 01 November 2009].

29. Hutzell, K., and Rico-Gutierrez, L. (2007). *Charm Bracelet Project 2006 Urban Laboratory Project.* Pittsburgh: Remaking Cities Institute, Carnegie Mellon University

30. Hutzell, K., and Rico-Gutierrez, L. (2008). *Hazelwood Studio,* Pittsburgh: Remaking Cities Institute, Carnegie Mellon University

31. Hutzell, K., and Rico-Gutierrez, L., 2007. The Urban Lab: A core curriculum of Carnegie Mellon University's School of Architecture. *43rd ISOCARP Congress on Urban Trialogues: Co-productive ways to relate visioning and strategic urban projects.* Antwerp, Belgium 16-23 September 2007.

32. Johnstone, K. (n.d.) Architecture Department, Records, 1905-1990 *Carnegie Mellon University Archives, Official University Records* Box1 Folder 18

33. Kaplan, H., 1963. *Urban Renewal Politics: Slum Clearance in Newark.* New York: Columbia University Press. [Online] Available at www.questia.com [Accessed 1 November 2009].

34. Kreiger, A. and Saunders, W., S. (2009). *Urban Design,* Minneapolis, MN: University of Minnesota Press

35. Krippendorff, K. (2004) *Content Analysis: an Introduction to its methodology.* Thousand Oaks, CA; London, England and New Delhi, India: Sage Publications

36. Kumar, A. Ed. (2009) "Challenges Facing Planning Education in India" in Changing *Planning Education and Practice in a Globalized World,* New Delhi: School of Planning and Architecture

37. Lewis, D. & Gindroz, R. (1982) Felicity/ City Project, Pittsburgh: Carnegie Mellon University

38. Lewis, D., & Simpson, A., 1991. *The Southside Community: Urban Laboratory project.* Pittsburgh: Carnegie Mellon University.

39. Lewis, D., 1979. "Listening and Hearing" *The entity from which ERIC acquires the content, including journal, organization, and conference names, or by means of online submission from the author. Journal of Architectural Education*, v33 No.1 Gaming (Sept., 1979), pp.27-29. [Online] Available at: Blackwell Publishing http://www.jstor.org/sTable/1424461 [Accessed on 3 October 2008].

40. Lewis, D., 2007. *Athena Medal Acceptance Remarks.* [Online] Available at http://www.cnu.org/lewis [Accessed 01 November 2009].

41. Lobsinger, M., L. (2002) That Obscure Object of Desire: Autobiography and Repetition in the Work of Aldo Rossi. *Grey Room,* No. 8 (Summer, 2002), pp. 38-61 [Online] from http://www.jstor.org/sTable/1262607 [Accessed] 17/02/2011

42. Lubove, R., 1996. *Twentieth-century Pittsburgh: Government, business, and environmental change.* [e-book] Pittsburgh: University of Pittsburgh Press. First Published 1969. Available at: Google Books http://books.google.co.uk/books?id=b5QQmDQKl5MC&dq=Roy+Lubove+Pittsburgh+publication+1996&printsec=frontcover&source=bl&ots=kmwoL3jlBm&si-

g=ZjgX_OhRiVIAO0ccHK2YfFS-7tto&hl=en&ei=LUkNS-OJHca-j4QbjmrGJBA&sa=X&oi=book_result&ct=result&resnum=3&ved=0CA8Q6AEwAg#v=onepage&q=participation&f=false [Accessed 30 October 2008]

43. McIntyre, M., R. (1963) *The Organizational nature of an Urban Residential Neigbhourhood in Transition: Homewood-Bruston of Pittsburgh.* Unpublished PhD Dissertation, University of Pittsburgh. In Hays, S., P. (1989) *"City at the point: essay on social history of Pittsburgh.* Pittsburgh, PA: University of Pittsburgh Press.

44. McKean, J., 2004. *Giancarlo De Carlo: Layered Places.* Stuttgart: Edition Axel Menges.

45. Nicholson, B. (1971) "Quotations" in Martin, J., L.; Nicholson, B., & Gabo, N. (Eds). *Circle: International Survey of Constructive Arts,* New York and Washington: Praeger Publishers

46. Nolan, J. (2008) CMU Students Use Wilkinsburg for Urban Lab. *Wilkinsburgsun* 15th December [Online] from http://wilkinsburgsun.wordpress.com/2008/12/15/cmu-students-use-wilkinsburg-for-urban-lab/ [accessed] 10 January 2011.

47. Rico-Gutierrez, L. (2006). *Herron Avenue,* Pittsburgh: Remaking Cities Institute, Carnegie Mellon University

48. Rosenblum, C., 2007. A Children's Museum design competition proposes remaking the North Side as a "Charm Bracelet." *Pittsburgh City Paper,* [Internet] 22 February, Available at: http://www.pittsburghcitypaper.ws/gyrobase/Content?oid=oid%3A23055 [Accessed 25 October 2009]

49. Sanoff, H., 1985. The application of participatory methods in design and evaluation *Design Studies,* 1985, Vol 6, No 4, pp.178-180. [Online] Available at: Elsevier B.V. doi:10.1016/0142-694X(85)90050-X [Accessed 28 November 2008].

50. Sanoff, H., 2000. *Community Participation Methods in Design and Planning.* New York, Chichester, Weinheim, Brisbane, Singapore and Toronto: John Wiley & Sons.

51. Schuman, S., 2009. *Thomas Jefferson on Information and Choice.* [Online] Available at

52. Scott-Brown, D., 2009. *Having Words.* London: AA Publications.

53. Sola-Morales, M., 1998. Scale not Size, More may be Less. *Paper presented at The Jerusalem Seminar in Architecture.* Jerusalem, Israel 21 - 23 June 1998. Reported by I. Klebanow [Online] Available at: http://www.jersemar.org.il/Files/1998%20-%20Manuel%20de%20Sola%20Morales.pdf [Accessed 13 October 2009].

54. Stephens, C (1997). As I was Going to St Ives, again, *Art History,* Vol. 20 pp. 622-626. [online] from doi: 10.1111/1467-8365.00086 [accessed] 10 January 2011.

55. Teaford, J., 2000. Urban Renewal and Its Aftermath. *Journal of Housing Policy Debate,* 11(2) 443-465, [Online] Available at: Fannie Mae Foundation www.mi.vt.edu/data/files/hpd%2011(2)/hpd%2011(2)_teaford.pdf [Accessed 1 November 2009].

56. Till, J., 2005. "Negotiation of Hope" In: P.B. Jones; D. Petrescu and J. Till, ed. 2005. *Architecture and Participation,* London and New York: Spon Press. Ch. 2

57. Toker, Z. (2007) "Recent Trends in Community Design: The Eminence of Participation" in Design Studies. Vol. 28(3), pp.309-323

58. Toker, Z. & Toker, U., 2006 "Community Design in its Pragmatistic Age: Increasing Popularity and Changing Outcome", *METU JFA 2006 (23:2), pp.155-166.* Mon, June 23 2008 [Online] Available at: *jfa.arch.metu.edu.tr/archive/0258-5316/2006/cilt23/sayi_2/155_166.pdf* [Accessed 24 December 2008]

59. Tuan, F. (1977) An Experimental Perspective," *Geographical Review,* 1975, Vol. 65(2), pp.151-165.

60. Urban Lab -Wilkinsburg (2008) Community Meeting ONE: Meeting Minutes. Weblog [Online] 8 October 2008. Available from: http://www.wilkinsburg-design.blogspot.com/. [Accessed 10/01/11].

61. Van den Heuvel, D. and Risselada, M. (Eds.) (2005) Jaap Bakema
(1914-1981) in *Team10 Online,* Rotterdam: NAi Publishers. [Online] from http://www.team10online.org/team10/bakema/ [Accessed] 10 January 2011.

62. Venturi, R., & Scott-Brown, D. (2004) *Architecture as signs and systems.* Cambridge, MA; London: Belknap Press

63. Watts and Hirst (1982) User participation in the early stages of building design. *Design Studies* Vol. 3 (1) pp.3-56

64. Zucker, C., 1995. The importance of interdisciplinary teamwork. *Urban Design Symposium,* Washington, DC, Library of Congress.

CHAPTER 3

Barcelona's *Laboratori d'Urbanisme*

This chapter looks at Laboratori d'Urbanisme de Barcelona at Universitat Politècnica de Catalunya, (UPC) examining the extent to which the historical context contributed to the methodological practices of the LUB. It gives some background information on Barcelona and Catalunya in Spanish context, followed by brief history of the laboratory and the founder the late Manuel de Solà-Morales i Rubio. The methodologies of UL are described and the strategies and tactics used are correlated to the historical context using of examples from case studies. These were taken from different exercises published in the "*Las Formas de Creciemento urbano*" (1997), "*El Projecte Urbà: Una experiència docent*" (1999) and "*A Matter of Things*" (2008). Each phase of the UL was investigated and linked to the sphere of influence that drove it.

3.1 Historical and Political Context

Historical context within which democracy arose in Spain after Franco's death can only be understood through the historical lens of what transpired in the previous decades (Palomares, 2004). She points out that after the 1936-39 Civil War that the Franco regime set about building a "...monolithic system in which the *Falange Espanola Tradicionalistas y de los JONS*, (FET y de las JONS) was the only dominant party..." (Palomares 2004, 23). However, the appearance of a united movement was not a true reflection of what was actually taking place. The National Movement (FET de las JONS) used drastic policies of autarchy in which Spain looked to itself in total exclusion of any other outside influence for socio-economic and political developments. In reality, the regime was actually excluded from participating in major international institutions because of the close links between Franco and the Fascist Axis of Mussolini and Hitler.

However, the fall of the latter two at the end of the Second World War brought important change to the regime: Spain became "...Less of a Fascist state and more of a Christian-coloured state…" that is a Catholic state (Palomares 2004, 11). In 1953, the US seeking to avoid communism getting close to Western Europe at the onset of the cold war after 1945, made deals with Spain in return for military bases. It provided Franco with a significant lifeline in that it signalled Spain's return to the international arena. The use of Spain as a strategic location for military deterrent brought American military personnel that benefited the Spanish economy and at the same time exposed citizens to a completely different way of life and thinking. A new consciousness was slowly being born. Prior to this, in 1951, the newly appointed Minister of Education in Spain Joaquin Ruiz Giménez had begun to reorganize the education system through the liberalization of the universities.

It resulted in 45% increase in the number of university students between 1962 and 1965. The students demanded for more say in the election of their leaders as opposed to the use of the official government approved channels. It has to be borne in mind that political parties had been banned in 1958 and participation in social and politics of Spain could only be carried out through the National Movement or associations sanctioned by it. Unfortunately for the students, participation was only allowed through the official unions (*Sindicato Español Universitario*, SEU). The leaders chosen by SEU were rejected by the students who went ahead and held their own elections in defiance of official policy. As expected the results were annulled by SEU that resulted in student's revolt, occupying university buildings, attacking SEU branches and organized massive demonstrations. However the student's activities were not the first opposition to the regime's policies; but were the most organized. The Franco regime acted by shutting the universities and refused to allow the students participation which merely entrenched the universities at the centre of opposition to the regime.

Between 1939 and 1950 all forms of political gatherings and organizations such as neighbourhood associations were prohibited. However, after 1950 business communities could meet and this quickly gained popularity giving them effective ability to contest major changes to their built environment (Boer and de Vries, 2009) Even the church that had been a bedfellow with the regime joined in the criticism of the state as demonstrated by the "…encyclical Mater e Magistra-published from the Vatican that demanded the establishment of democratic regimes and the restoration of basic freedom..." (Palomares 2004, 17). It is thus not surprising to note that the *Caputxinada* (uprising) by the students and their professors in 1966 took place in a Franciscan Monastery.

3.2 Socio-Economic Context

The period between 1957 and 1969 produced a lot of economic and social transformations in Spain partly due to the plan run by the technocratic team that collaborated with Opus Dei (elite Roman Catholic wing), academics and businessmen to reform the administration of the industry. The economy was liberated and the previous autarchic policies abandoned. The prosperity over that period resulted in massive rural-urban migration in search of not only employment opportunities but better life style. There was militancy and politicization that created a new consciousness among them. The increase in population in the urban areas correlated to rise in industrial related conflicts (Logan, 1978). It changed the social structure in urban areas and led to severe shortages of housing that were poorly built, lacked and green spaces, generating poor living conditions, social segregation and deep social conflicts (Calavita and Ferrer, 2000). The economic development was viewed as a way to social cohesion and peace instead an increase in conflict between the workers and the employers, workers and the state ensued because of the state control of the labour market that kept the wages low despite the growth. The workers started using other forums outside the recognized syndicates to stake their claims for more rights not just economically but also politically.

The historical context in Barcelona is unique to many places and different from the one in Pittsburgh and Copenhagen. The Spanish Civil War of 1936-39 played a very significant part in the development of the culture of discourse there. The political climate in Barcelona in particular post-civil war was very difficult. Sennott posits that the victorious Franco's regime (1939-75) "...had associated the country's various avant-garde movements with the left-wing political sensibilities and as consequence the architecture of modern movement was discouraged..." (2004, 112). This partly contributed to the stifling of development of theories or urban planning and the practice of architecture and the architects of *Modernisme* were confined to professional wilderness by repressive regime. The principal promoters, the *Grup d'Arquitectes i Tècnics Catalans per a la Realització de l'Arquitectura Contemporània* (G.A.T.C.P.A.C), that is group of architects and technicians for the accomplishment of contemporary architecture such as Lluís Sert, went into exile in the US and Josep Torres Clavé died at the front fighting as a Republican officer in the Franco's regime and no major works were commissioned in Barcelona.

The political crisis created a desire for strong national identity and as such the design of buildings and urban environment was informed by rational examinations of the locale, the context and the existing physical fabric. As such the international style of modernism did not take hold and "...the use of Le Corbusier's model and scale of modernism in urban design saw its demise in Barcelona..." (Solà-Morales 1998, 84). The country opted to close itself from the rest of the world with very little published materials from the USA and rest of Europe readily available. By mid to end of 1950s the isolationist tendencies of Spain began to dissipate and their contacts with other democratic nations resulted in an invigorated economy. The industrialization and growing economy led to rise in population of Barcelona from immigrants causing severe housing shortage.

A unique approach to tackling the problem of housing was developed by Barcelona's *Grupo R* founded in 1951 as a collaboration forum between *Colegio de*

Arquitectos de Cataluña and the Municipality of Barcelona. The founders to included architects "...Bohigas, Coderch, Martorell, Moragas, Pratmarsó, Sostres and Valls..." (Hernandez-Cros *et al;* 1977, p.16). The group wanted to promote architecture that was linked to the *Grup d'Arquitectes i Tècnics Catalans per al Progrés de l'Arquitectura Contemporània* (G.A.T.C.P.A.C.) and to the popular architectural traditions and the new organic tendencies that were growing in Europe and which overcame the confusion, isolation and futility of the country's architecture. Oriol Bohigas later became the director of the School of Architecture in Barcelona and head of urban design at the Barcelona Municipality between 1980 and 1984 (pre 1992 Olympic Games).

The *Grupo R* was a multi-disciplinary group whose forums were attended by not only professional architects, sociologists, town planners, geographers, engineers but also members of the public. They met to criticize each other's finished buildings and look to the future of architecture in the Catalonia region. The group rejected the neoclassical architecture promoted by the dictator Franco's regime and instead looked at regionalism that was underpinned on modernism, local craftsmanship, materials and rooted in what Sennott identifies as a strong "...belief that architecture should have social conscience to solve sociological problems..." (2004, 113). However, these were institutionalised and not voluntary organizations, while the one in Barcelona came not only out of circumstance of political oppression, but were also voluntary. The uniqueness comes from their culture of critique and analysis which operated as Mackay notes: "...they held exhibitions, ran competitions and above all, they retired to restaurants (informal places of gathering) after the site visits to reflect and discuss thoughts..." (2009, 100). The discussions were rather frank and passionate and were based on architectural issues that fostered the development of culture of critique and analysis that probably led to opportunities for cross-fertilization of ideas of design in architecture and urban environment was fostered.

The group also held lectures dedicated to topics ranging from sociology to urbanism's and interestingly even though one would have expected the attendees to be professional experts only, but the general public did attend as well in large numbers. The catalan people have a very close knit family unit and as such would often attend such meeting with their professional members of the family. This created opportunities for empowering the local citizens on issues related to sociology, economics and urbanism. By the end of 1950s the group is reported to have grown large and was reconstituted as the Barcelona School that later reject the modernist utopian ideals and instead looked at the regional architecture where traditional building practices, methods and pragmatic knowledge of local history was emphasized. In other words, architecture rooted on the local contexts, encompassing the historical, the political, the social, the physical and the cultural.

3.3 Laboratori d'Urbanisme de Barcelona (LUB)

The LUB also known as the Barcelona Urban laboratory was founded by Manuel de Solà-Morales i Rubio in 1968 in conjunction with the Head of School, Oriol Bohigas, Joan Busquets who later undertook his doctorate under de Solà-Morales. The laboratory is based at the Universitat Politècnica de Catalunya (UPC) in Barcelona as a research division that examined the growth of cities within the contextual: "...influence of the social and economic forces in which the urban elements (streets, houses, pieces of land, services, centres, etc.) are the fundamental subject of the theory…" (Domènech 2006, 4). The city thus become the object of intense study where all projects were important and were seen to contribute to the *shared* urban whole. This has been also known as the *plan versus urban project approach*; ideas are based on understanding of the traditional morphology of the city in new ways.

The *Escola Superior Tècnica d'Arquitectura de Barcelona,* (ESTAB) at UPC, looked to France and Italy for theoretical direction where Sennott points out that Aldo Rossi, Ludovici Quoroni, Carlo Aynomino and Vittorio Gregotti took the position that "…architecture should be a catalyst for significant social change and that the architectural practice should return to its traditional craft values…" (2004, 113). Manuel de Solà-Morales studied under Ludovici Quoroni in Rome, undertook a master's degree in urban design under Josep Sert at Harvard Graduate School and his doctorate under Oriel Bohigas at ESTAB. While in Italy, he must have been aware of the work of Aldo Rossi (*L'architettura della città*, 1966) and numerous critiques in the architectural journal *Casabella.* Rossi had also studied under Quoroni in Milan.

Barcelona's success in revitalization was the outcome of shared vision between "...the local government and the diverse needs and sense of identity of ordinary citizens and the civic society..." as pointed out by Rowe (1997, p.58-59). The strong civic consciousness developed during the years of economic growth between 1961 and 1973 that created a large and robust middle class who started to fight for a voice against General Franco. The economic growth created an influx of capital and exposure to foreign influences which had not existed during the early years of the regime. In addition, the expanded university access allowed for the development of a culture of hostility to Francoism among both the students and the academicians. Therefore a civic society slowly emerged as Franco lost grip on power creating a culture of resistance. The civic society is understood to be "...an organizational construct within the public sphere that depicts the banding together of people with common interest as opposed to depersonalized state authority..." (Rowe, 1997; 63).

The professionals at the school of architecture in Barcelona were very much at the core of civil resistance and Mackay reports that "on March 9th 1966, the *Caputxinada* (an illegal meeting) of about 500 university students and professors assembled in a Franciscan Monastery in Sarrià…" (2009, 104). The regime did find out and it was barricaded and eventually those involved were identified including Oriol Bohigas (who was head of ESTAB 1963-1966; 1977-80) and Josep Martorell, who were eventually expelled from the university along with 70 other professors. This act merely consolidated the participatory resistance against oppression. The school became politicized and was engaged with local neighbourhood associations to support their cause. Barcelona also had one of the blessed opportunities in history in that politics and theory met in real time through the Urban Social Movements, (USMs) called the *Asociaciones de Vecinos* or neighbourhood associations and the professional activists/advisors such as *Group R*. By late 1960s towards the end of Franco's life, organizations began to mobilize to demand public facilities and services that were lacking in the local neighbourhoods. They continually fought and achieved success in reclaiming more public services, facilities, and new public spaces in opposition to the proposed construction.

The USMs were socially and politically motivated and they organized demonstrations to achieve their goals and new democracy in Barcelona and the politicians responded. The approaches in Barcelona in transforming the physical, political and social landscapes was a *bottom-up approach* as opposed to *top down*, but were led by *visionary leaders* both at the city hall and at the professional level through the LUB at academic institutions at UPC. The direct actions and protests started by the collections of signatures, the building of consensus; assemblies, exhibitions and gathering around what ordinarily would have been perceived as normal every day events such as sports, music, etc. to the authorities. The political authorities did not respond as is typical in almost all places around the world and this further inspired them. The actions also include the invasion and occupation of public spaces, the formation of picket lines. The momentum was sustained through the existence of the networks between those concerned with the neighbourhood, clandestine unions, university students and professional organizations (Calavita & Ferrer, 1997).

The scope of things included in the action expanded to urban design and planning by the early 1970s and strong opposition to what was seen as supplementary tools called 'Partial Plans' that were part 1953 Comarcal Plan that was too general and increased densities without corresponding associated services like parks, paved roads. The partial plans had been used to satisfy the interest of the speculators during the long leadership of mayor Josep Maria de Porcioles (1957-1973). His removal from office came at the hands of the USM who led a confrontation in the city hall when there was an attempt to pass a partial plan that would have destroyed over 4300 homes. The event was publicized and the scandal forced the government in Madrid to remove him. The proposed plan was stopped; a victory and a testament to the transformative power of Barcelona's USM. The neighbourhoods involved formed an association called *Nou Barris*, "new neighbourhood," that later became one of the ten districts into which Barcelona was divided (Calavita, 2000).

With the passage of time the USMs acquired a greater voice and become part of a group of political opposition to Franco's regime. For example, the first version of the General Metropolitan Plan, (GMP) of Barcelona that was prepared in 1968 and approved in 1974 was part of the work that involved the input of the *Asociaciones de Vecinos*. It is important to note that the general features of the plan were maintained due to the defence by the city's group. Calavita & Ferrer (1977) point out that Barcelona has a history of the intense class conflict with several episodes of revolts at church and clergy which has contributed to fostering a suitable environment for the creation of an empowered community that would participate in their demands for collective goods and services.

The 1953 GMP for Barcelona was produced under political, social and cultural isolation from the rest of Europe as the result of the Civil War that stifled any attempts to develop the theories of the modern movement. By late 1960's the new crop of professionals joined the rest of Europe and the international links as a result of Franco's weakness and this, made it possible for the importation of books and journals from abroad. These brought the influences of Kevin Lynch (1960), Jane Jacobs (1961), Umberto Eco (1962), Christopher Alexander (1963), Robert Venturi (1965) and others that led to the rejection of the pitfalls that had befallen the modern movements worldwide. The publications from the US exposed the architects to the Social Usage traditions of Urban Design and Planning that were critical of the Urban Renewal programmes that were being carried out there and also to the Advocacy Planning Theories of Paul and Linda Davidoff (1962, 1965). This, coupled with the debates in other European Schools of Architecture, led to the analysis and criticism of the political and economic contexts of urban transformations.

In academia changes were taking place because of the need to respond to urban problems that emerged after the Second World War and the reconstruction of the European city following rationalism using CIAM's methodologies. The three developments led to interests in the "...historic urban form, the depreciations, demolition of medieval city walls, and processes of the inner-city reforms in some towns..." (Vilagrasa i Ibarz; 1998, p.36). The first development is related to the legal framework that led to changes in property ownership to public and private hands through the 1836 decree of Mendizábal. As a consequence of the change of use, many important buildings were demolished or destroyed and with it went the historic street systems that supported urban life.

The destruction of important historic buildings and traditional streets led to the emergence of conservation groups within academia and professional groups whose aims were to protest and demand the preservation of these assets. The response from the government was the formation of a Provincial Commission of Monuments charged with the keeping of an inventory and protection of these important assets. Unfortunately, it was not well funded and therefore ineffective, while elsewhere in Catalonia private organizations emerged. Ibarz identifies one such organization as the: "…Ramblers Association that played a part in the growing popularity of natural and historic elements and took on the propagandist role of defender of architectural and historic heritage…" (1998, 36). This was a locally based and bottom-up approach by the local citizens to fight for the protection of the historic urban forum and street through recognition of the important role the buildings and the streets play in the urbanity of a place. It is interesting to note that the organization is listed to have been multi-disciplinary in membership: among them were architects, historians, art historians, etc.

Later in the 1960s the interest in the conservation of historic contexts led to the development of the academic tradition of examination of the history of urban planning. This was very much in contrast to the approach encouraged by the CIAM movements where history was no longer important and only technological advancement and industrializations were to be looked to for progress. Important works in this period according to Ibarz are: "…re-examination of Cerdà's *Plan de Ensanche* in Barcelona (Martorell, Florensa and Martorell, 1960; Bohigas, 1963; Ribas Piera, 1964) and the contribution to the general morphological characters of Spanish cities…" (1998, p.37).

In the field of architecture and urban design there were new awakenings occurring, new consciousnesses that were aligned to developments in the academic field of geography and urban sociology. They developed interests in the roles of urban agents or stakeholders to the urban forum, published articles as a strategy to increase their influence: notable ones are: *Cap a una arquitectural realista,* (Bohigas, 1961), and *Los Ensanches* (Solà-Morales, 1978). Ibarz points to the work of LUB led by Manuel Solà-Morales on the "…urban landscapes of Barcelona and its metropolitan area that investigated the *Ensanche,* (Solà-Morales, 1978); self-built suburbs (Busquets, 1976) and public housing estates, (Ferrer, 1996) …" (1998, 40).

For a general discussion on this topic, see the classic work of Manuel de Solà-Morales. *Los ensanches (I): el ensanche de Barcelona*, Barcelona: Laboratorio de Urbanismo, 1978. A recent approach can be found in the Ph.D. of Laurent Coudroy de Lille, *L'ensanche de poblation en Espagne: invention d'une pratique d'amenagement urbain (1840-1890)*, Paris, Université de Paris X-Nanterre, 1994.]

The unique historical context in Catalunya and Barcelona in particular contributed greatly to the formation of the culture of participation and design thinking, discourse, and social and environmental justice. An example is that of the circumstances that surrounded the Ribera Plan which was eventually abandoned. The 1960s was a period in Barcelona when there were great housing shortages because of rural-urban migration in a large scale. This caused unprecedented real estate dynamics in the city because of the speculation on land values of industrial developments that were soon to be relocated to areas outside the city. Busquets points out that "...the transformations led to an increase in building levels without corresponding public services..." (2005, p.332). The government proposed further renewal programs through what is known as the Ribera Plan (*Figure 3.1*, following page) that started in 1965 proposing to relocate the population along the sea front of Barcelona. The plan was met with stiff opposition from the citizens who were already living in conditions that were not really suitable; they were congested, without clean air, open space, or amenities. The neighbourhood associations, the professionals using the LUB forum worked together using participatory design thinking to create a counter plan that halted the project.

A closer look at the Ribera Plan (*Figure 3.1*) reveals that the proposal relied on the *Tabula rasa* concept, proposing to completely eliminate the existing context and recreate a new community using large blocks without reference to the existing Cerdà grid. Ildefons Cerdà was an engineer from Catalunya appointed in 1855 to look at the future growth of medieval Barcelona (Aibar and Bijker, 1997). He proposed an open-ended extension plan that would grow beyond the then existing municipality boundaries. It contained straight streets abounded by regular block of 113 x 113 m within a geometric grid. The streets widths were between 20m while avenues were 50m. The blocks have 45-degree chamfers in the corner (*Figures 3.2 & 3.3*, following pages).

The transport infrastructure is clearly a divider between the new and the old. The proposal would have resulted in a different morphological organization from the existing context by using tall blocks that would have blocked the view to the sea that is of critical importance to Barcelona as a port city. In addition, it would have used a different typology of tall buildings surrounded by large empty grounds area reminiscent of the vertical city concept proposed by Le Corbusier and CIAM. Perhaps there was a link to his earlier Marcia plan proposal of 1932. The blocks would have created a barrier between the city and the port. The block in the plan departs significantly from the "*Manzana*" or block of the Cerdà Plan visible in the middle of the image (*Figures 3.2 & 3.3*). The proposed block lacked the definition of edge of the Cerdà plan, hence the street and public realm deemed important as drivers of urban growth.

The counter proposal on the other hand accepts and embraces the sea transforming the transportation infrastructure to a corniche. It also created three centres of activities at Montjuïc, La Barceloneta and at Glòries where the Avinguda Diagonal meets the upper ring road. The plan respects the existing Cerdà grid, it enhances and reinforces it. And most importantly it is the result of an empowered community effort to define their own representation of their view of how they would like to live. It recognizes and embraces the importance of clearly marked centres with the former industrial area on the LHS forming part of the great avenues of the diagonals. It is however interesting to note the compromise in the counter proposal in that Barceloneta is not destroyed but redeveloped using very large/ long block. This is perhaps remnants of the legacy of the modern movement. The plan gives the general view and leaves the particular to be developed at the intermediate scale unlike

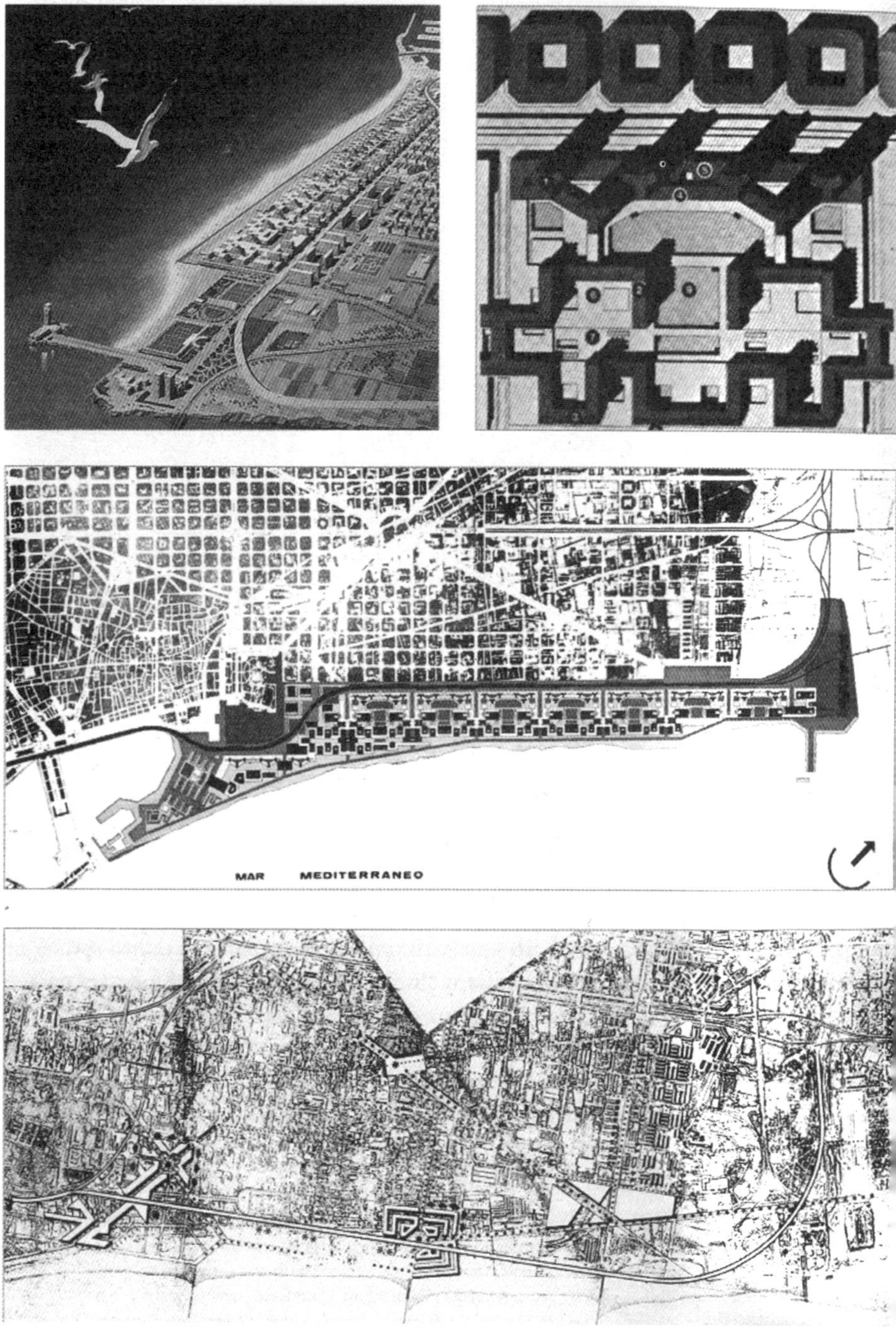

Figure 3.1: Ribera Plan and counter proposal (Busquets 2005, 333)

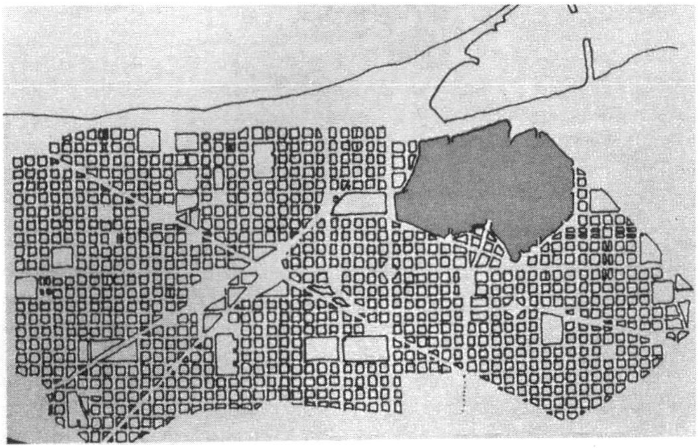

Figure 3.2: Cerdà plan
(De Solà-Morales 1997, 107)

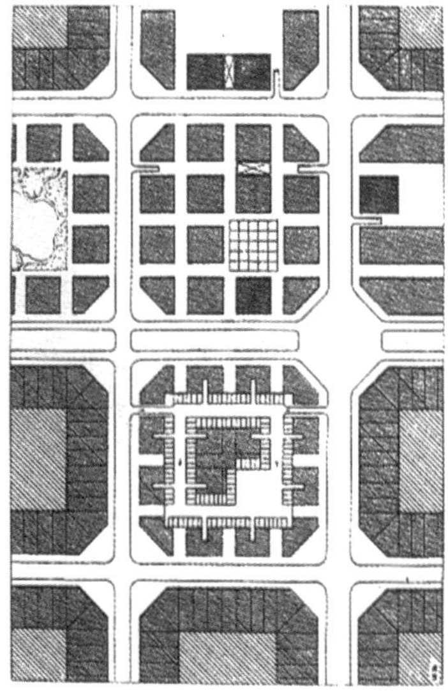

Figure 3.3: Cerdà block-*manzana*
(De Solà-Morales 1997, 119)

the Ribera plan that is complete. The strategy used in preparing the counter plan relied on the participatory design thinking through input by the professional and community USMs. It is a very powerful tool for urban transformation, education and community empowerment. Its publication in the local media allowed for a healthy discourse on the future of the city and its relationship to the citizens.

3.4 Design Process: Strategies and Tactics

The analysis of the work of the LUB reveals that the design process occurred in three key stages; the morphological study phase, the urban design framework and finally the place-making- urban project phase. The three stages are organized such that the school's curriculum objectives also met. These include enhancing skills in team-work and collaboration; analysis and communications. The process is summarized in *Table 3.2* and followed by detailed description. Urban design at LUB is taught from the perspective of radical modernism that is tied to the existing context where the interrelationship between the old/ historic and the new as established are important characteristics. The founder of the LUB, Manuel de Solà-Morales learned the trade from his modernist teacher Luis Sert at Harvard and the rationalist Italian Architect Ludovico Quaroni.

The Italian master Quaroni and Rossi were critical of the modernist approach that ignored the importance of the local place and human social values in urban planning as argued earlier. It led to the collapse of the distance between

PHASE	MORPHOLOGICAL STUDIES	URBAN DESIGN FRAMEWORK PHASE	PLACE-MAKING & URBAN PROJECT
	This phase mines and analyses 1. Economic data 2. Social Data 3. Physical morphology	1. Identifies crucial issues 2. Sets objectives 3. Looks at bench marks [use of typologies] 4. Finds relationships [building framework] 5. strengthens existing relationships between various area/ corridors	1. Details single area of focus 2. Explores typologies [how they can be applied appropriately] 3. 3D contents and representation 4. The area of focus must be at CRITICAL location of community 5. INSPIRES continued investments 6. Is the larger urban design goals for community investments
Skills acquired **Participatory Activity**	1. Gain communication skills [students] 2. Leadership skills [students] 3. Analytical Skills [students] 4. Learn importance of INTERDISCIPLINARY nature of design process [students, and professionals] **Observer**	1. Learn team-work / collaboration 2. analytical skills 3. Leadership skills 4. Relationship between buildings and surrounding 5. Learn about typologies as urban building block to be varied and repeated	1. Learn about team-work/ collaboration 2. Acquire creation skills for outdoor urban areas 3. Role of landscape architecture in urban design 4. Learn about landscape typologies to creation of public space
Products	1. Physical models [3 D large scale] 2. Maps [2 D] 3. Demographic data, diagrams 4. Photographic records 5. Publications/ Exhibitions	1. Strategic Vision 2. Creation of brief or programme for interventions 3. Typologies [building and urban]	1. Typologies [building and landscape] 2. Detailed design [architecture, infrastructure and landscaping] 3. Reports 4. Publications [journal papers, conference outputs, exhibitions]
Theoretical Framework	1. Social-Usage Tradition [Chicago School?] 2. Italian and French morphological studies	1. Visual-Artistic 2. Social-Usage Tradition	1. Visual-Artistic Tradition 2. Place-Making Tradition
Beneficiaries	1. Students	1. Students	1. Students 2. Community 3. Practitioners

Table 3.2: Stages of Urban Design Laboratory work: (Author)

Figure 3.4: Groningen. (Solà-Morales 2008, 63)

the urban design and architecture as argued by de Solà-Morales (2008). The teaching at the LUB placed emphasis on the need to "... learn from cities, to like cities as well as love creating them..." (de Solà-Morales, 1998; 86). He argued that learning from a city is done through studying, living, observing and loving the city by looking at it as the source material for the basic knowledge. This is an essential skill that designers need to be able to design at an urban scale.

In addition, de Solà-Morales taught the students to distinguish between scale and size; in other words, the urban does not always imply big objects, big schemes. In his view the "... question of urban scale even though is certainly large, does not mean it has to be expressed in large elements or large buildings..." (1998, 87). He illustrated the argument using the design proposal for a corner in the city of Groningen in the Netherlands where he was asked to change a corner of the central city surrounded by a ring canal that appeared misplaced in space. He approached the problem by looking at the corner as the key that would connect the old and the new external elements of the city as the point where the urban scale begins to change. It consisted of "...basic elementary line of observation of the place, the bench and the platform for music and the window as a point to look to the new from the old port..." (1998, 88)

The images (*Figure 3.4*) illustrate how the methodology that was underpinned on observation of the existing context at larger scale and intermediate scale is used to find resolution. The bench and the window are objects designed for immediate use at the intermediate scale yet have impact on the urban scale through the possible performance and observation of the city through the framed window. Solà-Morales argued that it is fundamental that the: "...architect's ideal role in the city is not necessarily the invention of forms or solutions of problems, but in the creation of meanings, the addition of relationships, and the clarification of the obscure and the enrichment of the muddled..." (2008, 64).

The work therefore, has meaning in as much as it experienced by people who use it. It becomes the mediator for the perception and the tangible. The interrelationship between the various parts of the urban elements is important to the design because the connection counts more than the individual objects themselves. For example, de Solà-Morales illustrated that: "...whereas size is an absolute measure (40x100x 30m), scale is a relative condition

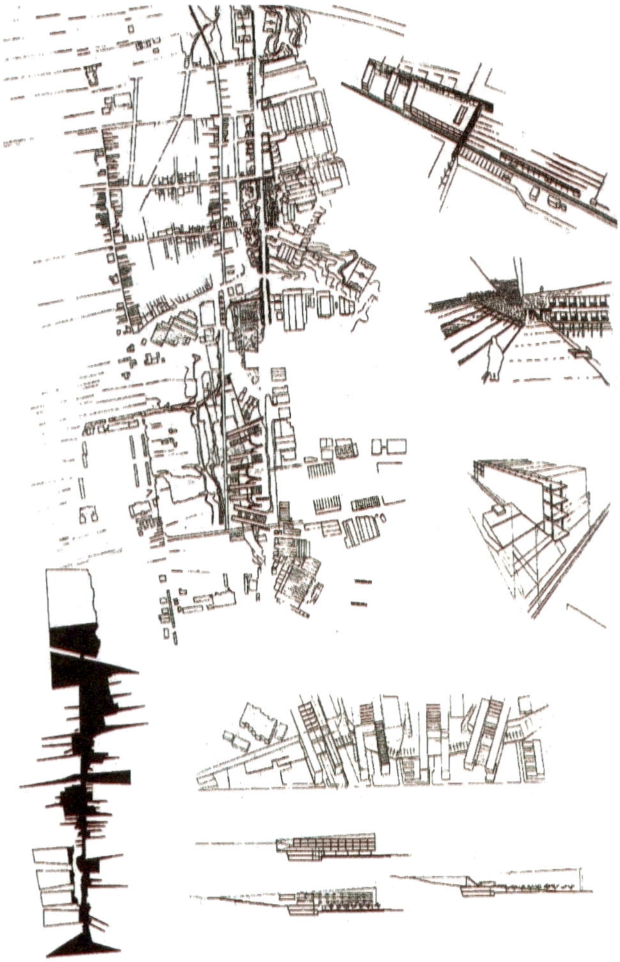

Figure 3.5: 1994-95 LUB project: *La línia ferroviària del Llobregat com a eix urbà* (de Solà-Morales et al 1999, 61)

which does not necessarily imply that bigger size has more relations than smaller things…" (1998, 88). This is notable at the level of attention paid to the elements that form the public realm in the students' work. In addition, the connections between the various elements at different locations of the city were examined and articulated at the intermediate scale (*Figure 3.5*).

At the LUB, the students are taught to avoid the division between the fields of architecture, urban design, and urban planning. Throughout the course they collaborate with other professionals because of the recognition that the architect has limited capacity (1998).

The students are encouraged to take a strategic approach, not too dissimilar to that at UL in CMU. Solà-Morales argue that it is important to take the approach because: "...by acting in one point of the city, one is constantly conscious of the physiological relationships that rely upon the whole body of the city thereby being able to somehow transform a wider field beyond the specific site itself in which one acts..."(1998, 89-90).

The process of making cities is a complex process of solving urban problems that are very specific in construction, are architectural yet have to be delivered on very tight budgets and time-scales. The solutions have to be broad yet very detailed at the same time a challenge that require the urban designer to be skilled to coordinate many competing forces.

3.5 Examined Cases of the Projects at LUB

Three cases were selected for detailed analysis of the methodology, strategies and influences to the projects carried out at the LUB. They were identified after discussion with the rector of the laboratory Professor Carles Crosas at the school. Unlike the UL at CMU which had three distinct periods (1963-68); 1982-92; and 1992 to date, the LUB had continuously carried out research on urban design in Catalonia since its inception in 1968.

The LUB has had a very well-established research centre as can been seen by the number of publications that include 244 journal articles, 133 conference paper presentations, 11 reports and 30 books, 108 book chapters and 32 doctoral dissertations (as of 2011) among others. In addition, the cases studied were those directly under the direction of the founder Professor Manuel de Solà-Morales. Also examined in detail are publications by de Solà-Morales that give indications of the methods and their sources of influence.

3.5.1 Case Study 1: Analysis of the Construction of a Street

The exercise on analysis of the construction of the street was used as the vehicle for understanding how the creation of the public realm is a result of network of forces and the work of many disciplines and community stakeholders. It required the student to select a street in any city they knew well that allowed direct interpretation with respect to or in relation to the whole city.

The emphasis on the exercise is the deductive method that relies on theoretical inputs from the other courses in urban history and theory during the semester by the professors. The intention of the exercise was to relate the themes and works developed throughout the whole course or year as the street, physical elements is common to every / all forms of growth. The theoretical orientations of the ultimate or final part of the course served as reference over the way they understood each of their relationship.

Required reading (main author)	Urban Design Tradition
1. Bacon, E. (1967). *Design of Cities.*	1. Visual Artistic Tradition
2. Bertrand, M., S. (1984). *Casa, barrio y ciudad. Arquitectura del habitat humano*	2. Social Usage Tradition
3. Giedion, S. (1978). *Espacio, tiempo y arquitectura (el future de una nueva tradicion)*	3. Modernists CIAM
4. Gomez Ordonez, J., L. (1982) *El Urbanismo de las obras publicos*	4. Social Usage Tradition
5. Lynch, k (1974) *La Imagen de la ciudad*	5. Visual Artistic tradition
6. Moneo, R (1978) *On Typology*	6. Visual Artistic Tradition
7. Rossi, A. (1968) *Consideraciones sobre la morfologia urbana y la tipologia de la edificion.*	7. Visual Artistic Tradition

Table 3.3: LUB reading list-1986 (de Solà-Morales 1997, 85)

3.5.1.1 Physical Context

The analysis of the exercise reveal that three major themes emphasised were: the physical, the economic and the strategy. The studio brief was very prescriptive on what the student would be looking for in the street as pointed out by Solà-Morales: "...relevant physical aspects that the theories and ecological models contained in your explanation of the configuration of the city, of its elements and its transformation..." (1997, 81). The readin**g list** ***(Table 3.3)*** reveals that the analysis was underpinned on theoretical models based on the Visual-artistic tradition (*Figure 3.6*). The definition of the city was examined by the means of accessibility i.e., roads, train lines and highways and how these affected the location of industrial developments, in turn location of housing. The topographic conditions and its impact on the growth of the city and how this affected the various layouts of streets and growth was also examined. The emphasis on the study of the physical context is related to the methodology underpinned on the culture of description discussed earlier. The morphological studies enabled the reading of the forces that create the relief in the city as snip shots of the life within.

3.5.1.2 Social-Economic Context

The analysis of the exercise also revealed that the urban project was considered in holistic way in that the economy is a driver of land value and acquisition was looked and how this affected the urban growth. It seems to follow same path as the work

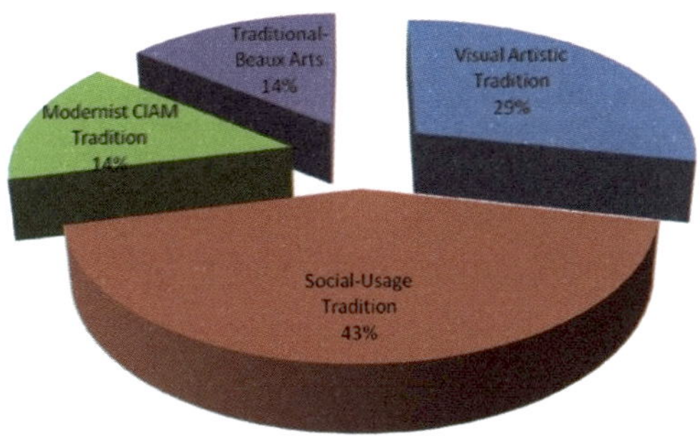

Figure 3.6: Distribution of LUB reading list-1986 by methodological approach (Author)

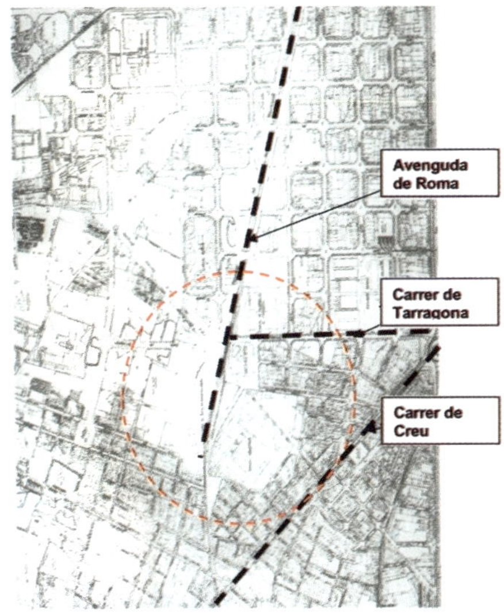

Figure 3.7: Map of Hostafrancs zone: Barcelona in 1945 (de Solà-Morales 1997, 84)

at the Centre for Spatial Analysis led by Michael Batty and use of Space Syntax research. There was also the examination using the social-usage tradition where Solà-Morales required that "....uses or functions, local, distribution, penetration/ entry of exit to the city, and the functional role of the street in the city regarding the activities it hosts (supports) residential, commenced, administration..." (1987, p.xx). The relationships between the existing activities and the land use, the street layouts, the urban space so formed was examined and used as a typology or data that would inform future designs.

The image above (*Figure 3.7*) is an example of the examination problem the students expected to solve. It is an area close to the University zone in Barcelona. It represents an area that had conflicting organization such as lack of clear grid and morphological order. It was a result of what had been left over from the post 1945 industrial history and had social consequences to the group of residences in the area.

The exercise the students were to make proposals for the subdivision for urban growth residential area from their state in 1945. The plan (scale of 1:2000 as the base) had to contain roads and pedestrian pathways established (in over a period of time), the alignments of properties for building and subdivision of these plots, according to proposals in the form of growth that considered appropriate in each area. These were as large developments as canary Warf in London; Olympic Village in Barcelona; Huerta del Rey in Valladolid in Spain, Cergy-Pontoise in Paris and Milano-Due in Italy that are examined in detail in next section.

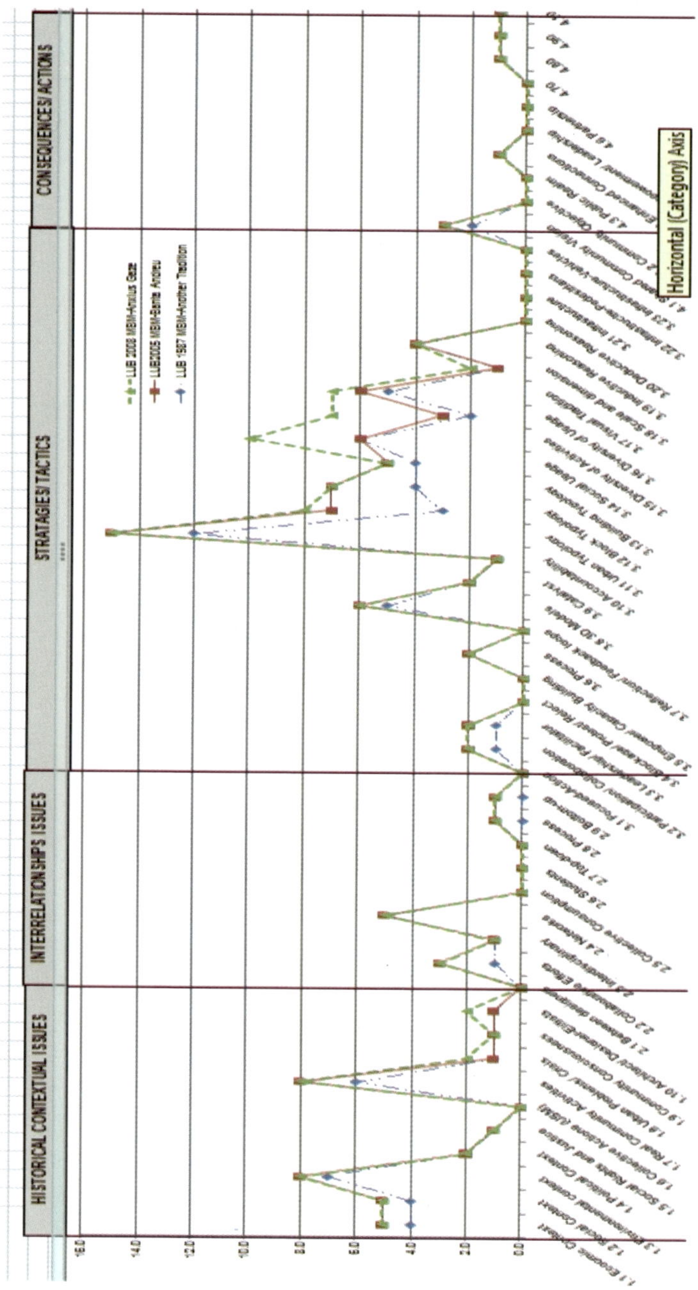

Figure 3.8: Content analysis of LUB.
Syllabi (Author)

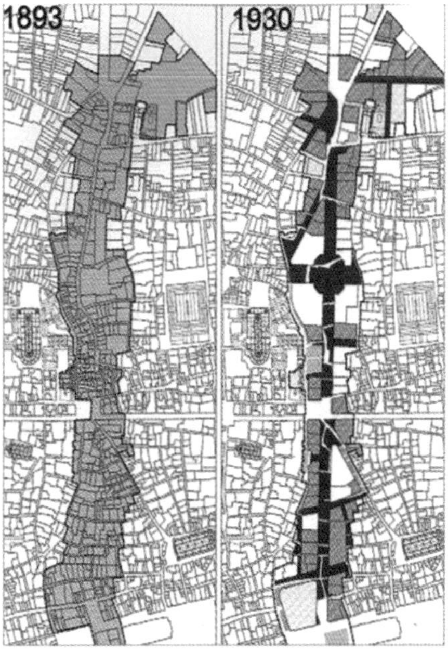

Figure 3.9: 1986 LUB morphological study of Via Laietana in Barcelona (Busquets 2005, 199)

Through the layout and dimensions of the parcel, division is as real growth would be set that would have combined the mall with the conditions proposed highway building and pre-existing subdivision. The accepted the hypothesis was a proposal containing only residential development.

The content analysis of the course syllabus reveals that the emphasis is on the importance and nature of the context, interrelationships and strategy using the "urban project." (*Figure 3.8*). The emphasis is placed on issues related to typological study (urban and building typology, 3D models) and on the importance of the support for diversity of activities in the place created. The urban project approach is based on the culture of description that developed over the years at the LUB. De Solà-Morales posited: "…is an alternative method of analysis, descriptive calligraphy that provides a way to avoid the project's arbitrary and eclectic nature... it is both analytical and projective, it narrates as well as describes the way of life of the people…" (1989, 19).

The view is supported by Parcerisa who argues that it is based on the historical analysis of the place that examines the relief of the city that are associated with the traits of the settlement. The relief are: "…the great figures or gestures formed by folds, panoramas or rivers that create the context in which the master strokes of the city – avenues, neighbourhoods and gardens – are enhanced (or in some cases are undermined)…" (1989, 28). The urban project is thus the vehicle through which the connection between the various isolated architectural objects as artefacts is established. The objects include parks, squares, residences, sports facilities, cultural amenities, infrastructures that are the building blocks of a city. It was carried out through what Cohen describes as "…policies associated with public intervention and spatial intervention that are related to particular moments of life in the Catalan metropolis…" (1998, 5).

The urban project is underpinned on the French and Italian models of urbanism rather than Anglo-Saxon one of town planning (Piccinato, 1978). It uses a technique of what Herbbert describes as "…physical urbanisms where morphological studies are used to repair, create the public realm, revise, create the block, the street etc…" (2008, 93). Therefore, it is essentially a strategy of reformulation and improvement rather than renovation of existing buildings thorough negotiated participation of the public groups and private players. The focus was on the making squares, streets or avenues and neighbourhoods as opposed to public spaces, thoroughfares and residential zones. It broke away from the functionalist modernism *Figure 3.9* is an example of a how the urban projects typology was used in the early Twentieth Century during the construction of the Via Laietana in Barcelona. The descriptive morphological study of the area was carried out and new square, streets created within the historical context. The streets were regularized and formalized and neighbourhood realigned.

3.5.2 Case Study 2: Urban Growth of Seville Expo

The second case study was of the Urban Design Course VI during 1992-93 academic year. It was under the direction of Prof Manuel de Solà-Morales in conjunction with professors Jaume Llobet, Jaume Carné, Oriol Clos and Miquel Roca. It looked at the area that was abandoned after the Seville Expo and how it could be regenerated to be part of the city of Seville. The expo occupied an area of about 259 hectares along the western margin of the Guadalquivir River. It resulted from the diversion of the train track which left an isolated strip of land (Isla de la Cartuja). The layout of the pavilions, the conservation of the monumental of the Cartuja, and preservation of the river by Park occupy space with uneven character. The Cartuja is a walled city, a restoration school of historic-artistic true value. However, the future of urbanization of the development in terms of the construction of streets and avenues, plantations, and drainage of the land, diversion of the river, etc. is uncertain, and becomes an important question of whether just planning for new is sustainable (*Figures 3.10 and 3.11*).

The exercise was to test proposals for the use of the development of the Expo through natural growth that is mixed use development growth of urban occupation. It departed from the hypotheses of voluntary specialized activities (Technology area, University City, Theme parks, Centre directional, etc.) as basis for development. The argument was that it seemed reasonable that the most common path would be to let it grow naturally with: housing, industries, multi-media city, decayed green spaces etc.), as a range of urban space, near the old town. The new ring roads were seen to pose a substantial change in the scheme of operation of the city, and a possibly introduced of new formulas (and forms) of urban growth.

3.5.2.1 Strategies

The students had taken theoretical courses on the processes of urban growth and were required to approach the proposal from three positions as: a dual city (new and old); extension to the existing fabric; and peripheral or suburban growth. The first alternative, the development considered the new area as autonomous city that was related to the historic core of Seville. They were reminded that the existing medieval Seville occupies an area of 300 hectares the same size as the current Expo. The

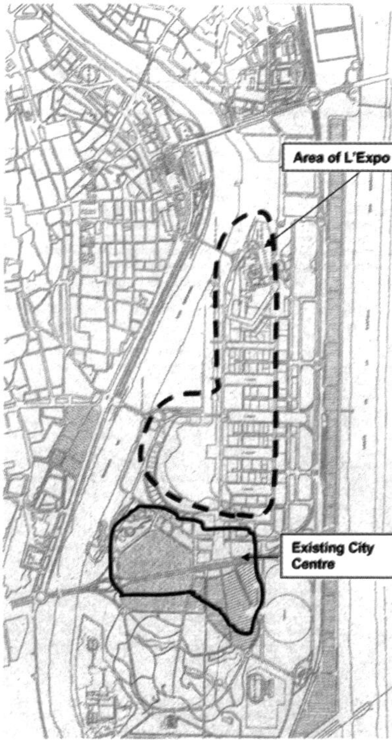

Figure 3.10: L'Expo de Seville in 1992 (de Solà-Morales 1999, 18)

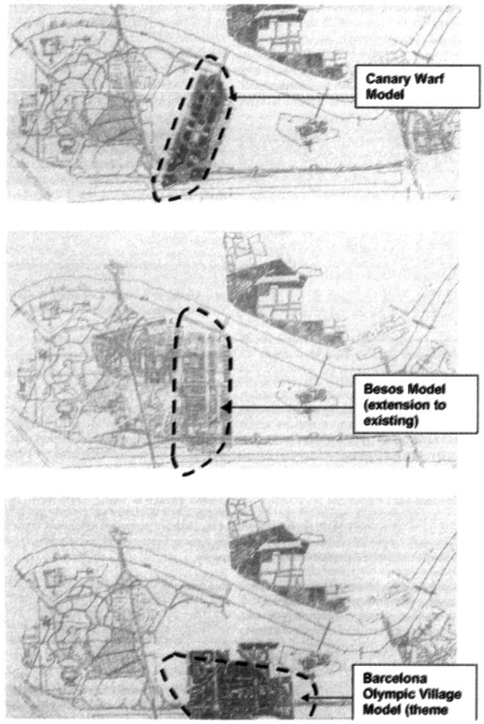

Figure 3.11: Proposals L'Expo de Seville in 1992 (de Solà-Morales 1999, 22)

approach would require well developed designs and precise forms that are tied to the existing typology of the city. Indeed, it considered questions like: What forms can this growth take? Should it be homogeneous or broken, should it remain different or constant? Different but remains constant? As a city or a periphery, as an autonomous district or a city? Or any city, but with open territory, half occupied and half free? A second alternative is understood it as an extension outside the city of today; as an extension of a residential (or industrial) or mixed. It was considered the most likely hypothesis. A third hypothesis was understanding growth as an open a periphery, i.e., as a free territory half full and half empty without conclusion or boundaries.

The students were free to select any alternative, which took the importance of access from the ring roads straight to roundabouts, is fast, and should consider what changes in the network in contact with the old. They were to draw and present the work at a scale of 1:5,000. The plan was accompanied by a couple of vignettes representing a perspective on the type of fabric, construction and images that characterize the proposed (visual artistic and social usage traditions).

The proposal shown below (*Figures 3.11a, b & c*) are examples of growth using three models indicated. The first: the Barcelona Olympic Village model (*Figure 311a*), is an alternative that shows a proposal that is developed as specialized theme area, separate and distinct from the existing city. It is similar to the previous proposal for the expo other than in scale. It occupies about the same areas as the old city. It is not clear from the drawings what would become of the buffer zone between the two, as one of the critiques is the decay caused by run down parks. The second: the Besòs model (*Figure 311b*) is an example of the second alternative as an extension to the existing city. The drawing reveals proposed growth of similar size to the existing city, distinct in character yet linked to it. It has linear block and yet separated from the existing core by the ring road/ motor way. However, it is difficult to establish what the buildings look like or heights due to the scale, the assumption are they would reflect the heights prevalent in exiting community if the historical analysis is the underpinning theory. The third: Canary Warf (*Figure 311c*) model that has semblance of coherent whole yet with functions woven together to form a *civitas*. However, it teaches the students the fallacies of such development of insular community of what Bird suggests are "a city within a city" (1993, 127).

3.5.3 Case Study 3: Redevelopment of the Area around Valencia Train Station: Urban Design VI

The third case study was of the Urban Design Course VI during 1995-96 academic year. The station (north) of Valencia, is still centrally located in an extraordinarily position. The Spanish Railway company (RENFE) has 40 hectares of land for roads, factories and warehouses that are hardly unused. There are several initiatives for the use of this space that include a change in the location and function of the station *(Figure 3.12)*. The General Municipal Plan provided for a large urban park with consideration of the possibility of relocating the RENFE station 600m back. This could create opportunity for a possible business centre (about 100,000m^2 of offices, and retail constructed under one roof). Another option was that the station could donate more land to the city if relocated to where the trains' lines arriving from the north, the west and south meet. There are 40 hectares located within continuity of the central extension. The current station is a modernist building of great architectural interest that was recently restored. The orthogonal angle blocks of the surrounding area of lands precisely reveal traces of the expansion of Valencia from Nicolas Marie Chapuy of 1844 painting. The access to the motorways of Alicante and Madrid, the continuation of the Great Street and other avenues coincides in the location of the station. The two neighbourhoods on the sides of the current station are especially popular and full of life: Russafa, and San Augustine in the west.

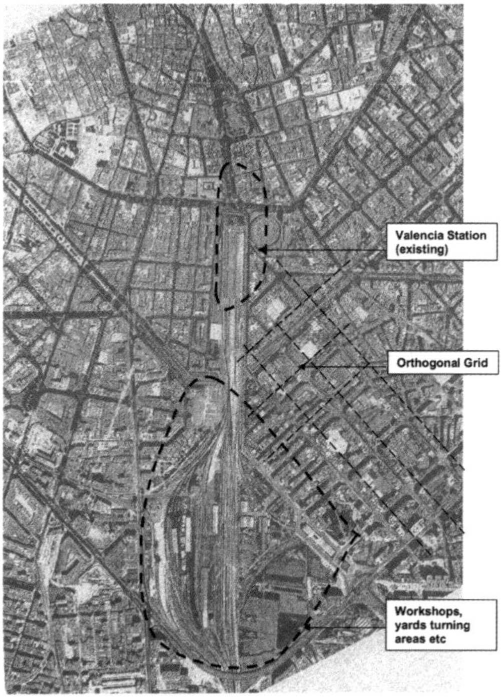

Figure 3.12: Proposal *Ordenació de l'àrea de l'estació de València* (de Solà-Morales 1999, 142)

Figure 3.13: Proposal *Expo de Sevilla* in 1992 (de Solà-Morales 1999, 164)

3.5.3.1 Strategies

The proposals were for the future management of this central area firstly, to indicate the position of the station, the city park and the new buildings to in the proposal. In addition, the size and shape of each of these elements in relation to town were to be clearly indicated and current description of the topography of the proposed changes. Secondly, the development of the scheme without consideration of planed commercial spaces, offices (100,000 m^2) typologically organized. They were to be presented through axonometric drawing that indicated the architecture. Thirdly, the proposal should also include road network supporting the above and connections to the rest of the urban and regional roads. Fourthly, the area zoned for residential housing with 3.000 units and finally the synthesis of the phased planning and defining the anchoring elements necessary during first phase (5 years) usually containing the infrastructure, and buildings (public and private).

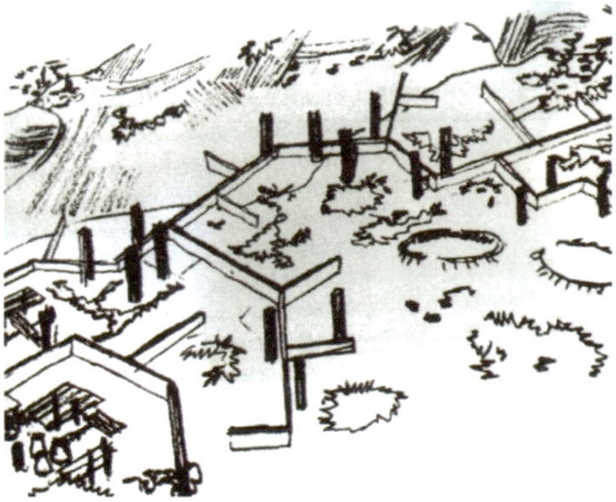

Figure 3.14: Sert and Wiener sketch project for Rio de Janeiro, 1946. (Mumford 2000, 82)

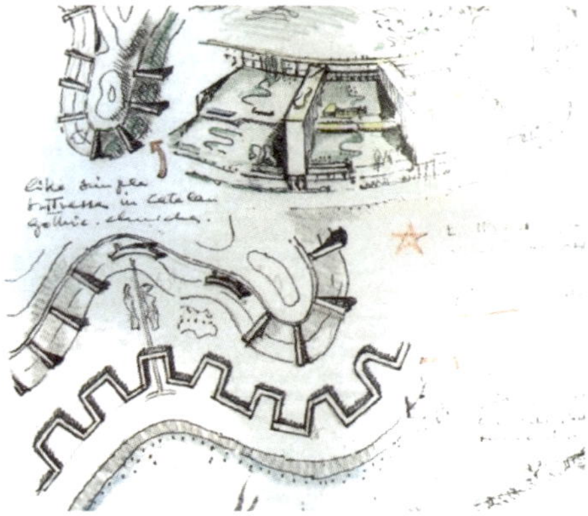

Figure 3.15: Allison & Peter Smith-Urban Reidentification Golden Lane Competition, 1952. (Mumford 2000, 235)

3.5.3.2 Consequences

The strategy adopted was reflected on the results of the work produced by the students. The LUB places emphasis on historical analysis underpinned on morphological studies. Even though the proposal was to look at the immediate station area, the "Urban Project" approach ensured that the wider context was looked at as evidenced in the *Figure 3.12*. The figure ground drawing reveals that the void left if the station were removed is as large as a quarter of the medieval Valencia. It was therefore fundamental that they considered the larger picture as opposed to narrow approach that is prevalent in conventional urban design.

It is interesting to note that even though de Solà-Morales is critical of functional modernism, the brief provided to the students suggest its use. In addition, the proposal suggests separation of functions by zones (*See Figure 3.13*). The commercial buildings and the public spaces are located on the spinal spine leading to the park. The 3D axonometric at the intermediate scale of the urban vision suggests emphasis on connection between the various parts of the city, infrastructure with less emphasis placed on the design of the buildings themselves. Even though urban typology relies on the peripheral block, the detailed drawings that would indicate the size of the units is lacking, perhaps a weakness in the strategy selected. However, in looking at details from other proposals reveal very large block similar to those proposed by Sert almost a century earlier (*Figure 3.14*). They are equally similar to work of the CIAM rebels (Team X) of Alison and Peter Smithson (*Figure 3.15*) around the same period underpinned on the idea of the grid.

Analysis of other proposals (*Figure 3.16*) reveal the two traditions of urban design: the visual artistic and social-usage. The large scales (1:2,000, 1:5,000 and 1:10,000) were used to give the urban vision with the 3D drawing. The proposals are not detailed enough to suggest the characteristics of the place. They reveal emphasis

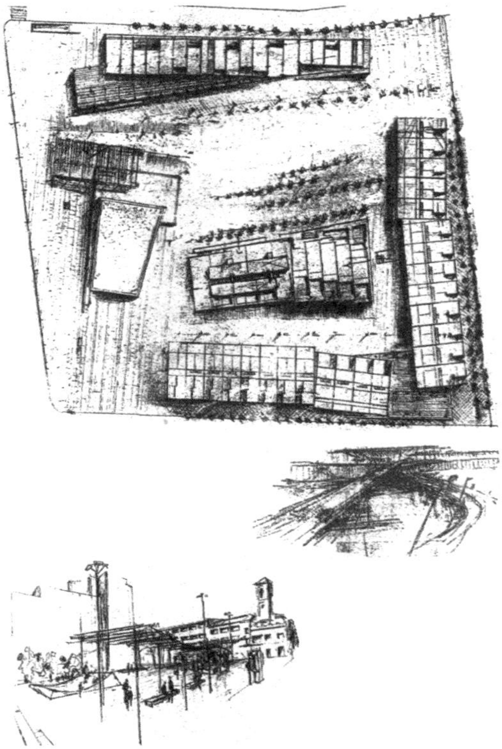

Figure 3.16: Tàctica Urbanística [Strategic Urbanism] (De Solà-Morales 1999, 191)

on strengthening of the urban edge that form the streets deemed important. The strategic use of the "Urban Project" ensured that the intermediate level of design that however reveal what appear as very large buildings. The images also suggest focus on social-usage tradition with the public spaces indicating places for socializing, meeting or networking.

3.6 Summary

This section summarizes the LUB model at UPC by type of organization and the methodologies adapted with their roots to contexts. It is based on the material provided from the websites, interviews with director of the LUB in 2008 and course materials and publications that have come out of the laboratory. The table below (*Table 3.4*) is a summary of the activities, the technique used to carry the activity and the influence or cause of the choice of the method. The analysis also revealed that the LUB process occurs in two key stages or phases as illustrated above. The theoretical leanings of the LUB are the Social-Usage and visual –artistic traditions. Three methods are used that could have arisen out of the circumstances in the political history of the place, the social and environmental histories and

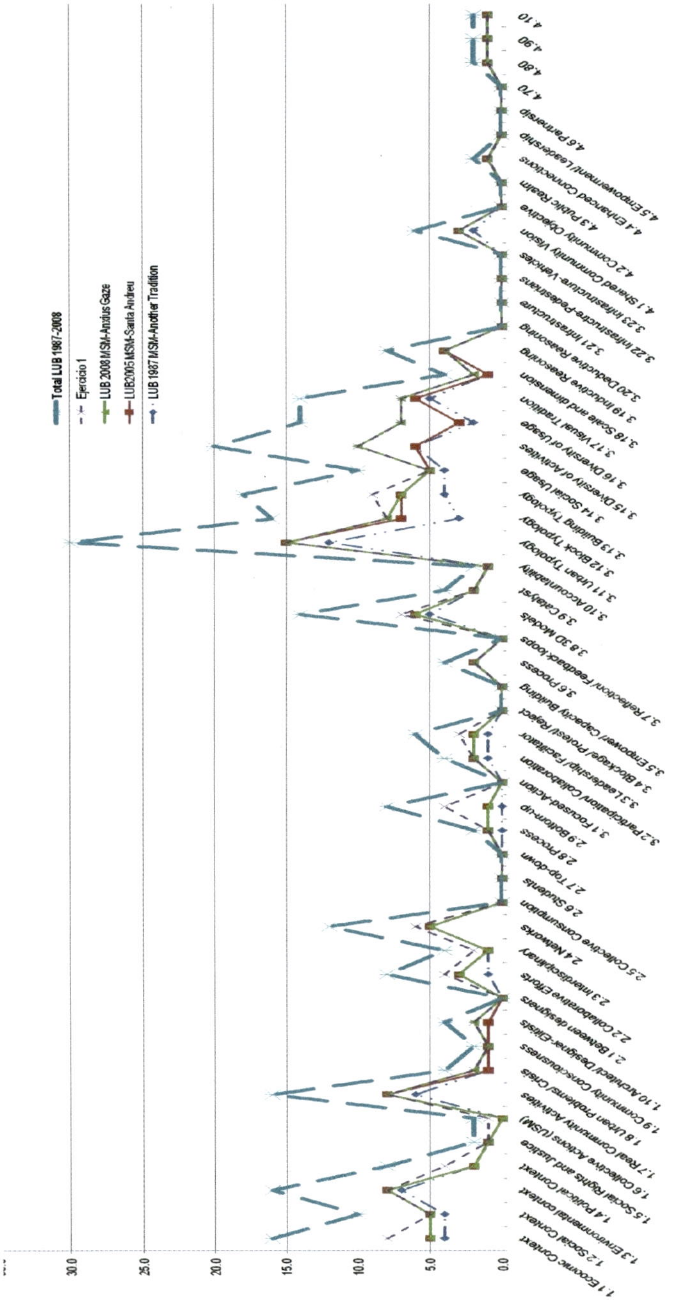

Figure 3.17: Content Analysis: Comparisons between LUB Syllabi of 1987, 2006 & 2008 (Author, 2011)

Phase	Methods	Influence/ cause
Critical Analysis	1. Awareness methods 2. Indirect methods	1. Rationalist approach: (Quaroni, Lynch, Gregotti, Jacobs, Venturi, Alexander, Rossi) 2. Visual Artistic Tradition (Bacon, Bertrand) 3. Urban Social Movements
Urban Project	1. Indirect methods 2. Group interactions methods	1. Rationalist (Rossi, Moneo,Gomez-Ordinez) 2. Urban Social Movements

Table 3.4: Summary of Phase, methods and influences

the academic traditions of the time. These are the awareness method, the indirect method, and the group interaction method.

Content Analysis was carried out on de Solà-Morales articles *"Another Tradition" (1987); "Sant Andreu"* (2005); *"Anxious Gaze"* (2008) and the assignment "Exercise 1" (1993). It reveals consistency between the LUB's work in the different periods as illustrated above (*Figure 3.17*). The analysis reveals that emphasis on two areas; historical contexts and strategies/ tactics. Within the historical context, the environmental issues and community activities have been highlighted most.

In addition, the analysis point to the importance of collaborative efforts and networks to their methodology. The success of the "Urban Project" is underpinned on the collaboration between the various professionals as well as with the community through *Associaciones de Vecinos* (neighbourhood's associations). The community network is therefore vital to its success. The awareness of the need to participate in the projects seems to be mainly through this network. The strategies highlighted as most important are the use of the urban and building typologies; designs that would foster diversity of activities; use of 3D models and inductive reasoning. These have been driven by the historical methods of analysis discussed earlier in the chapter that came from the French and Italian traditions.

The content analysis also reveals that as a consequence, the projects by both the professionals involved with the LUB and the student's work results in shared community vision. In addition, there are enhanced connections between the various sectors of the larger urban area because of the tactics or strategies that places emphasis on the morphological analysis (*Figures 3.13 & 3.14*). A detailed analysis of the historical context is illustrated by the radar diagram beside (*Figure 3.18*). It reveals that the work of the LUB was and is still driven by the forces of economic, social, political,

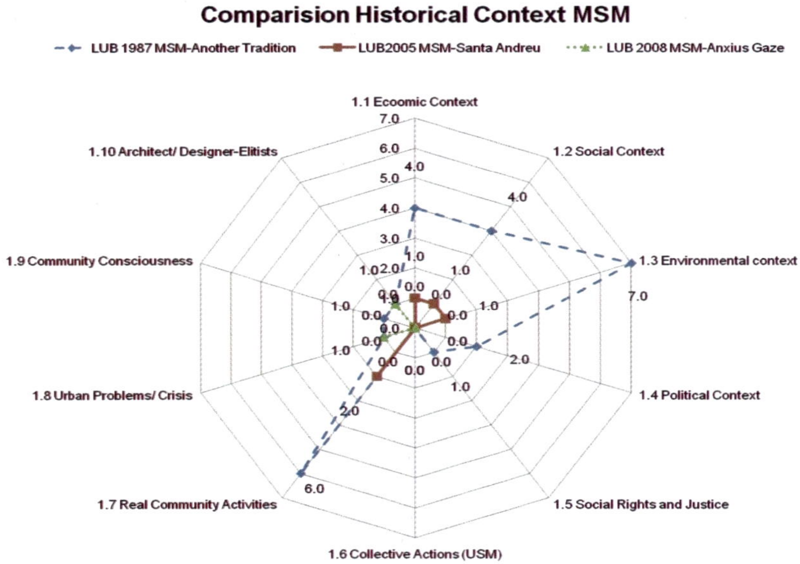

Figure 3.18: Comparison: Historical Context.

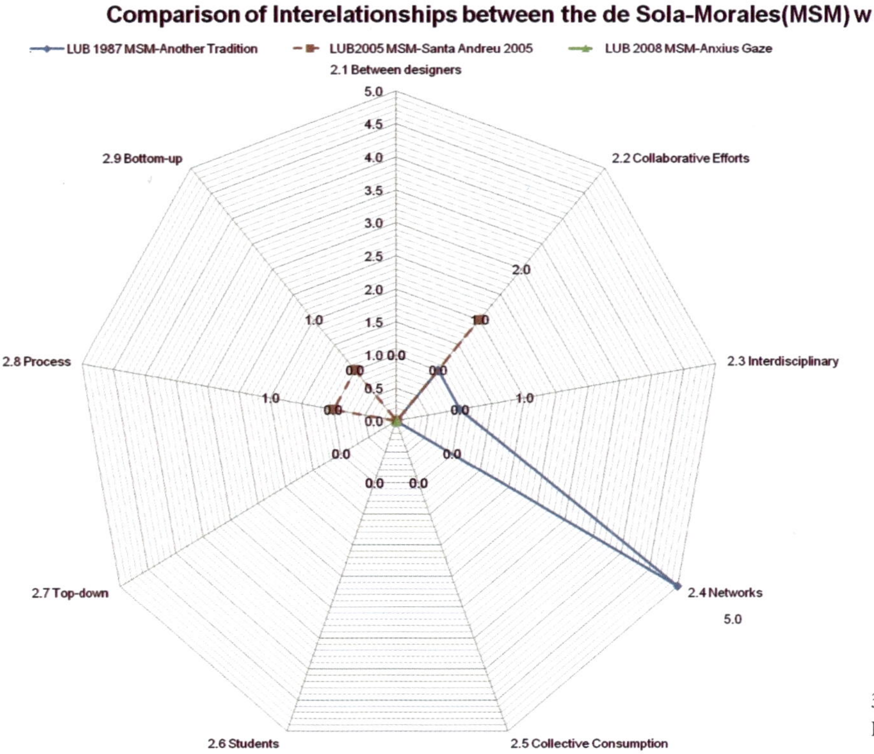

3.19: Comparison: Interrelationships

environmental contexts and the need for spaces for community activities. However, the most important aspects appear to be the degradation of the environmental context for the communities and the impact on the community activities due to the conditions of the urban spaces.

Content analysis of the data on interrelationships reveal that LUB methodology is depended on existence of a strong network within the community as illustrated (*Figure 3.19*). This is not surprising based on the history of repression that existed in Catalonia during the General Franco's dictatorial regime that outlawed any form of gathering other than for cultural reasons and there were no political parties. The community network was thus important in keeping abreast with developments across the area and in finding ways to get a new consciousness that allowed expression of views. It also reveals that collaborative efforts were important as well as existence of bottom-up approaches to the process. Even though it was difficult to establish how this was carried out specifically from the LUB reports, in an interview with Carles Crosas (the editor of the journal La Revista Quaderns d'Arquitectura i Urbanisme and a professor at the school), it was pointed out that the community had developed a great awareness and interest in projects that would affect their built environment and were very active in discussing proposals.

The LUB process is underpinned on morphological and typological studies as such the interdependence between the housing, road/ street and public realm is seen as the provider of richness and variety as pointed out by de Solà-Morales (1997). The process and bottom-up approaches are important to the LUB methodology as it provided the reflection by both the students and the community. It was however difficult to verify how the reflection took place beyond in the context of conventional studio presentation setting.

The figure at the precedent page is a radar representation of the detailed content analysis of the strategies used at the LUB (*Figure 3.20*). The emphases are on accountability, participation/ collaboration, leadership, capacity building and reflection. The issue of accountability is crucial to ensure the acceptability of a project proposal to any community. The participation by the community in the process is equally important and its success is dependent on an empowerment. This leads to opportunity to provide reflection to the process. It is however interesting to note that tactics like protests that were characteristics of the 1960s are no longer important as the community have been empowered over the years during the fight for democracy.

They have the power and do not need to protest but to negotiate the hurdles. Content analysis reveals that the expected consequences of the LUB were development of a shared community vision, community objective and enhanced connections (*Figure 3.21*). The strategy of using the "Urban Project" places focus on the public realm through the detailed study and understanding of the street and the interrelationships to the diversity of uses, connections to other forces that drive it such as economic, social, political, cultural and environmental.

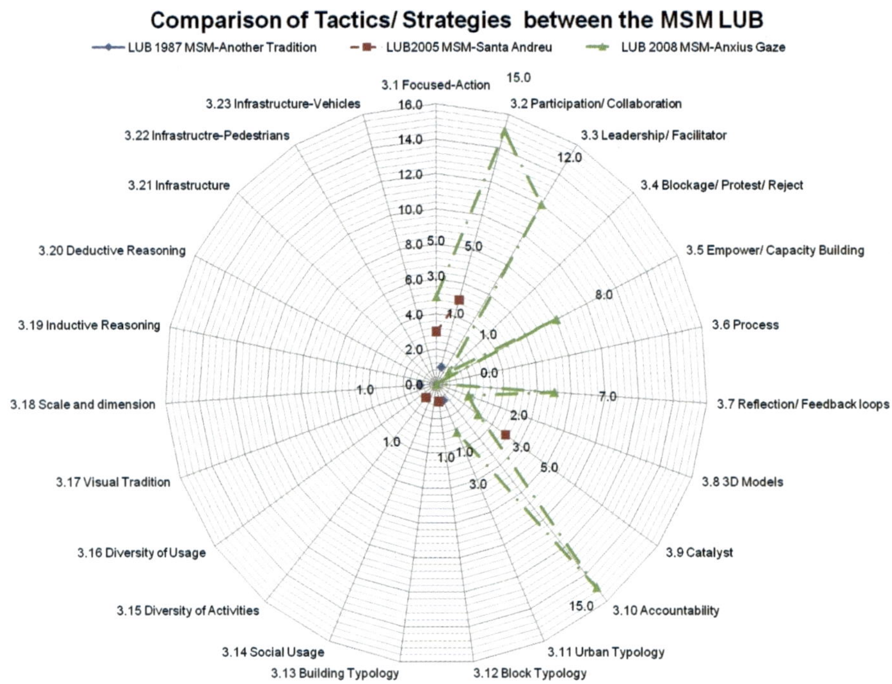

Figure 3.20: Comparison: Tactics / Strategies

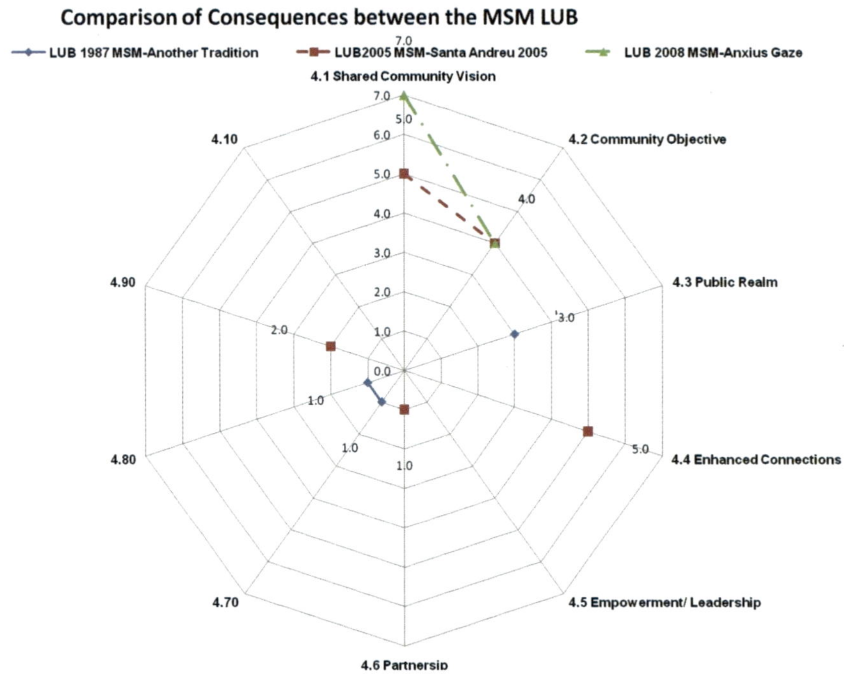

Figure 3.21: Comparison: Consequences

References

1. Aibar, E. & Wiebe E. Bijker, W. E. (1997) "Constructing a City: The Cerdà Plan for the Extension of Barcelona." *Science, Technology, & Human Values* Vol.22(3): 3-30. [Online] Available from: http://www.jstor.org/stable/689964, [Accessed 22 June 2022].

2. Bird, J. 1993. "Dystopia on the Thames" In *Mapping the Futures: local cultures, global change*, edited John Bird, Barry Curtis, Tim Putman & Lisa Tickner, 121-138. London: Routledge.

3. Boer, R. W. J. & de Vries, J. (2009). "The Right to the City as a tool for Urban Social Movements: The case of Barceloneta." Paper presented at the *4th International Conference of the International Forum on Urbanism (IFoU)* 2009 Amsterdam/Delft. The New Urban Question-Urbanism beyond Neo-Liberalism (2009): 1321-1330. [Online] Available from: http://ifou.org/conferences/2009delft/proceedings/9%20Changing%20Planning%20Cultures/full%20papers/F034-1_Boer_DeVries.pdf, [Accessed 22 June 2022].

4. Calavita, N. & Ferrer, A. (2000). "Behind Barcelona's success story: citizen movements and planners' power." *Journal of Urban History,* 26(6): 793-807. [Online] Available from: https://doi.org/10.1177%2F0096144

20002600604, [Accessed 22 June 2022].

5. Cohen, J. L. (1998). "Learning from Barcelona; twenty years of urban projects and their reception." In *Ciutat Real, Ciutat Ideal: Significat I Funcio a L'espai Urba Modern: Debat De Barcelona (III),* edited by Acebillo, Josep, and Subirós, Pep. Barcelona: Centre de Cultura Contemporània de Barcelona.

6. De Solà-Morales, M. (1989) "The Culture of Description." *Perspecta* 25 (1989): pp.16-25. [Online] Available from: https://www.jstor.org/stable/1567136, [Accessed 22 June 2022].

7. De Solà-Morales, M. (2008). *A Matter of Things.* Rotterdam: NAi Publishers

8. De Solà-Morales, M. (1997). *Las formas de crecimiento urbano.* Barcelona: Edicions UPC.

9. http://www.jersemar.org.il/english/speaker_Manuel_de_Sola_Morales.aspx.

10. De Solà-Morales, M.; Llobet, J.; Bellmunt, J.; Carne, J.; Clos, O.; Fiol, C. and Roa, M. (1999). "*El Projecte Urba: Una experiencia docent*" Barcelona: Edicions UPC

11. Domènech, L. (2006). *Barcelona: A quarter of a century in Town Planning,* Barcelona: Aula Barcelona

12. Hebbert, M. (2008). "Town Planning versus Urbanismo" In *Dialogues in Urban and Regional Planning*, edited by Harper, Thomas; Gar-On Yeh, Anthony; and Costa, Heloisa, pp. 150-170. London: Routledge.

13. Hernandez-Cros, J. E.; Mora, G., and Pouplana, X. (1977). "The Construction of the city of Barcelona 1716-1977" *Guía de arquitectura de Barcelona* 122(1): 12-18. [Online] Available from: https://www.raco.cat/index.php/CuadernosArquitecturaUrbanismo/article/download/121829/243538/, [Accessed 22 June 2022].

14. Logan, J. R. (1978). "Rural-Urban Migration and Working-Class Consciousness: The Spanish Case." *Social Forces*, Vol. 56(4) June, pp.1159-1178. [Online] Available from: https://doi.org/10.2307/2577516, [Accessed 22 June 2022].

15. MacKay, D. (2009). *A Life in Cities: An Architectural Autobiography.* Edinburgh, Scotland: The Royal Incorporation of Architects in Scotland.

16. Marzot, N. (2002). "The study of urban form in Italy." *Urban Morphology* Vol. 6 (1): pp.59-73. [Online] Available from: http://www.urbanform.org/pdf/marzot2002.pdf, [Accessed 22 June 2022].

17. Parcerisa, J. (1989). "The Relief of the City." *Perspecta*, Vol. 25, pp. 26-31 [Online] Available from: https://doi.org/10.2307/1567137, [Accessed 22 June 2022].

18. Palomares, C. (2004). *The Quest for Survival after Franco: Moderate Francoism and the slow journey to the Polls, 1964-1977.* Brighton and Portland: Sussex Academy Press. 2006 paperback edition.

19. Rowe, P. (1997) *Civic Realism.* Cambridge, MA: The MIT Press

20. Sennett, R. 1977. *The Fall of Public Man,* New York: Knopf.

21. Sennott, R. (ed) 2004. *Encyclopedia of 20th Century Architecture. Volume 2.* New York: Fitzroy Dearborn.

22. Vilagrasa i Ibarz, J. 1998 "The study of urban form in Spain" *Urban Morphology,* 2(1): 35-44, [Online] Available from: http://www.urbanform.org/online_

unlimited/um199801_35-44.pdf, [Accessed 22 June 2022].

CHAPTER 4

Copenhagen Center for Public Space Research

This chapter examines the Centre for Public Space Research (CPSR) at the Royal Danish Academy of Fine Arts and School of Architecture, RDAFA, Copenhagen by looking at the extent to which the historical context contributed to the methodological practices of the centre. It starts by giving some background information on Copenhagen and the Danish context, followed by a brief history of the centre. The methodologies of the centre are then described and how the strategies and tactics used correlate to the historical context was considered, using examples from case studies.

The examples are from professional work by the practice Jan Gehl Architects that involved students at the centre and those at the University of Melbourne including, an interview with Prof. Dr. Jonna Majgaard Krarup who was the director of the CPSR. It was very insightful in revealing some of the tensions that may have caused the need for transformation of the workings of the centre. Note that it has been difficult to obtain material on this case study in comparison to the others, since Jan Gehl retired from the school. In addition, his office has not been willing to share information, neither have the Institute, beyond letting me know they have restructured.

However before going any further into the work of Gehl and others at the centre, it is important to take a look at the historical framework that surrounded Denmark and Copenhagen around this period that could have contributed to the formation, interest in the methodology, and the new consciousness about the quality of the environment.

4.1 Historical Context

The Danish political system during the Twentieth Century is based on what is known as a consensus model. It is rooted in the population make-up of Denmark, which has historically been composed of workers and farmers. Jespersen argues that the political system was characterised by:

> "...a popular negotiated democracy between the farmers and the workers who respected each other and conducted a running political dialogue that stretched across all the boundaries of class and economics" (2004, p.31).

Several authors (Francis, 2000; Sanoff, 2000 & Toker, 2006 etc.) have underlined the importance of consensus to the participatory design thinking process; however, the crucial question in Denmark is how did it come about historically? The following next section traces its roots and in the next section relates it to the developments of the methodology used at the CPSR in Copenhagen.

The idea of the Danish model above comes from the description by an experienced Danish politician, Jens Otto Krag (1914-1978) who was the Prime Minister from 1962 to 1968 and 1971 to 1972. Krag pointed to the existence of a political symmetry between the farmers and the workers in Denmark who were not necessarily always opposed to each other. According to Jespersen, the model of political consensus is a collaborative democracy where the goals are achieved through:

> "...The understanding of issues and while respecting each other, being able to reconcile interests (competing at most times) to achieve an acceptable solution without creating destructive social conflicts..." (2004, p.31).

The collaboration is between the representatives in the interests of the whole society thus fundamentally pinned on the upholding of moral ethical values, therefore any developments are carried out along the lines of consensus rather than conflict as observed in other participatory political systems (I make reference to Alinsky's model seen in the initial periods of UL at CMU and of the LUB's model where the reactionary counter proposals were the order of the day against Franco's regime). The Danish model has roots linked to the political events that took place after the *Coup d'État* of 1536.

After the death of King Frederik I (r1523-33) in 1533 there was a 3-year violent civil war that was caused by the decision of the Council of the State, *Rigsrad,* to postpone the selection of a new king as was the practice, and to take control of the government. During this period in Denmark, the *Rigsrad* normally appointed an elected Monarchy from among the nobles and traditionally the eldest son of the deceased king ascended the throne.

In this particular case the problem arose because the oldest son, "...Duke Christian was a passionate adherent to the teachings of Luther...

" A protestant reformation leader, (Jespersen, 2004, p.33). However, most Danes and the *Rigsrad* feared that his ascension to the throne would jeopardize the existing social order. Jespersen further points out that the decision to postpone the selection of the new king until a suitable Catholic candidate was found was the spark needed to ignite the already "...existing social, religious and political tensions that had long been bubbling under the surface..." (2004, p.33).

Interestingly, Duke Christian became the stabilizing factor after using the military of German mercenaries and other loyal duchies to take control of the country. After his successful conquest, he set about systematically restructuring both the ecclesiastical and political structures of the country. The first key reform was the removal of the religious elements in the leadership of the state, to make it a purely secular matter for the king and non-ecclesiastical remnant of the *Rigsrad.*

It redefined the meaning of Sovereign in Denmark as "The Crown of Denmark" that was characterized by the collaboration between the king and council of noblemen. It elevated the Sovereign to a level of abstraction above both the king and the noblemen who could die yet it remained as the stabilizing element of Denmark. The new structure removed the previous political symmetry and created a body that consisted of complementary components.

The structure of "The Crown of Denmark" over the years has been transformed by two forces; firstly, changes in warfare techniques with less reliance on the use of the infantry that was previously provided by the noblemen. As a result, the noblemen were no longer able to provide protection to the citizens. Therefore, the general populace and clergy demanded more changes to the nobility's privileges. The King was too happy to decrease them, and instead collaborated with the commoners through elected representatives resulting in the second key reform, the removal of the inherited power of the nobility and replaces it with universal suffrage of able-bodied men.

The third reform arose because the Thirty Years' War bankrupted the state especially because in the previous structure, the nobles, who were less than 2000 out of a population of 800,000, controlled more than 90% of the land yet had paid no taxes. The change allowed for further "...negotiation over the royal charter of the new King Frederik III (r1648-70) to become totally dependent on the state council..." (Jespersen, 2004, p.39) thus shifting the centre of power.

According to Gutmann (1988) the Thirty Years' War was partly a civil war and partly an international war that began in central Europe and spread to other parts, including the Baltic States. It began as a conflict between the Catholic Habsburg emperor and his subjects but quickly extended to involve the Dutch, the Germans, the Spanish and the Swedes and Danish, mainly due to a fear of Protestant strength and the economic impact on the colonies.

It was manifested through the new constitution endorsed by the King so that the decisions were now taken though the collaborative work between "...the selected representatives of politically active sections of the population of the national assembly..." (Jespersen, 2004, p.61). In the new constitution, the King lost the absolute power to rule and had to share that responsibility with the parliament elected by universal male suffrage. In the new arrangement, the king no longer had the power to take action without the countersignature from the ministers responsible. The ministers were subject to parliamentary power for their conduct; previously they had reported directly to the King.

The transition from absolutism to democracy did not happen suddenly but took time, even though several events were decisive breaking points. However, though the King had yielded absolute power, in both cases the ruling framework was supportive of the will of the people and therefore ethics was central to the actions of both the king and the parliament.

The year 1830 was important in the democratic timeline of Denmark. The 1800s saw a rise in nationalist and liberal movements throughout most of Europe after the French Revolution and the Napoleon Wars. The liberals in Denmark began demanding a voice around 1830 and success came in 1834 when an advisory assembly was set up as a meeting point for the middle-class public.

4.1.1 Socio-economic and Political Context

Denmark was not at the centre of the Second World War; however, Germany occupied it for 5 years between April 1940 and 1945. The occupation left the country with a severe lack of both economic and financial resources (in foreign currency) that reduced its productive capacity. At the end of the War, the impact of the occupation and the cold war between the Western and the Eastern blocks that ensued, created a context where Denmark was not keen to integrate with the Western nations through the newly formed Northern Atlantic Nations Organization, NATO. The organization had objectives of protecting the smaller nations in Western Europe from possible attack by the Soviet Union-led Eastern block.

Denmark however, was willing to enter into the international capitalist system through the Marshal plan and the Organization for European Economic Cooperation, OEEC (Jamison *et al*, 1990). This arrangement benefited Denmark's production capacity as well as boosting its foreign exchange reserves through the exports in response to the demands of reconstruction of Europe from the devastation of the war.

In the period before the Second World War Denmark had a predominantly agrarian economy with a very limited industrial base that catered for the domestic market therefore, when it joined OEEC, economic growth ensued. However, Jamison *et al* (1990) also point to an increase in both unemployment and foreign exchange problems.

Denmark had the advantages over other European nations because most of its industries were small and family owned that gave them the flexibility and a differentiated production suitable for consumer items and semi-manufactured goods. The decision not to integrate fully into the OEEC enabled it to continue this system of industrial production as opposed to the large corporations that had dominated the rest of the world production system. By the 1960s Denmark's industrial production comprised of almost 60% of the source of foreign exchange income overtaking agriculture, according to Arentoft *et al* (cited in Jamison *et al,* 1990).

The reconstruction of Europe created demands for goods and therefore, for Denmark, the 1960s was a golden decade, however as previously pointed out, employment in the private sector did not increase, as almost 75% of half a million new jobs created between 1960 and 1972 were in the public sector (Hansen and Henrikson, 1984). This increased the welfare costs in addition to the breakdown of traditional social life like elsewhere in Europe, (Schildt and Siegfried, 2006).

In the political arena, reformations took place that resulted in the lack of a dominant party during this period. It meant that coalition politics were ensured and the initial socialist agenda by the Social Democratic party was abandoned. The economic growth however, continued to support the welfare system. The lack of a dominant party created an opportunity for smaller revolutionary parties, which, in partnership with the Social Democrats, impacted the Danish political culture significantly.

The tradition of co-operation between the political parties in the Danish parliament in the Twentieth Century goes back to the 1930s when the revolutionary parties rose to try to provide checks and balance to the existing established parties. Jamison *et al* point out that:

> "...The reformist policies of the Social Democrats provided space for more revolutionary socialist parties to emerge before the war..." created a dipole political relationship with the main parties. This played an important role in the growth of what he terms "...an authentic alternative political culture that had very significant influence on the environmental movement in Denmark" (1990, p.67).

The revolutionary parties attracted radical intellectuals from professionals like architects, artists, teachers, writers and debaters who defended the community against the great welfare state power and reasserted the rights of individualism. This was further fostered by the economic growth of the 1960s that allowed for the breakdown of the socialist collectivism and the transformation of the individualism.

The academics contributed a great deal to the culture of radicalism because the Danish social, cultural and political arena was very accepting of new ideas such as those of the psychoanalyst, Wilhelm Reich (1897-1957). He was expelled from

Austria for his radical ideas on sexuality and lived in Denmark between 1933 and 1939. His ideas are linked to the sexual revolution of the 1960s as posited by Allyn:

> "...Was an eccentric psychoanalyst who hoped to liberate Europeans from centuries of social, political, and psychological enslavement through the clinics he set up that distributed information about birth control and abortion..." (2001, p.4).

He combined political activism and sexual theory linking liberation from totalitarianism with sexual liberation. The acceptance of radicalism led to the transformation of the Danish educational system from an authoritarian one to one that had more experimental free schools.

Others such as the radical Villy Sorensen (b1929-2001) argued for freedom in society and saw the important role the artists and intellectuals played in a democracy and that the responsibility belonged to the individual rather than the collective as pointed out by Jamison *et al* (1990). The sphere in Denmark was similar to the contexts in Pittsburgh and Barcelona in that all joined the fight for individual rights but within the collective society, for the greater good of the society.

Sorensen lived in an era influenced by the Marxist philosophy and theories of Freud (whose major works had been translated into Danish in 1920). These became the dominant influence within cultural debates and literature, so that "... the idea that the arts, and not least, literature, should work to transform or reform society was not new to Danish literature..." (Stecher-Hansen; 1999, p.xvii). The Social Democratic Party won an election during the same period and embarked on a social reform agenda through the welfare state scheme.

Sorensen translated the works of Nietzche and Schopenhauer into Danish in the 1960s that contributed to the social and political debates of the period. He played a role in the introduction of European Modernism to Denmark through his writings and a laboratory in Danish Cultural life after becoming a member of the Academy in 1965. Rossell (1990) points out that Sorensen had advocated for the rejection of the older value systems and supported the welfare state as an alternative humane political system that would help modern man overcome the personal and social conditions that caused alienation because of the breakdown of the traditional value system. By the end of the 1960s, Sorensen was a regular contributor to the weekly *Politisk Revy* (Political Review) where he argued for the Utopian model of Danish Society. This further increased the heated debate on grass-roots democracy and the reduction of totalitarianism.

The radical subculture inspired by Sorensen and others through the Socialist People's Party (*Socialistisk Folkeparti*) played a "crucial role behind the relative strengths of the alternative political culture in Denmark" as pointed out by Jamieson *et al* (1990, p.68). The party had a wide support base in the industrial and the new public sector working class even though the leadership of the party was still composed of older generations.

Tensions arose between those who supported economic material growth as part of modernity and those who were concerned with human developments and social welfare. The problem was mainly due to the generation gap between those who had lived in the poverty of the inter-war periods and those who were growing up during the golden age. Therefore, the youth revolted, challenging the existing political framework.

There are two strands to the alternative political culture in Denmark that had an impact on environmentalism as a new consciousness and the development to the methodologies at the Centre for Public Space Research. The first comprised the approaches to participatory design thinking strategies seen in the context of Danish Social Housing Governance and the other considered environmentalism as a form of social and political critiques of the existing conditions.

Jensen (1995) sees a very close relationship between the concepts of citizenship, citizens and their participation in decision-making processes and he acknowledges Hill's (1994) position on the correlation pointing out that:

> "...Democracy articulated as process and structures is crucial, however the key questions are: what structure and procedures exist to facilitate people's involvement in decisions provides them with the adequate information and ensures quality and equity of the decisions..." (quoted in Jensen 1995, p.177).

Jensen (1995) argues that the way participants perceive themselves in relation to political decision-making is influenced by the context. He therefore interprets the participation as an exercise of citizenship with the product of competition between the different roles played by the participants seeking attention and legitimizing the process. His studies on the Danish political system of Social Housing identified two levels of representation: at the local level with direct election of the representatives and secondly at the housing association regional and national level, run by a combination of elected representatives and government appointees.

The participatory system within the Danish political landscape is historically well developed as pointed out by Torpe and Gundelach (1997). However, the levels of participation changed over time, and after the 1980s, when a conservative government was in power, there are noticeable restrictions in democratic participation. An accepted level of participation has become a problem that requires conscious strategic solutions even though promotional efforts are laudable; unfortunately, they actually result in the shift of power away from the citizens.

Between the late 1980s and mid 1990s there were various attempts at "promoting political citizenship among the housing tenants by placing *promotional teams* within the administrative bodies of large associations" as pointed out by Jensen (1995, p.179). This he argues is a top-down management strategy as opposed to a participatory strategy and as a result, stifled democratic participation.

Because of the move, the level of political participation within social housing had been declining and is blamed on social stratification, largely due to a lack of political resources. Jensen (1999) indicated that this limitation was in the educational, social and economic resources. Jensen on the other hand argues that the issue is beyond a social problem but is more widespread because of the problems inherent in the local democracy within the whole of the Danish political system.

Participation as a political process has two facets, the input and output according to Lundquist, (1976). The input side of politics has the recruitment and participation as a necessary first step that is influenced by the level of how the residents view themselves as "citizens (i.e., citizenships) who are part of a community as opposed to being merely fragmented individuals" (1995, p.180). However, the definition the term citizenship is fraught with problems as can be seen from Hill (1993), Arendt (1958), Andersen *et al* (1993).

Jensen (1995) however defines citizenship at the cognitive level where the public realm is a political system in which they regard the decisions made to affect their lives. Therefore, the process of decision-making must be adequate and legitimate: adequate in the sense of opportunities offered to make the decisions, and legitimate because the power to make decisions and to change them is vested in the citizens and not in the other party merely with interests such as developers.

He breaks the history of participatory governance within social housing in Denmark into three periods; the formation period from 1900 to 1945; the building or rationalization period from 1945 to 1970 and finally the management from 1970 to 1990 (I add to date). In the first period, community interests to fight for rights, to thrive on conflicts, underpin the role of the citizens. The participants take on the role of organizer, are extremely empowered and seeing a relevance to the political system, attempt to influence it and define the rules of the game while the State on the other hand responded by supporting the role through the provision of subsidies. The period historically coincided with a period when there was a balance of power between the Social Democrats and the Conservatives in the government. The organizational actions of the citizens keep the political attention on the housing problem.

The second period on the other hand witnesses the political manipulation by the state through the setting up of the Welfare state to provide the subsidies and eventually demand an administrative role in its use. The housing provision was now set from 1946 onwards as a political matter and the citizen organization mandated with the role of rationalizing and construction of the housing. The citizens began to lose power through the rationalization process and are seen as receivers of welfare outputs as products, becoming supporter citizen clients and with centralized voices.

The final period arose out of the changes to the roles played by the residents from consumers or receivers to clients reflecting the competitions in the market over the years for the provision of services. The key terminologies in use are services and individual solutions with the role of the citizen now legally tied to the assignment of lease. They no longer needed to fight for influence because once they received the keys to the tenancy; they received the freedom to modify their unit leading to the breakdown of the community spirit individualization set. In the process, the State had succeeded in by-passing the association or movements that organized the residents to work directly with the individual and thereby weakening both the associations and the citizen. The only output available to the citizens during the second and third period is exit rather than having a voice.

4.1.2 Growth of Environmentalism in Denmark

There are specific contextual factors that influenced the growth of the environmentalism in Denmark especially if looked at from the point of view of Jurgen Hebermas. The German sociologist took the perspective that social movements are organizations concerned with tactical successes and failures. Jamison *et al* on the other hand take a much broader view of social movements when looking at the formation of environmentalism. They argue that social movement exists when:

> "...A distinct set of knowledge interests is present in the consciousness of the activists and is reflected on the organization, when these knowledge interests form the basis not only for collective identity, but also coordination and co-operation between the organizations which identify themselves on that basis..." (1990, p.3).

They saw the USM movements as organizations or groups engaged in strategic actions in a political arena competing and bargaining with their counterparts from the established political culture as well as others. They point out that the formation of environmentalism, driven social movements, and conservation comprised the initial drive, however, this was transformed in the 1960s when science and technology provided the critique that the consequences would be to destroy the environment. They understood the environment to be "the meaningful arena for cognitive as well as political praxis" (1990, p.5) making it a new way of seeing, conceptualizing the relations between the society and nature. It involved locating pollution and defining harmony, balance and alternative technology within.

In Denmark environmentalism emerged from the alternative political culture of the 1960s and therefore, greatly influenced by the ideas of participatory democracy and the non-hierarchical organizational structure. The knowledge structure was initially tied to the student movements and the counter culture of the 1960s and had three dimensions: cosmological, technological and organizational.

The cosmological dimension related to the ordering of reality and the understanding of how and why it is structured that way, hence, our actions and activities in this dimension are understood through a system of meanings and interpretations according to activity theory. These meanings and activities are influenced by the cultural, political, social and economic praxis and hence are a critique of the existing worldview and offer an alternative view.

In the second dimension, the problem is not only identified but the scope and alternative means of intervention of the problem are suggested as was manifested in the 1960s as the negative consequences of technology over the development of natural processes, e.g., nuclear arms. The third dimension, the organizational, examines how knowledge is produced and distributed. It deals with social and societal relations and is rooted in the ethical values of how things should be carried out. Its focus are people, participation, and the decentralization and dissolution of barriers between the experts and the lay persons in the knowledge production.

Jamison *et al* argue, "…the construction of environmental knowledge interests is both a historical and an intellectual process…" (1990. P.6). The social processes; however, is tied to the particular through the unique cultural and political practices. Even though the movements may have global scopes and outlooks, the agenda is, however, framed by the local settings. The formation and growth of environmentalism in Denmark occurred in four distinct phases: 1962-1968; 1969-1973, 1974-1980 and 1980-1990 (Jamison *et al* (1990).

4.1.3 Phase 1: 1962-1968

The first phase coincided with the formation of a new environmental consciousness that started within the scientific community then the public through debates. During this phase, public education was taking place on the negative consequences of science on nature. The media played an important role through creating the awareness of the issues in relation to ethical values, and the state of the environmental degradation. This allowed for debates on these subjects. The issues were framed as problems and these turned into topics of social concern and conflicts.

4.1.4 Phase 2: 1969-1973

The second phase heralded the formation of environmentalism as a new kind of organization often by younger professionals from the fields of biology, environmental studies, and architects. They distanced themselves from the established conservative society and focused on dissemination of new knowledge interests as a group rather than as individuals. They occurred through media campaigns and demonstrations such as one against Vietnam War. The emphasis was on participation as a strategy to establish a following and the main contribution for the period was the clarification of the existence of alternative knowledge interests of the group to the established traditional society.

4.1.5 Phase 3: 1974-1980

The third phase represented the height of the environmental movement and is characterized by an increase in specialization where the work of the group had now been recognized socially and politically by the society and government. A strategic shift to a practical action-based group became a problem that split the loosely formed organization. The use of coercion and influence through the established channels of the political structures required accommodation and compromise and this led to division. Therefore, it reduced its strength of participation as a strategy that was dominant in the first two phases.

4.1.6 Phase 4: 1980 to date

This is characterized by the breakdown of the movement into a cluster of specialized organizations that are no longer related well to each other. They showed signs of the demise of the ideals with each sub organization developing their own tactics and group of activists.

4.1.7 New Consciousness in Denmark

In March 1969, the natural history society in Denmark, NOA, hosted a meeting at the University of Copenhagen and in attendance were several hundred people that included prominent academics. A group of about 20 students entered the meeting, locked the doors and "cut of the ventilation system, took the stage, talked about air pollution, poured water from the nearby factory on the fish tank and on the side walls showed films about cancer and pollution…" (Jameson *et al*; 1990, p.66). The ordeal lasted about an hour, after which they unlocked the doors and announced the intent to start an environmental movement, NOAH. It was rather dramatic but it succeeded in transforming the Danish society from one that had neglected the effect of environmental pollution to one that was critical of all actions that affect the environment. Therefore, the awakening happened through student activists.

The activities of the student revolt of 1969 at University of Copenhagen made two fundamental contributions to the Danish political culture. Firstly it "… opened a public sphere where institutional political aspiration was selected…and secondly, the adoption of an alternative political culture…" (Jameson *et al* ;1990, p.71). Unlike many student movements elsewhere in the world during this period, the Danish one was anarchistic in organizational principles yet rooted in the local contextual issues such as family politics and local democracy. This makes the movement locally grown and contextual in response but with a global outlook.

Their manifestation coincided with an increase in a number of cultural activities through the creation of places for music, dance drama, magazines that supported alternative sub-culture that continues to this day as witnessed in Christiania. The alternative culture used the organizational knowledge interest as a political strategy in the form of public information and communication via articles,

PHASE	FORMULATING VISION PHASE	PUBLIC SPACE NETWORK PHASE	PLACE-MAKING & BUILDING PROJECT PHASE
	This phase mines and analyses issue related to LIFE in the city through the: 1. Activities (necessary, optional and social) 2. Attractions (magnets) 3. Economic data 4. Social Data 5. Physical morphology	Is focused on the SPACE where LIFE occurs 1. Sets objectives (support for vision) 2. Looks at bench marks [use of typologies] 3. Finds relationships [building framework, scale, form and climatic factors] 4. Makes connections [supporting network]	Is focused on the BUILDING(S) 1. Explores typologies [how they can be applied appropriately] 2. 3D contents and representation 3. The area of focus looks at the possible building uses and their interaction with public realm.
Skills acquired Participation Activity	1. Gain communication skills [students] 2. Analytical Skills [students] 3. Learn importance of INTERDISCIPLINARY nature of design process [students, community and professionals] Participant Observer	1. Learn team-work / collaboration 2. analytical skills 3. Relationship between buildings and surrounding 4. Learn about typologies as urban building block to be varied and repeated	1. Learn about team-work/ collaboration 2. Acquire creation skills for outdoor urban areas 3. Role of landscape architecture in urban design 4. Learn about landscape typologies to creation of public space
Products	1. Behavioural Maps [2 D] 2. Demographic data, diagrams 3. Photographic records	1. Strategic Vision 2. Creation of brief or programme for interventions 3. Typologies [building and urban] 4. Policy tools/ mapping tools	1. Typologies [building and landscape] 2. Detailed design [architecture, infrastructure and landscaping] 3. Reports 4. Publications [journal papers, conference outputs, exhibitions]
Theoretical Framework	1. Social-Usage Tradition	1. Visual-Artistic 2. Social-Usage Tradition	1. Visual-Artistic Tradition 2. Place-Making Tradition
Beneficiaries	1. Students 2.	1. Students 2. Community leaders	1. Students 2. Community 3. Practitioners

Figure 4.1: Observation drawings in Copenhagen by Gehl Source: Gehl

meetings, debates and exhibitions and its success very much depended on support from friendly media.

4.2 Centre for Public Space Research at Royal Academy of Fine Arts in Copenhagen

The School was founded in 1754 as "The Royal Danish Painting, Sculpture and Building Academy" with the aims of providing interdisciplinary education to artists and craftsmen. In 1960s, it took the present form as The Royal Danish Academy of Fine Arts and has three subject areas for education and research in the fields of architecture, design, and conservation. The interdisciplinary nature has been kept intact and is perhaps one of the strengths of the academy.

The work of examining pedestrian schemes in Copenhagen was introduced in 1962 according to Gehl (2002). He however began studying the uses of public spaces in 1965 after receiving a five-year grant from Royal Danish Academy of Fine Art. Gehl and his wife Ingrid studied the interaction between the public space and public life, observations in Italy and correlate these to Copenhagen. This culminated in his seminal work "*Life Between Buildings*", first published in Danish in 1971, and then translated into other languages including the English edition in 1987. It summarizes the methodology developed by Gehl and his colleagues where urban design is an iterative process. Jan Gehl joined the Academy as a lecturer in 1971 after the publication of the book and continued research work culminating in the establishment of the Centre for Public Space Research in 1998, which he directed. The current director of the centre is Jonna Majgaard Krarup. In 2001, Jan Gehl opened a consultancy firm Jan Gehl Architects to practise what he had been advocating.

The methodology involves measuring, then reflection on the effects and gradually the making of incremental improvements to transform the quality of the urban environment and physical form. It is very much rooted in the scientific methodology of observation and measurements of different activities in public spaces, and making causal inferences to the quality of the spaces. However, it is not a manual on how to design a public space, but rather made arguments for observed factors that influenced the uses of public spaces, forms of public life and the spatial qualities or definitions of those spaces as starting point for reflections (Di Giovanni, 2007)

The work is a parallel development of the new consciousness that questioned the conventional planning and functional urbanisms underpinned on the Athens Charter of CIAM. It follows the development of interest in the morphological study and analysis of the city and architectural typology and is similar to the work of Kevin Lynch in Boston in USA. Lynch (1962) had observed that the users structured their perception of city spaces around five elements that recurred. Therefore, he reasoned

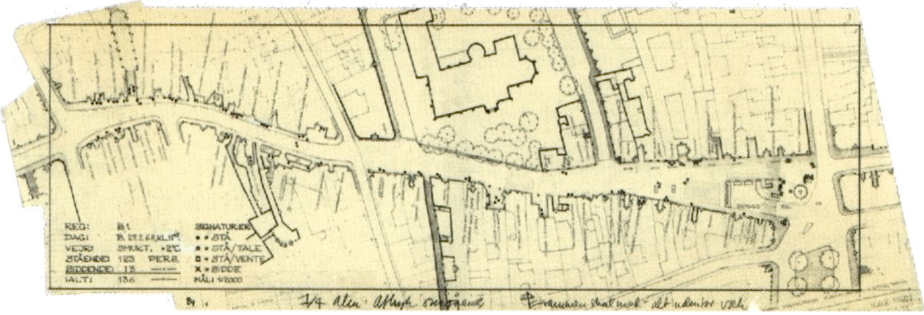

Figure 4.1: Observation drawings in Copenhagen by Gehl.
Source: Gehl

that if designers understood how users perceived them, then they would be able to create a more imaginable and psychologically good city.

The CPSR is co-funded by Realdania Foundation established in 2000 with the objectives of supporting projects that improve the built environment. The goal is the improvement of the quality of life through better-built environment. This continues in the positivist themes that Denmark as a whole is underpinned on, the welfare state, as previously pointed out by Stecher-Hansen (1999).

4.2.1 Design Process

The analysis reveals that the design process occurred in three key phases; formulating vision and programme of activities (LIFE); understanding of the public space networks (SPACE) and finally the place-making- building project (BUILDING) (Gehl, 2004). They focused on the human dimension through the activities that relate to life. In terms of pedagogy, the process provided opportunities for the students to enhance skills in teamwork, analysis and communications. These are summarized in *Table 4.1* and *Figure 4.2* and followed by a detailed description.

The first diagram (*Table 4.1*) is built from the descriptions taken from several publications by Gehl (1987, 2004), Gemzoe (2003) and De Giovanni (2007). It is used to identify the skills needed by the urban designer, as suggested by Kumar, (2009) and identifies different phases and what occurs within them. In addition, it indicates the products expected and who the beneficiaries are. The literature review reveals that the predominant theoretical underpinnings are the social-usage and visual artistic traditions.

PHASE	FORMULATING VISION PHASE	PUBLIC SPACE NETWORK PHASE	PLACE-MAKING & BUILDING PROJECT PHASE
	This phase mines and analyses issue related to LIFE in the city through the: 1. Activities (necessary, optional and social) 2. Attractions (magnets) 3. Economic data 4. Social Data 5. Physical morphology	Is focused on the SPACE where LIFE occurs 1. Sets objectives (support for vision) 2. Looks at bench marks [use of typologies] 3. Finds relationships [building framework, scale, form and climatic factors] 4. Makes connections [supporting network]	Is focused on the BUILDING(S) 1. Explores typologies [how they can be applied appropriately] 2. 3D contents and representation 3. The area of focus looks at the possible building uses and their interaction with public realm.
Skills acquired Participation Activity	1. Gain communication skills [students] 2. Analytical Skills [students] 3. Learn importance of INTERDISCIPLINARY nature of design process [students, community and professionals] Participant Observer	1. Learn team-work / collaboration 2. analytical skills 3. Relationship between buildings and surrounding 4. Learn about typologies as urban building block to be varied and repeated	1. Learn about team-work/ collaboration 2. Acquire creation skills for outdoor urban areas 3. Role of landscape architecture in urban design 4. Learn about landscape typologies to creation of public space
Products	1. Behavioural Maps [2 D] 2. Demographic data, diagrams 3. Photographic records	1. Strategic Vision 2. Creation of brief or programme for interventions 3. Typologies [building and urban] 4. Policy tools/ mapping tools	1. Typologies [building and landscape] 2. Detailed design [architecture, infrastructure and landscaping] 3. Reports 4. Publications [journal papers, conference outputs, exhibitions]
Theoretical Framework	1. Social-Usage Tradition	1. Visual-Artistic 2. Social-Usage Tradition	1. Visual-Artistic Tradition 2. Place-Making Tradition
Beneficiaries	1. Students 2.	1. Students 2. Community leaders	1. Students 2. Community 3. Practitioners

Table 4.1: Summary of design process at the RDA. FASA

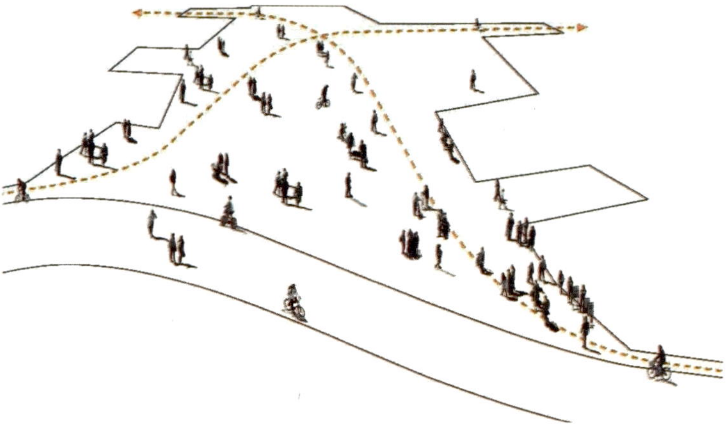

Figure 4.2: Activities representing LIFE
Source: Gehl (2010)

The image, (*Figure 4.2*) is the author's model of a reflective urban design thinking model and has been developed from the materials provided and the literature review on learning methods. The key text used to draw the diagram is Schön (1983) "*reflective practitioner*". The diagram reveals emphasis on an open-ended design process that has feedback loops embedded within it at every stage. The process is a linear iterative loop, however, the process at the CPSR does not have reflection embedded within it.

4.2.2 Formulating Vision Phase

The first phase used as the stage for the students to gain an understanding of the area under study. The focus is on life lived within the space and seen through the three activities; the necessary, optional and social. The activities expected are based on the type of lifestyle for the area, in addition, the things that act as magnets for the people are identified. They include local shops, cafés, parks, sitting areas etc. The argument that Gehl posit is that:

> "...The quality of a city is enhanced when planning and design solutions are based on the close relationship between people's use of public space and the physical characteristics of the space..." (Gehl, 2010, p.4).

The image below (*Figure 4.2*) is a representation of the analysis during the stage.

They use high tech digital animation to convey the idea, with the characters moving through the space and include what seems like all sectors of society, the old, the children, those in bicycles, others sitting etc. It is interesting that there is no

Figure 4.3: Mapping diagram
Source: Gehl and Gemzoe (2004, p.11)

representation of vehicular mode of transport, which was seen as negatively affecting the environment.

The image above (*Figure 4.3*) illustrates the map of Copenhagen and the locations where the studies were carried out. The numbers 1-8 are pedestrian count gates, while the letters represent spaces where the activities were observed. The selection of gates matches the key entry points to the city centre while the gates are located along the busiest shopping areas.

4.2.3 Public Space Networks Phase

The design itself begins during this phase through the development of the network of spaces within the area that would support the life expected or desired there carried out through investigating the appropriate scale of the spaces, the form of buildings that frame them, and most importantly, bearing in mind the climatic factors. The illustration in the following page (*Figure 4.4*) is a representation of those attributes that includes the addition of magnetic elements such as pool, sitting areas, avenues of trees. The vehicular movement is kept to the edge, as they are equally essential to life in the city however, the space depicted is intended to support different sizes and modes of transportation. Urban typologies taken from other spaces worldwide deemed successful are used as precedents to aid the visualization. They are based on a study previously carried out by Gehl and Gemzoe "*New City Spaces*" (2003). The representation would include unifying elements like types of paving, wall treatments, lighting themes etc.

Figure 4.4: Activities representing SPACE. (Gehl and Gemzoe, 2010, p.4)

4.2.3.1 Space Making and Building Project Phase

This is the final phase where the buildings are placed within the space in a way that supports the vision of life within it and the investigations take into account the height of buildings, massing and scale. In addition, the building uses that would support the activities especially on the ground and first floors are interrogated. The threshold between the building and the public realm is thus important (*Figures 4.5, 4.6 & 4.7*).

The stylistic issues are not critical, however the need to have people present for longer periods is suggested in several cases. These include schedules that would allow late opening of shops, the presence of students within the city centre area and balconies on at least first floor areas. These correspond to research that indicated that levels of contacts are enhanced by the perimeter conditions as well as those of the immediate floor above.

4.2.4 Strategies, Tactic, Methods and Influences

The work of the centre during Jan Gehl's tenure was underpinned on the basis that design undertaken with the human dimension in mind would produce durable high-quality solutions since they are framed by the street that provides the space for various activities enhanced by the quality of the spaces (Gehl, 1971). The street typically has pedestrians on the sidewalks, children playing near the front doors and in yards, people sitting on benches on the street, groups engaged in conversation, others just sitting and watching the comedians on the street.

From a positivist viewpoint, the activities are influenced by several mitigating conditions that either enhance or suppress them. Gehl points to the existence of:

Figure 4.5: Activities representing BUILDINGS
Source: (2010, p.4)

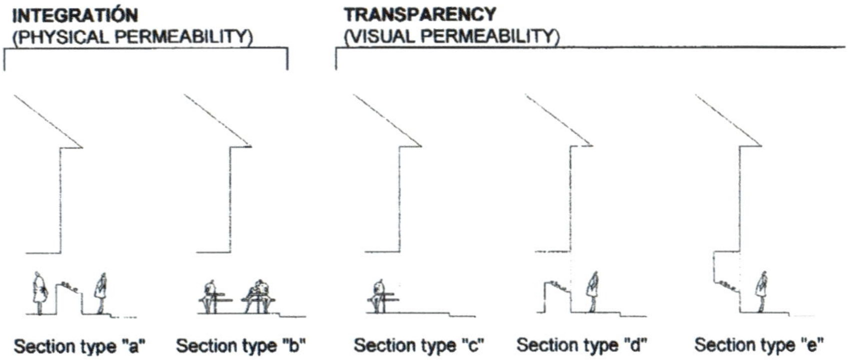

Figure 4.6: Activities representing BUILDINGS
Source: (Sullivan, 2006; p.40)

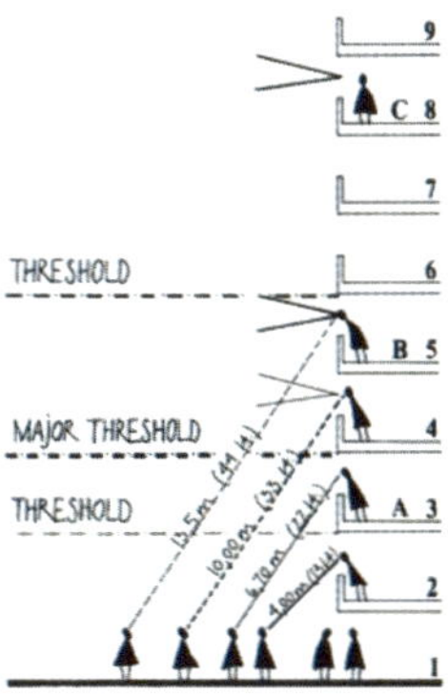

Figure 4.7: Activities representing BUILDINGS .
Source: (De Giovanni; 2007, p.1)

> "...Three kinds of outdoor activities that have different demands on the physical environment; the necessary activities, the optional activities and the social activities..." (1987, p.11).

The necessary activities are those that are essential for the livelihood and sustenance of the residents of a place, such as going to work, to school, shopping, thus there is little choice on opting out of them. They take place all year round regardless of the exterior conditions such as weather, or crime on the street.

Optional activities on the other hand are those that would only take place when the exterior conditions are favourable such as the weather, and depend on the time available to the user of the space. These include activities such as opting to linger around on the streets on the way home, going out for a leisurely walk (roaming), sitting in the park and reading a book.

The last categories, the social activities, are those that develop from others already in the place. They include the greetings and conversations that go beyond the *hello there* and are very much a resultant from the first two kinds of activities. They are spontaneous; however, their character varies with context and most activities and discussions occur in areas of common interests such as residential streets, places of work or school. According to Gehl "...people will talk to each other for no other reason other than they know each other..." (1987, p.15).

The public realm of the cities on the other hand is full of strangers thus making contacts very passive. Therefore, the very act of seeing and meeting is important in architecture, as the design of the built environment will influence by either enhancing creative ways of making contact or discouraging. Gehl argues that the:

> "...Lives between buildings encompass beyond the pedestrian traffic but includes the intertwined spectrum of activities and rituals that make the public realm important..." (1987, p.16).

The spectrum includes social, economic, cultural, political, and educational activities among others and both local residents and visitors are stakeholders who contribute greatly to its successes.

The level of intensity of social activities varies from low to high with the former corresponding to "see and hear" passive contacts typical of life in the public realm while the latter corresponds to very close friends and family. The image below (*Figure 4.8*) illustrates Gehl's view of the changes that have occurred in the public realm over the years in Copenhagen. It reveals a decrease in the public realm and uses of those spaces that need addressing. Emphasis has been placed on the importance of supporting the optional activities that he deems to be crucial in urban life (see Wirth, 1938).

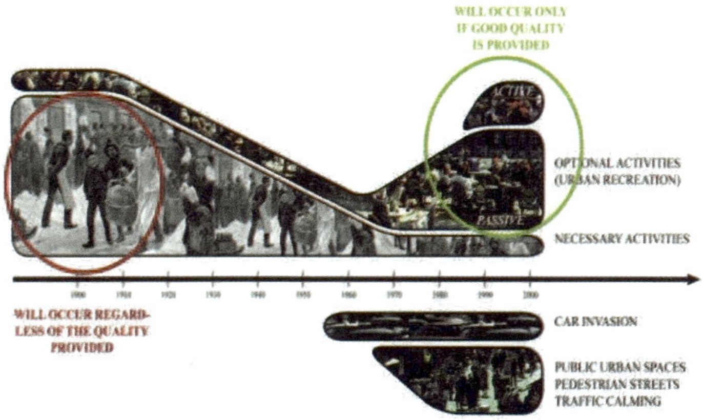

Figure 4.8: Changing role of public life
Source: Gehl (2004, p.2)

The approach by Gehl has a history in the works of the revolutionary-surrealist movements identified with the Situationist International (SI) and the Lettrist of 1950s and 1960s that was published in the journal COBRA (Copenhagen-Brussels-Amsterdam). The SI, was formed in "...July 1957 by eight delegates in a drunken state..." as pointed out by Sadler (1998, p.4). McDonough posits that the SI group included:

> "...Writers, painters, and architects from England, France, Algeria, Denmark, Holland, Italy and Germany who developed a revolutionary idea of the dérive or playful walk about to discover the lost intimations of real life lost in the modernist society..." (1999, p.7).

Debord defined the dérive as "...a form of spatial and conceptual investigation of the city through roaming..." according to Costa and Andreotti (1996, p.20). It was a method used to examine the effect of the urban environment on the individual's state of mind, hence linked to happiness. Other names are psychogeography, which Coverley (2006) suggests is the interaction between psychology and geography and the emotional and behavioural response of the urban environment.

Fontana-Giusti (2007) argues that in the process of urban strolling, the dérive, the quality of the spaces unravels gradually through the experiences read within the larger urban landscape. The experiences are rhythmic in that the regular movement or patterns of movements or change and everyday life in the city centres is composed of the unhindered *to-ings* and *fro-ings* of the people feeling their way through the day as they undertake various activities or gratifications that impact the quality of their lives. Some of the activities are repetitive, while others are onetime events, but all inform part of the daily life in the city centre, giving meaning to life. The everyday life is bounded by the space and time with the latter viewed in two strands, as "clock time and as lived time" (Lefèbvre; 2004; p.x).

The quality of the experience comes from the notions of change and repetition, identity and difference, duality, contrasts and continuity; the opposites that form the dialectics of division, which Bachelard saw as a "duality of yes and no whose geometry is binding in the metaphorical domain" (1964; p211).

In Copenhagen the Danish painter Asger Jorn who was among the founders of SI had collaborated and produced a folding map of Paris in 1956 and 1957 (Newman and Bird, 1999, p.31). The image below (*Figure 4.9*) of the "Naked City" of Paris is interesting in that it represented the totality of the city of Paris in fragments related to the situationist experience of the everyday life.

In the map, there are areas that seem fixed and linked by the red arrows representing the paths for the dérive. Jan Gehl was a university student in the 1950s graduating in 1960. He must have been aware of the work of Jorn, though makes little reference to them. However, an interview with Makovsky of Metropolitan Mag reveals that he was:

> "...Married to a psychologist Ingrid Mundt, and they had many discussions about why the human side of architecture was not more carefully looked after by the architects, landscape architects, and planners..." (2002).

The meetings would have discussed the methodologies of dérive which can be seen from illustrations of his work (*Figure 4.10*).

Figure 4.9: Dérive Map of Paris by Jorn and Dubord. (Costa and Andreotti; 1996, p.56).

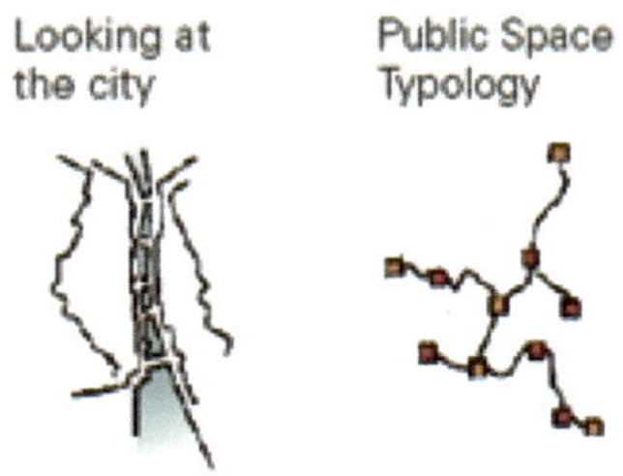

Figure 4.10: Design Process: Source: (Gehl Architects, 2010).

The methodology adopted by at CPSR was driven by the emergence of ecologically motivated citizen initiatives that later become a political force according to Webler and Renn (1995). The methods of political anarchist that used large demonstrations, boycotts and the blocking of environmentally controversial facilities had shaken European countries including Denmark. It is not surprising that the focus of the work at the Centre was on the environmental conditions of the public realm of the streets and squares used daily by pedestrians.

The literature review reveals that the methodology adopted consists of observational, behavioural mappings of most public spaces. It relied on two methods for the analysis of the uses and morphology of public spaces. The first was a description of the physical conditions that provided the basic support ingredients that support pedestrian activities. The second was a survey of the pedestrian activities that occurred in the public spaces in the city centres.

4.2.4.1 First Method: Mapping Exercises

The first method relied on textual and image taxonomies of maps and written data of the streets being studied with the various land-uses, the locations of steps, seats, short walls, and lamp post, etc., are marked out. The elements that affected how the spaces are used, where people stood and sat were mapped. In addition, the configuration of the streets, height of buildings, the visibility, and nodes, were mapped and drawn. The maps were keyed with information on the sizes of areas available for the pedestrians and public life and where they were situated, the conditions offered for walking and staying and finally the traffic conditions (*Figure 4.11*). The image by Di Giovanni is a representation of the typical mapping plan as used by Gehl at CPSR (*Figure 4.12*).

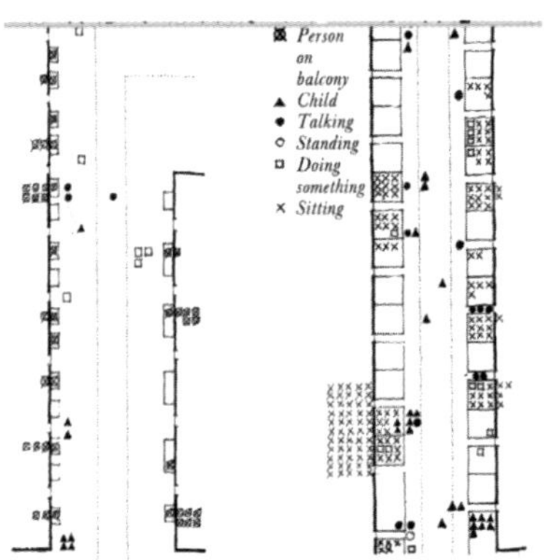

Figure 4.11: Typical Mapping. Source: Di Giovanni (2007)

Figure 4.12: Typical Mapping . (Gehl, 1971). See page XX

4.2.4.2 Second Method: Traffic and Pedestrian counts

The second method correlated the intensity of both the pedestrian and vehicular movements through the site to the level of activities within. It examined the pedestrian traffic volumes, and their locations; the number of people stationary, in groups or singles and what they did within the spaces. The pedestrians were counted in the selected public spaces for 10 minutes every hour between 10:00am and midnight. The figures were then extrapolated to get hourly rates. The amount of people staying was counted every second throughout the study. The surveys were carried during the various varying seasons and weather conditions during the week and weekend both at day and night. Gehl's methodology has weakness in that it does not unravel reasons why people are attracted to the city by not asking the users, and is very labour intensive.

4.3 Examined Case of the CPSR Projects

As pointed out earlier at the beginning of this chapter, the researcher encountered difficulty in obtaining records of student's projects from CPSR due to circumstances that occurred in 2007 when Jan Gehl left the centre to concentrate on his practice. However, the methodology is similar to what he uses at his practice as well as when teaching abroad. A review of several of the projects (Adaleide, 2002; London, 2004; and Copenhagen 2007) revealed that the methodology has been standardized as a tool kit and therefore only one case study has been examined as it is representative of the rest.

4.3.1 Public Spaces and Public Life: City of Adelaide, 2002

Gehl Architects carried out the study of the public spaces and public life in Adelaide in conjunction with students from the University of Adelaide to highlight the fact that changes can happen over a longer time frame with examples taken from Copenhagen. The study was of the central area of the city that contained most of the public and commercial activities. Its objectives were to identify problems and potentials within the city and to make strategic recommendations for the improvement of the quality of spaces.

It started by giving the physical descriptions of the environment that were provided for the pedestrians who were the focus of all Jan Gehl's studies (*Figure 4.13*). The focus was less on the building, but more on people and what they do within the spaces through pedestrian counts, surveys of stationary activities and behavioural mappings. It is not clear from the study what the participation by the users was besides the researchers acting as participant observers. The power of decisions here still lies with the expert who identifies the problem and proposes a solution.

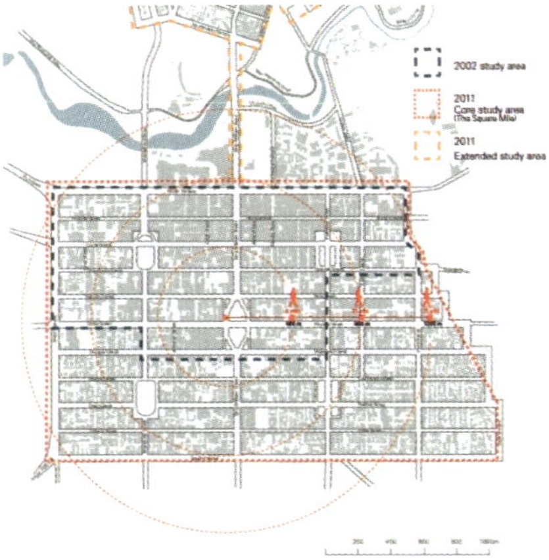

Figure 4.13: Adelaide City Centre (Gehl; 2011, p.8)

4.3.1.1 Contextual Issues

The content analysis of the report revealed that there was more emphasis on addressing the environmental contexts than other forces by a large margin (*Figure 4.14, following page).* This is related to the political, social and economic history of Denmark discussed previously. It responded to the environmental consciousness that was heightened during the 1960s by the radical student groups which they linked to the urban problems and political posturing by the parties.

4.3.1.2 Interrelationship Issues

The project was carried out by an interdisciplinary team of students at the University of Adelaide, the staff from the City Council and professionals from Gehl Architects in Copenhagen, however the process itself was managed top-down with the decision made by the experts without involvement of the community.

4.3.1.3 Tactics and Strategies

The content analysis revealed that the strategies or tactics focused on the social and physical attributes highlighting great emphasis on building typology and uses of the spaces through activity mapping. This was driven by the positivist approach taken by Gehl that perhaps comes from his contact with his psychologist wife. This would not be surprising as developments in psychology had carried out studies that linked behaviour with environmental causal forces; (Mead, 1934 and Kelly, 1955; quoted in Canter; 1977, p.2).

Canter's work (1977) is similar to Gehl as it uses the methodology that deals with the cognition of places, followed by the understanding of the structures of the systems, i.e., one that enables the capturing of the experiences. In order to interrogate the second, recording and measurements have to be carried out. He suggests a variety of methods that include recording of the everyday activities through photography, maps, textual taxonomies, caricatures, etc

4.1.3.4 Consequences

The consequences of the project were recommendations that focused on the physical improvements to the urban fabric in direct contact with pedestrians. These included reduction in through vehicular traffic; connections between the city and the river; pedestrian networks; sidewalk improvements; safety in the street through lighting and an increase of diversity of activity over longer periods. They do not specify the

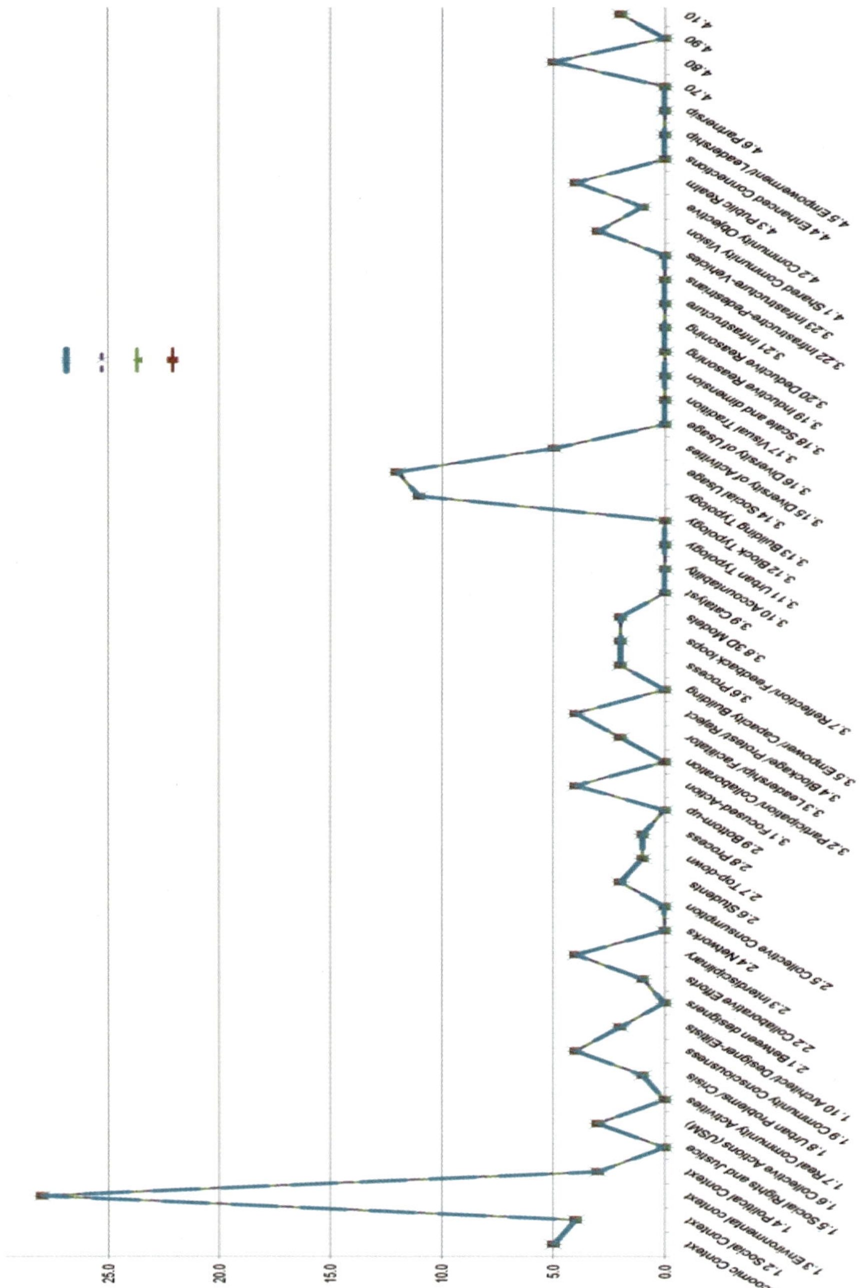

Figure 4.14: Content analysis-public spaces and publiclife in Adelaide

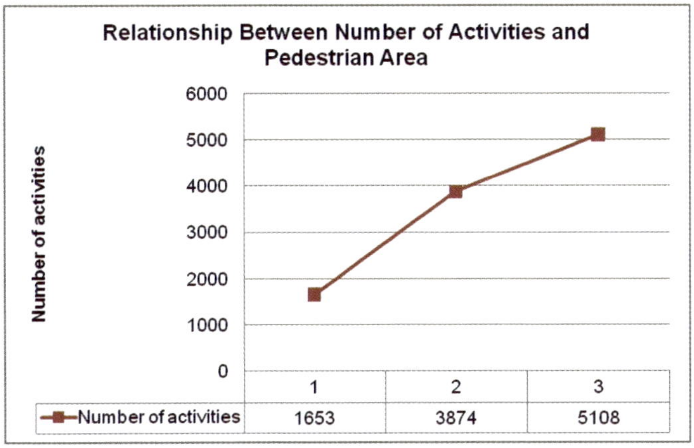

Figure 4.15: Relationship between pedestrian activity and area available in Copenhagen (1=1968, 2=1988 and 3=1995)
Source: calculated from data given in Gehl and Gomzoe

design intent and are left to the client body to implement. Therefore, it would be difficult to ascertain how successful this would be other than to rely on data from Copenhagen where Gehl has been very actively involved.

The image below (*Figure 4.15*) is from the study of the impact of the pedestrianization of the streets in Copenhagen with the numbers 1, 2 ad 3 corresponding to the years 1968, 1988 and 1995 respectively. The first image reveals that even though the area available to pedestrians has increased three-fold over the period, the area used by the pedestrian per activity has remained constant. It suggests that the design of a successful city using the Copenhagen model would need an average area of 13.5 m². It should be noted that increasing the area of pedestrian area per activity beyond the threshold size does not translate into an increase in umber of activities. The second image reveals a positive correlation between the pedestrian areas and the number of activities observed. If one takes the number of activities as the measure of quality of the place, then the study suggests that the consequences of implementing the recommendation would result in a better environment.

Phase	Methods	Influence/ cause
Formulating Vision and Programming of Activities	1. Awareness methods 2. Indirect methods	1. Rationalist approach: (Jorn and Situationists, Lefebvre- Rights to the city),
Public Space Framework	1. Brainstorming among team members	1. Collaborative context
Place-Making and Building Project	1. Visual artistic/ social usage	1.

Table 4.2: Summary of Phase, methods and influences

4.4 Summary

The *Table 4.2* is a summary of the activities, the technique used to carry the activity and the influence or cause of the choice of the method. The work of the centre is characterized by its interdisciplinary approach within the team members and underpinned on personal observation of the activities within it as a measure of subjective quality of the space. There is very little if any public participation in design thinking process, which is not surprising given that the level of engagement has fallen over the years according to Jensen (1995).

The analysis also revealed that the process occurs in three key phases as illustrated (*Table 4.1*). The theoretical leanings are the Social-Usage and Visual Artistic traditions. Three main methods are used that could have arisen out of the circumstances in the political history of the place, the social and environmental histories and the academic traditions of the time. These are the awareness method, the indirect method, and brainstorming methods.

A content analysis of the historical contextual force within the report reveals the physical condition of the built environment as the most important driver to the formation of the centre (*Figure 4.15*). The level of emphasis is more than five times that of the nearest important issues, economic context and community consciousness. However, the literature review points to the developments of environmental consciousness as driven by political and economic parameters.

In addition, examinations of the importance of interrelationships in the process reveal an emphasis on interdisciplinary procedures between the participants in the design process (*Figure 4.16*). The students are equally important to the process as they provide cheap labour in addition to learning the techniques developed by Gehl over the years. However, the most revealing drawback is the top-down nature of the process, which is contrary to the historical context that framed it.

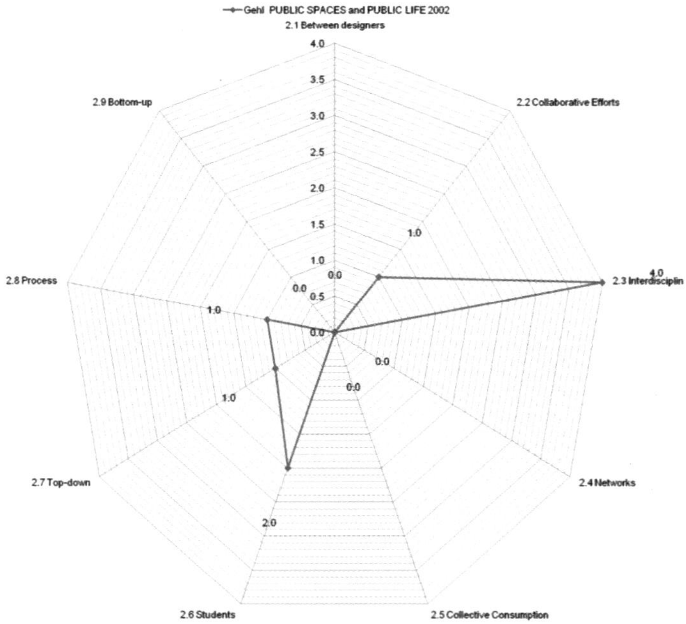

Figure 4.15: Historical Context

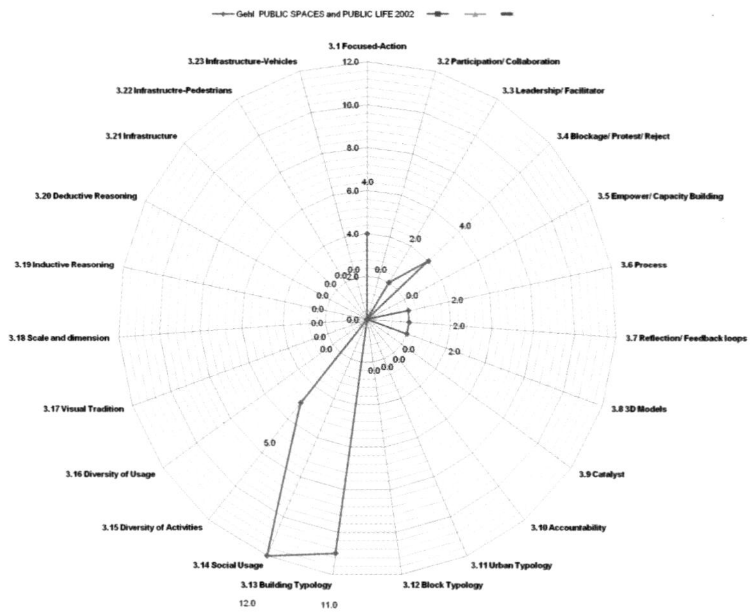

Figure 4.16: Interrelationships

References

1. Allyn, D. (2001). *Make love, not war: the sexual revolution, an unfettered history.* New York: Routledge.

2. Arendt, H. (1958). *The Human Condition,* Chicago: University of Chicago Press.

3. Bachelard, G. (1969). *The Poetics of Space,* Boston: Beacon [originally 1958].

4. Canter, D. (1977). *The Psychology of Place,* London, England: The Architectural Press

5. City of Adaleide (2002). *Public Spaces and Public Life,* Adelaide: Planning SA. [Online] from www.adelaidecitycouncil.com/.../publications/.../public_spaces_public_life.pdf *[Accessed] 10 June 2008.*

6. Coverley, M. (2006) *Psychogeography,* Herts, England: Pocket Essentials

7. Di Giovanni, A. (2007). "Jan Gehl. Public space public life". *Planum-The European Journal of Planning on-line,* (March). [Online] from http://www.planum.net/topics/main/m-gehl-e.html [Accessed] 10 November 2010.

8. Fontana-Giusti, G., K. (2007). "Urban strolling as the measure of quality" *Architectural Research Quarterly.* Volume 11(3-4), pp. 255 -264 [Online] from *http://journals.cambridge.org/action/displayIssue?-jid=ARQ&volumeId=11&seriesId=0&issueId=3-4* [Accessed] 10 January 2010.

9. Gehl, J. (1987). *Life Between Buildings: Using Public Space,* Trans. Jo Koch, Van Nostrand Reinhold, New York, USA, London, UK; Melbourne, Australia, Agincourt, Canada.

10. Gehl, J. (1989). "A Changing Street Life in a Changing Society". *Places,* Volume 6(1). [Online] from http://escholarship.org/uc/item/46r-328ks [Accessed] 8 July 2009.

11. Gehl, J. (2010). This is where we are, *Company Profile,* Copenhagen: Gehl Architects

12. Gehl, J. and Gemzoe, L. (2000). *New City Spaces,* Copenhagen: Danish Press.

13. Gehl, J., Kaefer, L., J. and Reigstad, S. (2006). "Close encounters with buildings". *URBAN DESIGN International* (2006) Vol. 11, pp.29–47. [Online] from www.palgrave-journals.co.uk/udi [Accessed] 10 January 2010.

14. Gutmann, M., P. (1988). "The Origins of the Thirty Years' War". Journal of Interdisciplinary History, Vol. 18(4), (Spring, 1988), pp.749-770. [Online] from http://www.jstor.org/stable/204823 [Accessed] 7 January 2011

15. Hanse, P., H. (1999). "Activation of the Unemployed in Denmark since the early 1990s. Welfare or Workfare?" *Centre for Comparative Welfare State Studies (CCWS),* Aalborg: Aalborg University (January) [Online] from http://www.politiquessociales.net/IMG/pdf/1999-1-ActivationoftheUnemployedinDenmark.pdf [Accessed] 10 January 2011.

16. Hill, G. (1993) Citizenship and Ontology in liberal States, *Review of Politics,* Vol. 55 pp. 67-84 [Online] available from http://dx.doi.org/10.1017/S0034670500016739 Accessed] 15 November 2011.

17. Jamison, A; Eyerman, R. & Cramer, J. (1990). The Making of the New Environmental Consciousness: A Comparative Study of the Environmental Movements in Sweden, Denmark and the Netherlands. Edinburgh: Edinburgh University Press. [Online] Available at http://www.questia.com/read/94197654 [Accessed] on 05-August 2010

18. Jensen, L (1995) "Challenges to Citizenships. *Journal of Housing Theory and Society,* Vol 12 (4) pp.177-194 [Online] from http://dx.doi.org/10.1080/02815739508730

388 [Accessed] on 9th March 2010

19. Jespersen, K. J. V. 2004. *A History of Denmark,* Hill, I. (Trans.). Basingstoke (UK) and New York: Palgrave Macmillan.

20. Lefebvre, H. (2004). *Rhythmanalysis: Space, Time and Everyday Life,* Elden, S. and Moore, G. (Trans.) New York and London: Continuum

21. Newman, M. and Bird, J. (1999). *Rewriting conceptual art,* London: Reaktion Books Ltd.

22. Rosell, S., H. (1991). "Villy Sorensen: Mythologist, Philosopher, Writer", *World Literature Today,* Vol. 65(1) (Winter) p.41-45. [Online] from http://www.jstor.org/stable/40146117 [Accessed] 10 November 2010.

23. Sadler, S. (1998). *The Situationist City,* Boston: MIT Press.

24. Stecher-Hansen, M. Eds. (1999) *Twentieth-Century Danish Writers,* Detroit, San Francisco,

Boston, Woodbridge, CONN., London: A Bruccoli Clark Layman Book.

25. Sullivan, R. (2006). "The Architect's Changing Role in City-Making: A Survey of Contemporary Danish Urban Design Practice" Conference Paper *Agents of Change Symposium Nordic Association for Architectural Research* on 20-22 April 2006 [Online] from *www.sparkssullivan.com/Sullivan%20Paper%20-%20Changing%20Roles.pdf* [Accessed] 8 November 2010.

26. Torpe, L. and Gundelach, P. (1997). "Social reflectivity, democracy and new types of citizen involvement in Denmark", in Van Deth, J., W. *Private Groups and Public Life: Social Participation, voluntary associations, and political involvement in representative democracies,* pp.48-64

27. Webler, T., and Renn, O. (1995). "A Brief Primer on Participation: Philosophy and Practice" In Renn, O.; Webler, T.; and Wiedemann, P., M. (eds). *Fairness and competence in citizen participation: evaluating models for environmental discourse.* pp. 17-34.

28. Whyte, W., (1980). *The Social Life of Small Urban Spaces,* Washington DC, The Conservation Foundation.

CHAPTER 5

Discussion and Conclusions

The research for the book was guided by a central hypothesis that if the model of urban laboratory was used in the education and practice of architecture, then the future designers are likely to be rooted in the ethical values of building or serving the nation through sound-built environment. The book started with a key question; how and why did urban laboratories come about, addressed through looking at several secondary questions that emanated from it. These include to what extent did the historical context contribute to the formation and design thinking methodological practices of the Urban Design Laboratory at Carnegie Mellon University in Pittsburgh? How do the methodologies of the urban design laboratory model at CMU in Pittsburgh compare with others in the European continent (i.e., in Barcelona and Copenhagen)? What constitutes urban laboratories and how can an 'ideal model' of urban design laboratory be replicated elsewhere in the world?

This chapter summarizes the historical contexts that framed the founding of the urban laboratories at Pittsburgh and Barcelona. It examined the impacts of the transformations in the social and economic conditions and the political realignments on the collective action and participation. It looked at the tactics used by the communities and professionals to respond to the changing landscape conditions mentioned above.

The literature review linked the deteriorations of the physical environment to the rise of new approaches to urban developments. The CIAM dealt with urban problems caused by socio-economic changes because of industrializations among others. In addition, worldwide, there were changes to the methods of design due to perception that the corrupt and tired older hegemony of the *Beaux-Arts.*

The complexities involved in solving these urban problems were recognized and new methods of analysis were developed by academics from Frankfurt School of Sociology and later Chicago School of Sociology. The new methods meant that solutions came after the experts had studied the city with public interests at heart.

However, the approach was elitist and on the other hand, they claimed all was to be done in public interests.

The designer/ expert worked with the concern of the user in mind. The new methods however had shortcomings because it had separated human activities of dwelling, working, leisure and travel in addition to reliance of the idea of the minimum dwelling. It proved to be short-sighted. In academia developed an interest in the morphological study and analysis of the city and architectural typology that impacted the teaching in schools of architecture across both the USA and Western Europe.

5.1 Historical Comparison between the Cases

The industrialization led to an increase in population in Barcelona and Copenhagen due to rural-urban migration while in Pittsburgh. It was due to both rural-urban migrants from southern states and immigrants from Poland, Germany, Italy and Ireland. These increase demand for new housing was not matched by the supply. In Pittsburgh, the renewal efforts were directly linked to the housing shortage, but unfortunately provided only to those with access to finance, while the majority were left out.

In Spain, large urban centres like Barcelona experienced a doubling of the population between 1950 and 1970 and giving rise to concentration of consciously aware industrial workforce because of the conflicts between the workers and employers. However, due to the ban on any form of gathering other than through the mandated syndicates by the dictatorial Franco Regime, the workers opted to use forums outside this to fight for their rights both politically and economically.

The study revealed that even though no major historical events occurred in USA in the 1960s, however, major pieces of legislations were enacted such as Voters Act of 1964, the Employment Act of 1967, and the Fair Housing Act of 1968 that framed local events in different regions. These gave rise to the civil rights movements, the women's liberation, anti-war movements and the challenge of the alternative energy culture. A new consciousness, an alternative culture of demanding a say in all affairs affecting the future of not only the young people but also the local communities developed. The students' free speech movements came out of this period as well.

The study revealed that in both Spain and USA, the political conditions during the 1950s and 1960s had created both social and environmental injustices. These led to the formation of the forums outside the official syndicates and the Civil Rights movement respectively to fight for the rights of those without voices. However, in Denmark, the situation was different, in that decision making through a consensus model though universal suffrage had been established by 1600. By 1930s, the Danish parliament had revolutionary parties that got elected to provide the check and balance to the existing traditional parties.

The revolutionary party attracted radical intellectuals such as architects, artists, teachers who defended the community interest against the government welfare programmes. The radicals led to the growth of an alternative culture in the 1960s that influence participatory design thinking in non-hierarchical way. This is contrary to the USA where the various Acts enacted in 1960s were supporting welfare programmes and providing the framework from which the advocacy groups grew. However, it has to be pointed out that all the three cases are similar in that in Copenhagen, Pittsburgh and Barcelona the fight was for rights but within the collective society and the better good of the society.

However, in all the three places, USA, Spain and Denmark; the students' revolt opened up debates and involvement of more people in the alternative culture. In USA, it occurred in 1964 and 1968 at University of California Berkeley and Columbia University in New York respectively. In Barcelona, it occurred in 1966 through the *Caputxinada* (uprising) by the students and their professors that took place in a Franciscan Monastery; in Denmark, through the activities of the student revolt of 1969 at University of Copenhagen.

The research reveals parallels; in Barcelona as early as 1951, collaborative approach to tackling housing problems had developed through the formation of *Grupo R.* It used a multi-disciplinary design thinking approach open to not only the professionals like architects, sociologist, town planners but also to the members of the public. In Pittsburgh, ACTION-Housing was formed in 1957 as a non-profit organization that worked with professionals to provide the best solutions to the housing shortage. They collaborated and worked with low-income residential groups that had risen out of the Acts that had been passed in 1960s to provide self-improvements. The work of these organizations depended on goodwill from within the government bodies that was open to manipulation and abuse. It is therefore not surprising that by 1970s, their activities had declined through the co-opting into the top leadership.

However, the main differences between the two places were that in Pittsburgh the citizen design thinking participation and organization actually came through the government funded initiatives such as Community Revitalization Plan, while in Barcelona, they were voluntary, in opposition to government ban. In Pittsburgh, the focus was mainly on providing the needed financial support and opportunities for collaboration, while in Barcelona it was focused on the development of national identity through the culture of critique and analysis. The *Grupo R* held lectures that were open to all and well attended by the public because of the close-knit formation of families among the Catalans. In addition, the lectures were on wide ranging topics from sociology to urbanism, which in effect built the capacity of the community to participate in design thinking process.
In USA, activism against the demotions of the New Deal and revitalization programmes fostered new thinking within the academia and the ethical stand to

support those communities that they deemed were unjustly treated. The academic community came up with new design thinking methods of analysing the city that was not mainstream at period by approaching the residents to help them find aspirations, identify the problems that they faced beyond the demolition, identify the course and target for action. Equally in Barcelona and Copenhagen new thinking emerged from the political and social contextual challenges, which led to the design thinking methodologies developed by the designers and academics. In all cases, the students were used as a pool of raw talent, energy, creativity and activism, the young always want actions against the established authority.

The research of the book has revealed a connection between the founding of the UL, LUB and CPSR at Pittsburgh, Barcelona and Copenhagen respectively to different contextual circumstances. In Pittsburgh and Barcelona, the context was a fight for injustice focused mainly at the social and political levels, while at Copenhagen, it was on environmental issues that were none the less linked to global events such as the anti-nuclear movements, anti-Vietnam War etc. The founding of the UL at CMU by David Lewis appears coincidental rather than driven by specific events at Pittsburgh, in particular to the Civil Rights Movement as there were very little record of direct involvements by students at CMU in the protest movements.

5.2 Comparison between the Methods and Techniques

The research revealed that the design thinking process in the laboratories occurred in three key stages that were fundamentally similar at UL and LUB and is summarized in *Table 5.1* which are organized around the pedagogy of the various schools and in some cases at the UL provided support for the meeting community objectives.

The laboratories at Barcelona and Copenhagen used what is known as a linear design process strategy where one phase follows another directly in a "…sequence of actions that are dependent on the previous one, but independent of the output at later stages…" as pointed out by Jones (1992, p.76). All the three laboratories started their design thinking processes at phase one, move to two and complete in phase three without any commitments to continue the work further with the community making the work focused mainly on advocacy rather than provision of consultancy services. The UL at CMU however, relies on what they claim is a reflective strategy as previously discussed, but a close analysis reveals that in actuality, it is a branching out strategy as illustrated in *Figure 5.1*.

The figure is a superposition of what the model design strategy and actual process ought to look like from the descriptions of syllabus, published material and interviews with the faculty at the UL. It suggests an open-ended system that is allows for the community to continuously amend the design, yet in reality this is not done due to compressed pedagogical logistics, but also complete empowerment of the community has not really been fully realized. As would be expected, there is a lot of animosity, anger, suspicions of the intents of those proposing the meetings

Stage	UL at CMU	LUB at Barcelona	CPSR at Copenhagen
1st Phase	Systems Analysis	Morphological Studies	Formulating Vision
2nd phase	Urban Design Framework	Urban Design Framework	Public Space Network
3rd Phase	Place-Making	Place-Making and Urban Project	Place-Making and Building Project

Table 5.1: Summary of stages

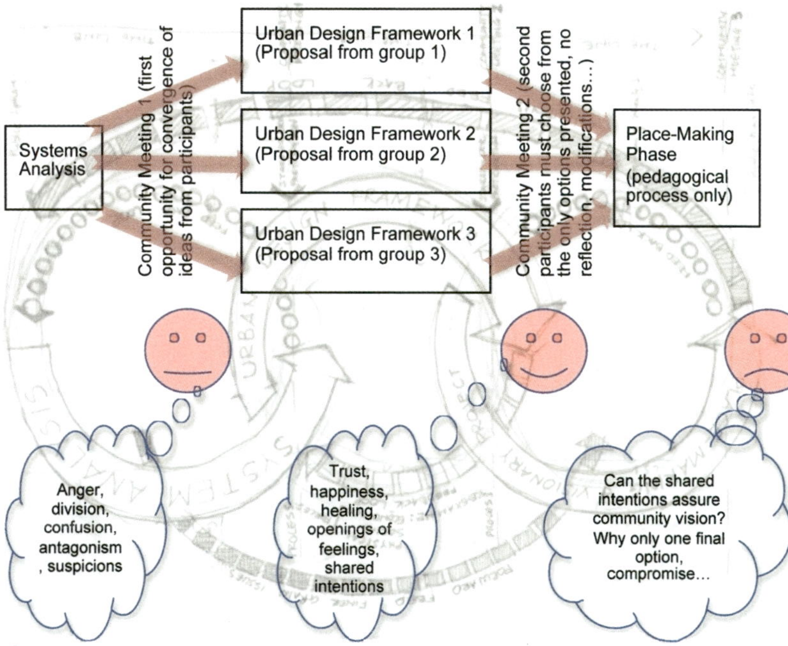

Figure 5.1: Summary of stages

as they controlled the agenda, were on payroll of the client owners, are outsiders to the community and of elitist background. However, it seems like the curiosity of the community drove them to continue attending the meetings, seem to see opportunities, had high expectations which were dashed when they are presented with only 3 options to choose from during the second meeting. There was little evidence of follow-up in the communities to see if the proposals have grown legs subsequently.

At the UL, advocacy was the most important driver in the 1960s, as the context then called for communities such as the Hill District to be empowered with a voice to fight against the destruction of their community through what was called the renewal or development efforts to rid the city of blight. Over time as the community become more aware of the rights, levels of participatory design thinking seem to have dropped to passive at best as passion decreased with availability of other options such as relocation to other areas due to what they perceived as upward mobility.

At the UL, the study of threshold was done through the use of urban and block typologies that seem critical to the process and arise out of the French and Italian traditions of urban design. In this sense, morphological analysis to understand the activities within the spaces and the connections to other surrounding contexts are fundamental. The study revealed that in the cases, examined the main drivers for community involvement were the degradation of the built environment and the protests against the destruction of their communities. These informed the methods and strategies used by the laboratories more than the ethical stance of the designers, except in the case of Barcelona where the design professionals had started critiquing own work and supporting communities through support for alternative visions, the design thinking methodologies.

At CPSR, the focus was mainly on the usage of the spaces between the existing buildings in redevelopments, or the kinds of activities that the client and the designers desire to foster in the places made (a top-down approach). The strategy though may look similar to those at LUB, but is fundamentally different in that there is less emphasis on the building (what Morales called the Urban Project), but more on how the spaces are used or could be used, before deciding on ways to enhance them. At both the UL and LUB, the initial phase looks at the spaces through systems analysis and urban design framework while at CPSR only through the second phase, public space network.

Therefore, the research for the book revealed that the methods and tactics adapted were very much driven by the theoretical traditions that underpinned the laboratory more than the desire for community participatory design thinking. At UL at CMU, the participation comes from the history of advocacy but the design thinking methods were driven by the emphasis to the social usage and visual artistic traditions of late 1950s and 1960s. The LUB emphasised the morphological study of the relationships between the street and the buildings, the connections between the various existing public realms and the rationalist historical growth strategies. At CPSR, the designers took a utilitarian ethical stand, deciding that the quality of the life in the public space is a measure of the quality of the built environment, hence the decision for the designer to make the places as they ought to be, an elitist value judgment and not much on participatory design thinking methods.

5.3 Does Participatory Process matter to Urban Design Education and Practice in Built Environment?

Chapter 1 and 2 discussed the importance of participatory design thinking processes where I argued that they are fundamental to not only getting a chance to be involved with the design of live / real projects, but also addresses the issues of ethics. The levels and kinds of involvements will inevitably vary depending on the pedagogical needs of the individual school, however, at the UL at CMU there was little evidence that participatory design thinking process was fundamentally important to the design education given that it comes late in the learning stage a well as not emphasised all throughout. In addition, the levels of community involvement appeared very low, with majority of participants at the community meetings being the students, client body representative or faculty. Where participation occurred, the power of decision making during the design thinking process still resided with the student designers who drove the agenda, made proposals based on their system analysis of the context then merely asked the community to respond (see *Figure 5.2* where blue represents passive stance by the community on design thinking)

There were however, attempts at design thinking during the *charrette,* using 3D models, which were mainly used to check if the student designers understood the physical elements of the community better. This was corroborated by analysis of meeting minutes as well as interview with both student and faculty participants making the session more about information exchange, consultation and tokenism.

The proponents of the UL have constantly argued that the participatory design thinking process is fundamental to the education of the urban designer and hence making their programme unique. In reality, the position is not too dissimilar to what Bourdieu argues:

> "...Defined in relation to the space of possibilities and its distinctiveness arising from its negative relationship with the co-existing positions takings to which it is objectively related and which determine it by delimiting it..." (1993, p.30).

In other words, the UL at CMU tries to define itself outside the norm of existing positions taken by other schools of architecture, which is to give it distinctive value of difference! An interview in November 2010 with Prof. Bruce Lindsay of University of Alabama, an alumnus of CMU and student of David Lewis during the early phase of the UL points out that pedagogically, it was viewed within the school as weak in academic and pedagogical rigour, which is what led David Lewis and Ray Gindroz to leave in 1968 and go to Yale. It is not surprising as the curriculum was completely changed at the start of the second phase.

On the argument of position taking, a question that arises is what would happen to the UL programme at CMU if other peer schools of architecture

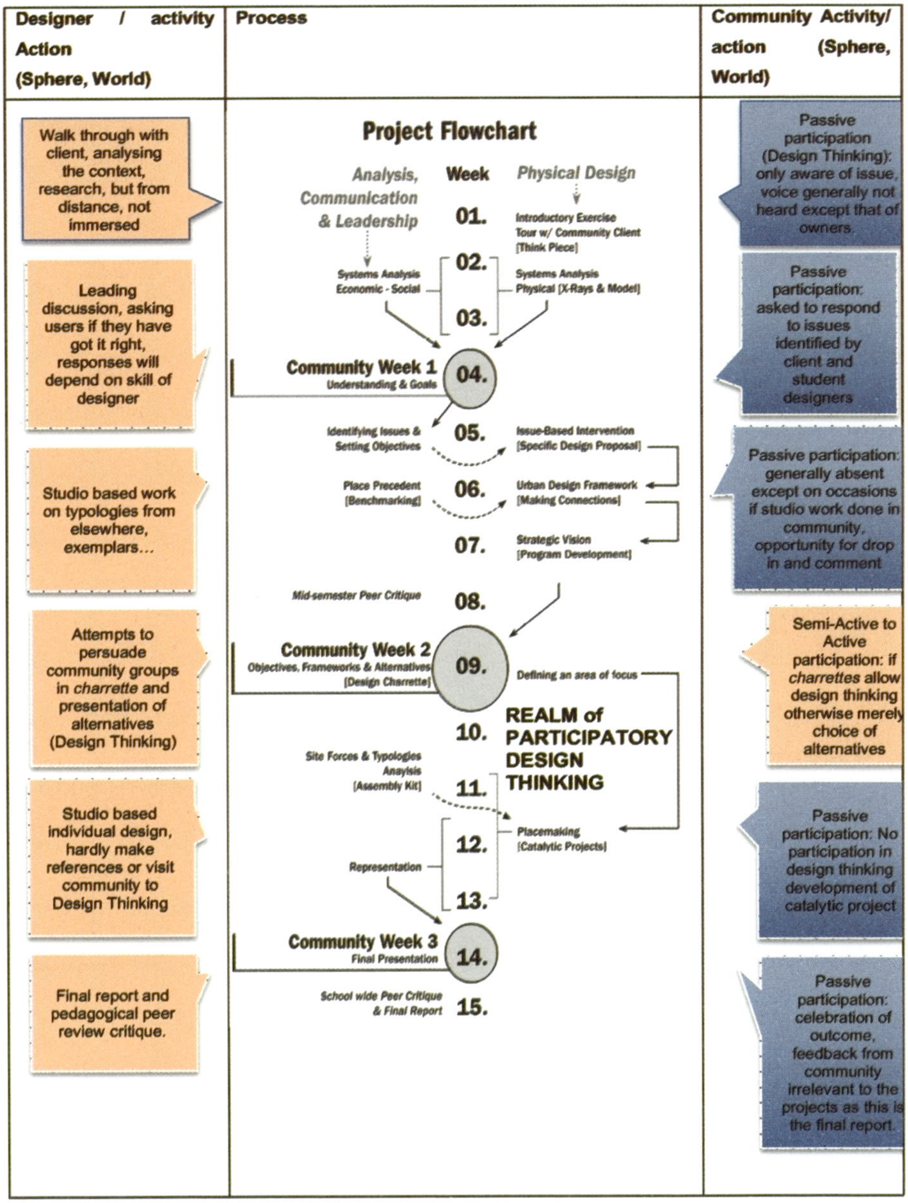

Figure 5.2: Matrix of process activity versus level of participation
(Chart taken from Rico-Gutierrez & Hutzell; 2006)

start taking similar positions, will its position remain the same or will it shift to maintain the distinctiveness? I argue that it would probably shift looking at the transformations that took place over the years as other schools like University of Miami, University of Notre Dame, University of Alabama, University of Cincinnati have started their own in order to maintain the culture of production.

The culture of production in a capitalist society is supported by an educational system because it imposes the legitimate mode of production as pointed out by Bourdieu (1993) who argued that symbolism of work of arts exists only if they are known and recognized, in other words, because they are socially instituted works of art and received by spectators capable of knowing and recognizing them as such.

The work and methodology at the UL at CMU has meaning mainly because of the strong relationship that exist between the school and the benefactors, Andrew Mellon and Richard King, both who were very important in the renaissance of Pittsburgh in 1950s. Their wealth and influence has continued the propagation of the culture of production and distribution of both the social and economic capital, it is therefore not surprising to note that the social agents involved in the field of urban regeneration in Pittsburgh are intimately involved with the School (Don Carter, Ray Gindroz among others).

At both the LUB and CPSR, participatory process Is not explicitly mentioned nor depended upon as a strategy, however, the consequences reveal little differences to the outcomes of the laboratories, place created to faster and support urban living, feeling of ownership, safety, beauty, among others. They all vision the communities where they have been involved wit and their students are trained to have the ability to carry out designs that call for ethical stand based on hard choices that have to be made.

The graduates of the LUB over the years have been engaged with the city of Barcelona and are credited for the success of the Barcelona model of managed development and growth without destruction, of creating strong communities that continue to inspire others, while Gehl's methodology appears to be gaining ground worldwide as different cities compete to stem decay and focus on people. The same cannot be said of the UL at CMU that has been in existence longer, shout louder yet it is difficult to establish the impact of the training as their methodology are those either employed by the firm founded by David Lewis (Urban Design Associates) or working at the university to continue to propagate the system.

So, one would wonder if participation really matters to the processes of the urban laboratory methods? Fundamentals to at least the UL at CMU is the issue of advocacy that it actually came out of, the desire to support communities that lack ability or are not empowered to challenge or even decide on the how their community development would occur despite rights being conferred by the US constitution.

The concept of empowerment is tied to the issue or ethics and moral sensitivity which Deutch defines as "…the recognition that is informed by knowledge and understanding of an action or act of the causes and the consequences of the action…" (1992, p.185). The participatory process of the UL at CMU takes the community through the discovery and understanding of the causes of stress and blight in their environment [be they cultural, economic, social or political] and the actions and the consequences that would result from them at the end of the design visioning.

Therefore, through the process of participation use their knowledge of ethical awareness by being morally sensitive to the contextual situation, as it is locational and not universal. The term ethics here is not applied in terms of good or bad, right or wrong dichotomous relations, but in a subtle way that accepts and recognizes that the relativity of success or failures of the acts against its realization and promotion of freedom of those affected.

> *One would therefore be left to wonder if there is a proper or model participatory processes or activities that are related to a project? This is negative looking at the way each school developed their own methodology in response to their contextual needs. It has to be pointed out here that the crux of the matter is not really about judging the merits of the issues that are raised during the meeting, but rather is about the examination, discussion, exploration with the objectives of trying to resolve the difficult sticky points of the design decision, that is the collective dialogue.*

This introduces an interesting cycle to looking at ethical acts of the UL approaches that constantly raises other questions such as; do their actions make the moral designers or good persons by their expertise offered? Deutsch points out that it is not the case as he postulates "…that the moral actor does not possess special branch of knowledge or body of truth called morals nor have specially tuned intellect that give them privileged ability to reason to the correct moral conclusions…" (1992, p.190).

Therefore, the education provided to the students does not bring about some kind of intuition grasp of the ethical principles apart from their involvement in the specific actions; it however does cultivate in the students the situation awareness and its uniqueness. It enables them to do that which as best as can be determined, embodies and promotes the self-identity, confidence and freedom of the individual participants from the community, i.e. builds their capacity to act for the benefit of the whole group.

The other approach taken at the LUB and CPRS does not explicitly use participatory process as a methodology, but seem to be based on another ethical approach to the built environment as utility or artefact. It is an old idea that has in the past been associated with the "…public principles and common good…" as pointed by Whiteley (1999, p.190). For example, in post war Britain it was once an approach to design that exposed a belief in the higher role for beyond profit as a way to improve the life of citizens and the ethos of society. At the heart of this design thinking is the idea of existence of the ethical dimensions that is both above and in judgment on any design manifestation. This argument linking morality of the designer/ builder and their artefacts or design have been put for example by John Ruskin:

> "Great art is the expression of the mind of great man, and mean art, that of the want of mind of a weak man. A foolish person builds foolishly, and a wise one, sensibly; a virtuous one, beautifully; and a vicious one, basely. If stonework is well put together, it means that a thoughtful man planned it and a careful man cut it and an honest man cemented it. If it is too has too much ornament, it means that its carver was too greedy of pleasure; if too little, that he was rude, or insensitive, or stupid and the like..." (1865, quoted in Clarke; 1967, p.168)

In the traditional view, ethical and aesthetic informed design with the objectives of focusing on the improvement of human conditions along timeless lines. The idea of applications of good design principles was first mooted in the Nineteenth Century and were "...not involved in the cause of an ethically superior society, but to improve the tastes of the public..." as argued by Whiteley (1999, p.192). It suggests that the public were deemed ignorant, lacked knowledge of good taste, and had to be taught how to appreciate what was good. The elite designers were therefore making value judgments on the basis of what they considered their moral/ ethical responsibility to do for the collective good of the community at large. William Morris and the other proponents of the Arts and Crafts Movement for example deplored capitalism that they blamed for the creation of an ugly environment (Morris, 1885 quoted in Denvir, 1986).

The above raises fundamentally important arguments on the ethical ideals of the relationship between the designer and the operating contextual social conditions. The advent of Modern Movements in Architecture ignored the relationship as it focused on the object and the commitment to social progress through design only as pointed out by Loos (1908 quoted in Conrads, 1970). It is interesting to note that in early modernism, ethics and morality centred on the object of design, seen as truthful. The tough deprivation of the war period provided the opportunity for the advancement in the social and cultural spheres through the raising of design that Russell "...would give people something better than they might have expected to demand..." (1946, p.184), in other words, showing them through exemplar projects what the community might actually look like, vision the place to aspire for something much better.

5.4 The impacts of the Urban Laboratory versus Traditional Approaches

In Barcelona, there is evidence of the impacts of work both the LUB's Urban Projects whose model is being studied intensely as ways to succeed in regenerations and redevelopment of cities without destruction through catalytic step-by-step process of little spaces as part of the overall project strategy which is additionally continuously studied and monitored and modified as contextual circumstances change.

The same can be said of Gehl's work at Copenhagen over the years that has transformed the quality of life in the city through targeted changes to the pedestrian environment and infrastructure that supported life on the streets. The strategy of first focusing on the envisioned life in the space, then the supporting framework and buildings turns the traditional process on its head where the buildings are the first focus and in most cases the only focus, while the public realm is the spaces that are left over. Little is done to understand what the impact of those buildings might be and in comparison, the strategy by the LUB to look at every project as an urban project has been critical to its success by taking the importance of scale and impact of a little change over a wider area of influence through the analogy of acupuncture.

The work of UL at CMU even though has been extensive in terms of the number of projects or studies taken, the impact is not as wide or as far reaching as those of LUB at Barcelona and CPRS at Copenhagen. I argue that one of the reasons being is that the strategy is still very much tied to and liked to the urban regime coalition system where those in positions of power are still holding the pan by the handle.

However, having said that, the urban laboratory model in its various forms definitely has an impact on the design process, design education and the built environment. In the three case study locations, the impacts have been significant enough to make a case for consideration of the model as a method of teaching urban design at universities as well as perhaps as outreach using master classes as Jan Gehl has now started in Copenhagen.

5.5 Limitations of the Study

This research has been limited to examinations of three urban laboratories at Carnegie Mellon University in Pittsburgh; Universitat Politècnica de Catalunya in Barcelona and the Centre for Public Space Research at the Royal Danish School of Architecture and Fine Arts in Copenhagen. The period of study of advocacy and founding of the laboratories and the end cut date that the published materials were available.

It was limited to documenting and critically examining the impacts of the revolutions of the 1960s on the participatory decision making and specifically in the transformation of the urban design processes through urban design laboratories. It focused on the assessment of various methods and tactics used at the laboratories in addressing the complex issues of urban design education and practice. The research will finally suggest aspects that have universal application that may be incorporated in the use of the urban design laboratory model as a tool for educating future designers especially in emerging economies, where democracy is still developing and building on the Arab Spring uprising. This is especially important for places where urban populations are rsing unlike in the western world where some countries are facing different challenges, increase in percentage of older people white at same time facing an overall dwindling population.

5.6 Policy Implications

The research revealed the importance of genuine participation in the promotion of place and ascribing meaning to place that would occur only if the community's capacity to participate has been built. In addition, it should not be taken as a given and that will occur merely because of legislative measures as can be seen from the case of Pittsburgh, and perhaps a better approach is one taken in Scotland with the publication of Planning Advice Note 81 that "advises planning authorities and developers on how communities should be properly engaged in the planning process" (Scottish Executive, 2007, p.8).

In addition, the study revealed that participation might be omitted if the focus is on the quality of the built environment (aesthetics). Examples from Barcelona and Copenhagen indicate that if the designers take an ethical approach to design, one that recognizes that their have positions of responsibility to community at large beyond their immediate client, then the urban laboratory methodologies selected if targeted on the development and improvement of the public realm positive results are likely to be achieved. The model is useful here in regards to imparting skills in leadership, and the acknowledgement of the importance of collaboration with other professionals, interested parties in the urban design process.

Finally, the studies revealed that success requires long-term commitments to monitoring the transformations in the life in the public realm as the built environment is changed over the years due to various spheres of influences from the economic, social, cultural and political fronts.

5.7 Expanding knowledge in Urban Laboratory Process?

The research has contributed to the understanding of the methodologies and tactics used at the various urban laboratories and how they have risen from the contexts. It is the first study that has documented the comparisons between the methodologies in three urban laboratories of similar age from different parts of the western world and contributes to the area of urban design education, practice and process that would enable a model urban design laboratory to be developed that responded to the local context anywhere in the world.

5.8 Future Research

The study has been limited to the understanding of the influence of historical context in the founding of the urban laboratories and the influence on the methodologies adapted. It examined only three urban laboratories from USA, Spain and Denmark; however, it has to be pointed out that over the years there has been an increase in the number of schools that have adapted participatory methodologies as part of their pedagogy.

Future work could look at comparing the differences in the models used at universities in the same country that have similar historical origins, for example, MIT URBLAB, Dallas Urban Laboratory, University of Washington-Chandigarh Urban Laboratory were all established in 2006; Glasgow Urban Laboratory, Queens University-Live Projects Studio, University of Sheffield-Participation studio (after 2007) among others.

5.9 Conclusions

The research has contributed to the understanding of the methodological framework of best practices of urban design education and practice that may be applied to improve the quality of designed places, build capacities of local communities under study, highlight and build partnerships with developers, foundations and local authorities and perhaps establish and build networks with schools of architecture in other non-western countries. It is however important to point out that a universal model laboratory would be difficult to achieve as the methodologies, strategies and tactics are context dependent. This suggests that the first step would therefore be the undertaking of historical study of the place, changes to the current traditional working practices to one of collaboration and eventually slowly involving communities to support the work.

References

1. Bourdieu, P. (1993). *The Field of Cultural Productions,* Cambridge, UK: Polity Press.

2. Deutsch, E (1992) *Creative Being: The Crafting of persons and World,* Honolulu: University of Hawai Press,

3. Graham, K. (2006) "Imposing and Embracing Collective Responsibility: Why the Moral Difference?" In French, P., A. and Wettstein, H., K. *Shared Intentions and Collective Responsibility,* Boston, MA & Oxford, UK: Blackwell Publishing,

4. Jones, C. (2007). *Design Methods,* New York, Chichester, Weinheim, Brisbane, Singapore and Toronto: John Wiley and Sons Inc.

5. Loos, A. (1908) Ornament and Crime", In Conrads, V eds. (1970) *Programs and Manifestos on twentieth Century Architecture,* Boston, MA: MIT Press.

6. Morris, W. (1885) "The Workers Share of Art", In Denver, B. (1986) *The Victorians,* London: Longman (p.72),

7. Russell, G. (1946) National Furniture Production, *Architectural Review,* December, 1946, p.184,

8. Sadler, B.; J. (2006). "Shared Intentions and Shared Responsibility" In French, P., A. and Wettstein, H., K. *Shared Intentions and Collective Responsibility,* Boston, MA & Oxford, UK: Blackwell Publishing,

9. Scottish Executive, (2007). *Planning, Community Engagement, Planning with People: Planning Advice Note 81.* Edinburgh: Crown Publications.

10. Whiteley, N. (1999) "Utility, design principles and the ethical traditions," in Attfield, J. Ed. (1999) *Utility Reassessed: The role of ethics in the practice of design,* Manchester & New York: Manchester University Press,

Author's Biography

John Odhiambo Onyango, PhD., is an Associate Professor at the School of Architecture, University of Notre Dame. John has taught and developed over 40 architecture and architectural engineering courses at all levels since 2002 and has an extensive and solid professional background in architectural practice.

At Notre Dame, he leads an interdisciplinary lab Buil+Perform@nd that aims to understand causes and consequences of design decisions and their impact on the environment and people's health and well-being. It uses evidence-based research to study the design, construction and operation of Sustainable Traditional Buildings and Cities. John has been a PI and CoPI in over 13 research projects securing over $527k in competitive research grants.

John's research focuses on understanding influences behind design decisions and impacts of such decisions upon the built environment and human health and happiness. It asks: *(1) How do design methodologies influence sustainable place-making in the built environment? (2) What impacts do design decisions and methods have on sustainability in energy and environmental performances at the urban and building levels? (3) How do design decisions of the built environment promote human health, dignity and integral development?*

Acknowledgements

I would like to give the glory to God Almighty for all that I am and for the opportunity to serve Him while working on this book. I thank my family (Natalia, Eduardo & Juan) for the time their patience with me while working on the book project, in addition to for their criticism, reflection and prayer.

I want to thank Dr. Robert Procter, University of Bath, England, for comments and guidance, Dr Lorens Holm, Dundee University, Scotland, for encouragement to publish the research in a book when I started year ago. Finally, I would like to appreciate the financial support from the School of Architecture (Dean Stefanos Polyzoides, Jennifer Hoover and Jennifer Parker for title suggestions). The editors at Actar for all their diligent work in getting the book published on time and for going through rigorous peer review process.

Participatory Design Thinking
in Architecture & Urban Planning

Published by
Actar Publishers, New York, Barcelona
www.actar.com

Author
John Odhiambo Onyango

Edited by
John Odhiambo Onyango

Graphic Design
Marga Gibert Valls

Copy editing and proofreading
John Odhiambo Onyango

Printing and binding
Gràfiques Jou

Distribution
Actar D, Inc. New York, Barcelona.

New York
440 Park Avenue South, 17th Floor
New York, NY 10016, USA
T +1 2129662207
salesnewyork@actar-d.com

Barcelona
Roca i Batlle 2
08023 Barcelona, Spain
T +34 933 282 183
eurosales@actar-d.com

Indexing
English ISBN: 9781638400714
Library of Congress Control Number:
2022946044
Printed in Spain
Publication date: September 2023